MIDNIGHT TRAIN

Midnight Train

*An All–Southeastern Conference quarterback's ride
from the football fields of the South to enshrinement
in the Songwriters Hall of Fame in New York*

Jim Weatherly

with Jeff Roberson

Yoknapatawpha Press
in association with
the School of Journalism and New Media
at the University of Mississippi

Published by Yoknapatawpha Press, P.O. Box 248, Oxford, MS 38655,
and the School of Journalism and New Media, P.O. Box, 1848, University, MS, 38677

ISBN 978-0-692196-21-2

For Brighton and Zack
My wife, Cynthia
And all of my family

Jim Weatherly
Brentwood, Tennessee

For the children of James Samuel and Elsie Shannon Roberson –
Edith, Billy, Jean, Mary Ann, and Richard. And for their
thirteen grandchildren, of which Jimmy and I are two.
And for Mississippi, where the train ride began.

Jeff Roberson
Oxford, Mississippi

"I'm just grateful our spirits met and we got a chance to give to the world the best of both of us."

— Gladys Knight talking about Jim Weatherly

"A lot of kids grow up in Mississippi dreaming of playing quarterback for Ole Miss on championship teams and in Sugar Bowls. And a lot of kids grow up in Mississippi dreaming of a successful career in music. Jim Weatherly got to do both."

— *Billy Watkins, Clarion Ledger, Jackson*

Preface

In 1971, I was living in a tiny apartment in Los Angeles trying to make it as a songwriter, just one of the countless, faceless writers pitching songs to seemingly indifferent music executives in hopes of hitting the jackpot. I was disappointed and depressed and just about ready to give up. I had poured my soul into song after song, only to see them rejected. I was on the verge of taking what was left of my money – and my songs – and going back to Mississippi to finish my teaching degree at Ole Miss, become a football coach in some small town, and forget about music.

I wandered up and down Hollywood Boulevard in a blue funk, looking in store windows to kill time between phone calls and appointments. Sometimes I would go to an afternoon movie at Grauman's Chinese Theatre just around the corner from my apartment. It helped me forget my troubles for a couple of hours. I would eat a chicken salad melt at the Hamburger Hamlet across the street from Grauman's and then head on home. Sometimes I would just sleep.

One afternoon I went to a movie hoping to relieve some stress, but this time it only seemed to add to my loneliness. When I got back to my apartment, I sat down on the bed feeling kind of empty inside. I picked up my guitar and started to strum.

Suddenly, a song poured out of my soul. I sang the whole first verse without even thinking about what I was doing. I didn't have a title. I didn't have a melody. I didn't have a lyric. I didn't have anything but deep, overwhelming sadness. I wrote in a stream of consciousness, as if I were in a trance. It was as if God was writing the song and giving it to me.

It's sad to think we're not gonna make it
And it's gotten to the point where we just can't fake it
But for some ungodly reason we just won't let it die
I guess neither one of us wants to be the first to say goodbye

In time, legendary soul group Gladys Knight and the Pips would take "Neither One of Us" to the top of the charts. It was their first No.1 hit record. And mine. It was a long time coming and tough getting there. The road was paved with hard work, heartache and luck.

And no small measure of the grace of God.

1 ——⁊⁊

Songwriter

I didn't set out to become a songwriter. I had planned to be a football coach. When I was a little boy, I always said I wanted to be a professional football player. Sports always came naturally to me.

Something else came naturally to me as well. Around the age of 12, I realized I could write songs. It was an incredible feeling. Even if they were just words strung together which didn't always make good sense, it felt satisfying to me. I didn't know what I was doing but I kept doing it and never stopped.

I was influenced by the music on radio in the late 1940s and during the first decade of rock and roll in the 1950s and by songs from movies. It took many years of writing to feel like I was making some headway.

For a long time when people asked me what I did, I would tell them "I write songs." I never said, "I'm a songwriter." I think there's a distinct difference. Writing songs is something you do. A songwriter is something you are. Something internal. I felt I hadn't earned the right to call myself a songwriter, because I hadn't reached a point where I was consistently accomplished at it.

Some people are songwriters and some people write songs. It's kind of like quarterbacks. There are quarterbacks and there are guys who play quarterback.

Songwriting is very mysterious to me. I believe it's a gift. Sometimes a song will appear out of thin air like you had nothing to do with it except put the words down on paper. Sometimes it comes to you in a dream. I wrote a song called "White Castle Station" like that. I heard the whole thing in a dream. Sometimes you pick up your guitar or sit down at a piano and your hands just automatically go to the right chords. That just amazes me.

Most of the time for me, melodies and lyrics come at the same time. Some songs come more slowly than others and can be a struggle. Some come fast. Songs come to different writers in different ways because there's more than one way to write a song. Getting it right is what counts.

My philosophy of songwriting, once I found who I was as a writer, has been to write simply for the listener. I try to write the kind of song that when you have your car radio turned down, you immediately turn it up because for some reason, melodically or lyrically, it catches your attention. I try to write with the kind of emotion and feeling that hopefully touches the listener the way it touches me when I write it.

Simply put, I'm trying to communicate with the listener. The singer is the vessel that communicates the emotion, similar to an actor playing a part. And when the right artist records the right song, what makes it a hit is when the audience relates to it or feels it on a personal level. They can put themselves in the song.

Another aspect of songwriting is that it's subjective. Other people get to decide if a song is good or bad or worthy of being recorded or becoming a hit. When you write it, you never know if anyone's going to like it. If an artist likes it, will the producer like it? If they both like it, will the record company like it? And if they all like it, will they record it? And if they do record it, will it make the album? And if it makes the album, will the record company like it enough to put it out as a single? And if it is a single, will radio play it? And if radio does play it, will people like it enough to buy it? And if they do buy it, will it make the charts? And if it does make the charts, how far up will it go? Will it reach No. 1 or stall?

That's how it was when I came along in the early 1970s. I have to say the music business has changed dramatically since then.

Songwriters are at the mercy of a lot of people. The momentum of a song or a record can be stopped in its tracks at any point if anyone in the long line of decision makers says no.

But if it does get recorded, makes it through all the potential naysayers, gets on the charts and then hits that magic No. 1, you breathe a sigh of relief and thank God you have a major hit record and some money coming in. Then you hope you can do it again and again and again. And if that happens, you might have finally achieved enough credibility to call yourself a songwriter.

Not every great song is a hit and not every hit is a great song. But sometimes they are one and the same. The writer writes a great song and the public makes it a hit. And sometimes it becomes a timeless classic. Paul Simon's "Bridge Over Troubled Water" is a good example.

Year after year, struggling writers painfully pour their souls into songs only to have them end up collecting dust in a storage room somewhere. There are thousands of great songs lying dormant in publishing houses that no one has recorded or that time has passed by and that the public will never get to hear.

It's a tough business and getting tougher.

Some people have asked me how to have a songwriting career. I know how it happened for me, but that was a long time ago. Every path is different, and music is constantly changing. But one thing I know for sure. It takes perseverance. If you don't keep trying, it will never happen.

My pathway was sometimes rocky. When I look back, I can see so many little miracles that kept putting me where I was supposed to be, just when I was losing hope and about to give up. Something kept telling me I was meant to be a songwriter.

2 ——❧

Pontotoc

On March 17, 1943, the United States was at war with Germany and Japan. The people in my hometown of Pontotoc, Mississippi, were affected just like Americans everywhere. Boys from towns large and small, many mere teenagers, left home for Europe and the Pacific as World War II dragged on. Some would never return.

On that day at the Pontotoc County Hospital I was born breech with the umbilical cord wrapped around my neck. I've been told that for a while it was "touch and go." But the doctor, John Rayburn – Dr. John as he was called by the townsfolk – quickly got me untangled and my life began.

They named me James Dexter for my two grandfathers – James Samuel Roberson and Ira Dexter Weatherly. I was the first of four children born to Ira "Ike" Burdell Weatherly and Edith Roberson Weatherly, the first of 13 grandchildren on my mother's side. A lot of family members were at the hospital that day, which isn't surprising. Mom's brother, Billy, hitchhiked home from college to see his new nephew.

But my dad wasn't there. He was on a battleship in the treacherous waters of the Pacific fighting for his country.

When I went home from the hospital, Mom and I lived with my grandparents in a house built by my grandfather James. The house is still there on Roberson Street, which was named for our family.

I was born into a football family. Starting with my dad there have been more than ten high school quarterbacks in our family. My younger brother, Shan, and my son, Zack, as well as uncles, cousins and a brother-in-law, all eventually played quarterback. Mom's brothers Billy and Richard were quarterbacks. Richard was only eight years older than me. When I was old enough, Richard

Getting ready for football at a young age

would play football with me. He'd kick the football and then run and tackle me as hard as he could. I guess he was trying to toughen me up.

My dad had been a star high school football player. For years after he graduated, people around Pontotoc said he was "the best." When he was in the eighth grade, he made the high school team because he was bigger than most players.

Uncle Billy, a teammate of my dad, told me that in a

game against Tupelo, Dad was injured pretty badly when he was kneed in the stomach. They carried him to the hospital and found out his stomach had been paralyzed by the blow and he couldn't digest food. He stayed there several days until he was able to eat again and eventually fully recovered. In a game

Me and Mom

against Corinth when he was a senior, he badly injured his knee. In those days they didn't have the knowledge and skills to repair that kind of injury, so he never played again. That injury bothered him for the rest of his life. At times it would jump out of place and was really painful. He would have to walk with a cane when that happened.

The week after the Corinth game, Pontotoc was about to play Fulton. Uncle Billy told me that before the game, school superintendent H.R. Carter addressed the team and talked about my dad. He told of the hardships he endured growing up, how he'd worked on a farm and got to school somehow each day while also being a good football player. He talked about the seriousness of his injury. My dad was in the locker room with the rest of the team listening, and Mr. Carter became emotional, shedding tears as he spoke.

If it hadn't been for that injury, Dad would have probably played college football. Everybody said he was that good. He taught me how to throw a football when I was very young, trying to help me avoid future bad throwing habits. He really loved the game.

Right after graduation from high school in 1941, my dad married a cheerleader, his high school sweetheart, Edith. Shortly after that he enlisted in the Navy. Even with his bad knee – Dad called it a "trick knee" – he was accepted.

And then the miracles began.

In that uncertain climate, my mother recalled how Dad was given a choice between two ships headed for the Pacific. One would return to the states sooner. For some unknown reason, he chose the ship scheduled to stay in peril longer, subjecting himself to even more danger. I have always wondered why he would do that. Then one day he watched the ship that he could have taken – the one that was supposed to go home sooner – get blown up. It quickly sank to the bottom. It turned out that he made a wise choice after all. Was it divine intervention?

I've always heard you don't remember things that happen when you are very young, but I have a vivid image of at least one such moment. The first thing I remember about my dad was that he leaned over my baby bed and put a football in there with me. He must have just come home from the Navy, or maybe he was home on leave because he had his Navy uniform on. I was probably close to two years old, but I remember it.

As I grew a little older I was always frightened of war.

People talked about it all the time because it affected everyone. When I was about four years old I remember asking my mom on more than one occasion if I would ever have to go to war. She would always reassure me by saying, "Your dad went to war so you wouldn't have to."

After he got out of the Navy, my parents built a little white frame house on Warren Street, just a dirt road at the time. It cost

Mom and Dad

around $3,000. It's still there. It was probably 600 square feet, with a full, unfinished basement. My dad wired the house himself.

We were only about five minutes from my grandparents and about the same distance from the courthouse square in downtown Pontotoc by car. I grew up in that small house and lived there until I went to college.

I felt safe and secure in that little house. Sometimes on rainy nights I would lie in bed right next to the screened-in window in the dark, snuggled under a warm blanket. The window was raised just a little bit and I would listen to raindrops hit the windowsill as they softly splashed on my face. It was a comforting feeling as I lay there wondering what was going on in a world beyond my little town. Even today I sometimes close my eyes and drift back in time to listen to those raindrops.

Over the next few years Mom and Dad had three more children – daughters Sherrie and Elise and a son, Shan, shortened from a great grandfather's family name, Shannon. My dad got a job working for his father-in-law, my grandfather James. Daddy James taught my dad all about being an electrician. Dad repaired and delivered electrical appliances.

We always had family all around us. Our neighbors were our friends. All the storekeepers and businessmen knew me and my family. I was almost like a pet dog in that town. Everybody looked after everyone else's child. I look back on those idyllic small town years and I feel so blessed to have grown up there when I did. It was kind of like Mayberry.

All the grandchildren called my mother's parents Daddy James and Nanny. On Sunday afternoons our family would go to their house and join more family and friends there. They lived in a classic Southern house, a big white structure with large rooms and tall ceilings and a long front porch. It was situated on a small rise above Oxford Street, the main east-west thoroughfare.

The house belonged to Papa Shannon, Nanny's father. She and Daddy James had moved in with him to help take care of the house after Papa Shannon's wife passed away.

On warm summer days with a slight breeze rustling the leaves, the grownups would sit in rusted white metal chairs or the lattice swing with the paint peeling off, the huge oak tree in the corner of the yard next to the big house serving as a shady canopy. They'd talk and laugh, drink Cokes, eat watermelon or homemade ice cream and enjoy each other's company.

Some of the kids and even the adults would play croquet,

baseball, football, and anything competitive and fun. When twilight descended we'd catch lightning bugs, put them in fruit jars, and pretend they were lanterns. As the sun faded and shadows fell across the big front yard, everyone would move into the big house to eat supper. It was a warm, comforting place.

Pontotoc was a small farming community, one of those "everybody knows your name" places of a few thousand souls. People spent weekdays and even Saturdays working, while Sundays were for church, family, and rest. Trees lined the streets and sidewalks, and just outside the city limits lay wide open spaces, pastures, and fields of corn, cotton, and beans in every direction.

On lazy spring and summer days, I would lie back in the plush green grass of my grandparents' front yard and study the sky. Clouds seemed magical to me as they slowly floated along, gently pushed by a warm Southern breeze. I would try to find faces in them. I would lie there and think about all sorts of things – heaven, where it was, what it looked like. I wondered who I was and what I was going to be, and what was I going to do tomorrow, and what was for supper. There seemed to be all the time in the world to do anything – or nothing at all. My roots in Pontotoc still run deep.

One of my great-grandfathers, James Richard Roberson, was a pastor who presided over the First Methodist Church on two different occasions, finally settling there with his wife, Mary Ann Bigham, and their family for the rest of his life.

Another great grandfather, Papa Shannon – Dr. Marcus Lee Shannon – was an optometrist and a staunch leader in the community. He set up shop in 1895, one of the first, if not "the" first, optometrists in Mississippi. That he became an optometrist might have been considered unusual since Papa Shannon had only one good eye. When he was a boy he shot an arrow straight up, and it came down and hit him in his right eye. Doctors replaced it with a glass eye, which fascinated me as a child. He would take it out and let me hold it. No wonder he was always telling me to be careful with a bow and arrow or a BB gun.

Papa Shannon also promised that if I didn't smoke until I was 21, he would give me a gold watch. That made an impression on me. He died when I was 12, so I never got the watch. But just the fact that he promised it was the real gift. I've never smoked.

He was on the board that oversaw the construction of the First Baptist Church building in Pontotoc, still used today as the sanctuary. I was baptized in that church when I was around 12 years old.

Even before all that, when the railroad came to Pontotoc in 1888, Papa Shannon had opened a telephone and telegraph office. He was instrumental in bringing both to Pontotoc County. We had relatives in Tippah County, Union County, Pontotoc County, and Chickasaw County, all of whom helped establish telegraph lines that ran from Tennessee south into those areas of Mississippi.

I was born into a musical family as well as an athletic family, between Tupelo, where Elvis Presley was born, and Oxford, where William Faulkner lived. So I guess you could say I had a head start as a songwriter.

My paternal grandfather, Ira Dexter Weatherly – we called him "Daddy Deck" – was a farmer who wrote gospel songs and sang with a gospel quartet that traveled through north Mississippi and north Alabama on the weekends performing in churches and all-day singings. He was one of the first music teachers in Pontotoc County and held "singing schools" in the summer. His wife, my dad's mother, died when Dad was just a young boy.

My mother and her brothers and sisters, Billy, Jean, Richard, and Mary Ann, could all sing. My dad was a really good singer, too. He sang bass. They would all gather around the old upright piano at Nanny and Daddy James' house on those late Sunday afternoons after an early supper and sing gospel

My dad, Floyd Brandon, Rayburn Lambert

songs. My Uncle Billy's wife, Jane, really knew how to make that piano talk. Sometimes I would try to sing with them, but mostly I was just in the way.

My dad had one brother, Leon, who lived in Pontotoc, and he had three sisters – Louise, Juanita, and Floyce. They lived in other towns, so we didn't get to see them as much. To my knowledge none of them had any musical talent.

Daddy James' store on the town square, called Roberson's Electric Supply, was right next door to Papa Shannon's optometry office and jewelry store. He sold appliances, radios, TVs, record players, and – most importantly to me – records.

As I grew older, I loved to spend time in the back left corner of the store, where racks of phonograph records were displayed. Daddy James let me pick out the records to buy on his monthly trip to Pop Tunes record store in Memphis. When he would return, he'd let me pick out the records I wanted first. Those would include rockabilly, R&B, pop, country, and all the hits of the day. He also brought home some pretty obscure ones that I had asked him to buy for me.

Since he sold them, Daddy James always had the latest stereo record player at his house. I was really lucky to have the newest model and a constant flow of new records to listen to all the time.

Uncle Billy told me that Daddy James installed the first TV antenna on a house in Pontotoc on Thanksgiving Day in 1948. Uncle Billy helped him. When the NBC affiliate from Memphis – the first TV station we could pick up – came on the air, Daddy James put a television in his store window. The sidewalk filled with locals who stopped to take a look at this curious new invention, its small screen and black and white snowy picture fascinating all those peering over and around each other to see what all the fuss was about. On some nights a few of the men would gather at Daddy James' house after supper to sit and talk and watch the test pattern on TV until wrestling came on at 8 o'clock. Some would fall asleep while watching.

He also owned the only public address system in town. When I was 10 or 11 he taught me how to set it up and work it. When it was time for the local elections I'd run it for the candidates who were giving their political speeches, and Daddy James would pay me. That P.A. system came in handy when I later formed my first band. We used it as our sound system.

On the same side of the court square as Papa Shannon's eye clinic and Daddy James' electric supply store was the Joy Theater, one of Pontotoc's two indoor movie houses. I called it the "new show" because it was built later. On Main Street just a couple of blocks away was the "old show" which featured old black and white cowboy movies on Friday nights and Saturday mornings. I spent a lot of my childhood watching those cowboy movies, and they influenced the music I would later write and sing, songs like Gene Autry's "Mexicali Rose" and "You're the Only Star in My Blue Heaven." I learned a lot of cowboy songs watching those old movies. I soaked them up like a sponge. Sometimes I'd come home from the movies singing a new song I'd just heard. Nanny once told me that when I was around five, I would sit on the front steps of her house and make up cowboy songs.

Those simple cowboy movies were a big influence on me in other ways as well. The good guys, like Roy Rogers, Lash LaRue, Gene Autry, Hopalong Cassidy, and Wild Bill Elliott, were always honest, loyal, and truthful and did things the right way. The bad guys always lost in the end. Simple message, but it stuck with me. In today's super-heated media market, some people laugh and poke fun at those black and white Westerns. But they encouraged kids like me to grow up to be like the good guys, with a strong sense of right and wrong. Today's TV heroes are often more complicated, the boundaries between right and wrong not nearly so clear.

Ray Bedingfield has been a close friend of mine since grade school. Every Saturday morning Ray and I and our buddies would go to the Joy Theatre to watch a cowboy movie. We'd stuff ourselves on popcorn and Cokes sitting in the front row. Sometimes we'd wear our holsters and toy guns. One day we were sitting in the first row, Ray had a balloon and was cutting up pretty good. Everybody had their guns out shooting the Indians and bad guys on the screen. Ray kept blowing the balloon up and letting the air out toward the rest of us and it would make this weird, irritating noise. You know what I mean. He did it one too many times and I came across with my gun and there went his middle tooth, right in half. I didn't mean to; it was an accident. He'll tell you to this day he's still got a crown on that tooth. Most of the time we all had fun and came out unscathed.

It wasn't just Westerns. I loved all kinds of movies – comedies, mysteries. I also loved the Technicolor musicals of the 1940s and '50s. The color was a vivid and brilliant tone that you don't see in movies anymore. Going to the show, as we called it, always lifted my spirits. Those early movies had a mystique about them that drew me in. In the darkened theater, new worlds came to life right before my eyes, exciting places so very different from my little town. I sat there and marveled at the magic of movies, mesmerized by the ability to create entire lives on the silver screen.

I thought, "When I'm older I might go to Hollywood and see what they're all about."

In the spring and summer farmers brought their crops to town and sold them out of the backs of wagons and trucks. Men in well-worn overalls and straw hats gravitated to the courthouse square, where they sat on the benches and whittled, traded knives, or just killed some time. And there were always dogs running around.

Years later, I put my memories of that simpler time in a song. It was 1970. I was living in California and thinking of home and "Misty Mississippi Morning" was born.

MISTY MISSISSIPPI MORNING

Rows and rows of houses line the neatly laid out streets
All the yards are silent 'cause the kids are still asleep
The streetlights all grow dimmer as the sun begins to streak across
the haze
The six o'clock whistle tells the town it's time to rise
A distant passing train echoes faintly in reply
People stumble from their beds wiping sleep from their eyes
to start their day

It's a misty Mississippi morning
The dew is still hanging in the air
Sunshine's dripping from the sky like honey
There's not a cloud to be seen anywhere
The breeze seems to blow straight from heaven
Scented with the honeysuckle vine
Those misty Mississippi mornings
Come back to me in pictures and rhymes
To linger soft as summer in my mind

Shadows touch down softly as they skip across the lawns
Playing hide and seek with the brand new silky dawn
If you listen closely you can hear the day's first song
In the morning chimes

The harmony is sung by a peaceful meadowlark
As the picture comes to life dogs begin to run and bark
While the old men sit and whittle on the benches in the park
Just killing time

Many of the songs I wrote were significantly influenced by home, that sense of place you get growing up in a small town with a large and loving family and community. I loved to write about the little meaningful things of life most small town people cherish, universal experiences that can strike a chord in the hearts of people living in a world sometimes left cynical and bruised by the constant changes. I've always remained rooted in the postage stamp world of Pontotoc and my home state of Mississippi.

When I was a small boy, a passenger train called "The Rebel" would leave Tennessee and travel through small country towns down into Mississippi. Late on Friday nights it would arrive in Pontotoc at 11:25 to drop off and pick up passengers and then head on down to New Orleans or Mobile. There was always a crowd waiting to meet the train. It was local entertainment for the townsfolk. A song I wrote in the early 1970s tells how I felt about those special Friday nights.

THE REBEL KEEPS ON ROLLIN'

I remember when I was just a boy
Daddy would take my hand
And say come on son it's Friday night
And the Rebel is gonna roll in
It's gonna bring folks here from Memphis
And take 'em down to Mobile.
Come on let's go down to the depot
And get ourselves a thrill

The Rebel keeps on rollin' down the line, down the line
Ridin' on the rails of yesterday and down the tracks of time
Leaving a string of memories danglin' in my mind
the Rebel keeps on rollin' down the line

Everyone in town would be there
standing out in the cold
listenin' for the whistle and lookin' for the smoke
And when that ol' red streamline
Came rollin' into sight
It was like the 4th of July every Friday night

The Rebel keeps on rollin' down the line, down the line
Ridin' on the rails of yesterday and down the tracks of time
Leaving a string of memories danglin' in my mind
the Rebel keeps on rollin' down the line

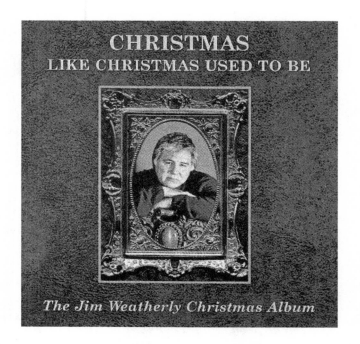

My earliest memories of music were hymns, Sunday School songs, and Christmas songs. My mother took me to Sunday School at an early age and the words of those old Baptist songs stuck with me. "This Little Light of Mine," "Jesus Loves Me," "Deep and Wide." The kinds of songs with words you can't forget, songs that remain special in my southern soul, the kind of music that is with you throughout your life. That's where I heard "Silent Night" and "O Little Town of Bethlehem" at Christmas. Sunday School was also where I met some of my future classmates.

Christmas was always magical to me. It was a warm and happy time with all the decorations and presents under the tree. And family and Nanny's gumdrop trees. And Christmas carols. We always went out in a pasture and cut down our own Christmas tree. I remember one Christmas my dad made a star to put on the top of our tree. I thought that was really special, and later in the early 2000s, I wrote a song about it.

THE STAR AT THE TOP OF THE TREE

I remember a Christmas long ago
We went and chopped our tree down in the snow
We tied it on top of Dad's old Chevrolet
Hauled it home, put it up, began to decorate

Mom and Dad strung all the colored lights
We hung ornaments of every shape and size
There were bells and balls and Santa in his sleigh
And when it was done Dad gave us a gift he'd made

He put a star at the top of the tree
To remind us what Christmas really means
He carved it out of wood, put a small light in the center
He painted it with silver and sprinkled it with glitter
It was just so magical to see
The star at the top of the tree

I can still recall that Christmas Eve
The red ribbon bows and holly leaves
We all made a wish on that star so bright
Then we ate some Christmas cake and all sang Silent Night

He put a star at the top of the tree
To remind us what Christmas really means
He carved it out of wood, put a small light in the center
He painted it with silver and sprinkled it with glitter
It was just so magical to see
The star at the top of the tree

Even now I see the shimmer of that star
A vision that will always be forever in my heart

I remember hearing my dad get up early in the mornings and turn the radio on to gospel music while he dressed for work. He loved The Statesmen Quartet and the Blackwood Brothers Quartet. Gospel music was a really strong influence on me from a young age.

My mother and her sisters, Jean and Mary Ann, had all the latest records by stars of the day like Frank Sinatra, Perry Como, and Frankie Laine (who would record one of my songs – "You're the Best Thing That Ever Happened to Me" – in the 1970s). I used to play those records over and over, losing myself in the music.

When I was in the fifth grade, some of the older guys started getting ukuleles. It looked like a lot of fun so I talked Mom into buying me one. I taught myself to play it. I would take it to school and play it for my classmates during rest period after lunch. I was already preparing for a career in music without even realizing it.

But music wasn't my only interest. Sports were destined to be a big part of my life. Before I started playing organized football, my buddies and I would choose sides and play pickup games on the huge lawn in front of the Pontotoc Community House. For generations it has been a gathering spot, situated next to the old high school and tennis courts and where the city swimming pool was at the town's busiest crossroads, Main and Oxford. Sunday afternoons drew the largest crowds of kids and teenagers for football on the front lawn. It's a longstanding tradition for the town and its people.

It was there on December 7, 1941, in just such a football game that Uncle Billy and some friends were playing on the lawn of the Community House. He told me that a friend of his, J.B. McCullough, drove up, stopped his car and yelled "the Japanese have bombed Pearl Harbor." Billy said they didn't even know where Pearl Harbor was, but they were pretty sure their lives were about to change forever.

3 ——⋙

From Rockabilly to Rock & Roll

When I was in the seventh grade, a friend and football teammate, Jerry Young, played me some songs by a young Memphis singer named Elvis Presley. Songs like "Lawdy Miss Clawdy," "Tryin' to Get to You," "Blue Moon."

"Bug," as we called Jerry, probably didn't know it then and neither did I, but it was one of those life-changing moments for me. I was hooked. I became a huge Elvis fan right then and there and fell in love with his music, especially the rockabilly years when he recorded for Sun Records in Memphis as well as his early years on RCA.

Elvis was born 15 miles away in Tupelo. By the time I heard his records he was living in Memphis, a two-hour drive from Pontotoc. Situated on the bluffs of the Mississippi River, Tennessee's largest city became an important star in the music universe. Sam Phillips had started the Sun Record label, mainly to record black blues artists from around the South, especially Memphis and the

Mississippi Delta. He wanted to capture their raw talent in the most natural setting he could provide. He always said if he could find a white man who could sing like a black man, he could make a million dollars.

Around the country some radio stations in the 1950s had begun to evolve from a big band sound and a more easy listening repertoire to the new phenomenon called rock and roll, which included a lot of music with a black influence. I remember being really excited about these changes. I was not alone. A lot of young people, especially in the South but really all across the country, seemed to feel the same way. Sam Phillips soon found himself riding a comet.

The 1950s became the first decade of rock and roll. Up until that point you couldn't hear "race music," as they called it, on pop or mainstream radio because certain stations wouldn't play black music. After Elvis came along, the dam broke. Suddenly, black artists had no trouble getting on mainstream radio. Chuck Berry, Fats Domino, Little Richard, Ray Charles, as well as groups like the Moonglows, the Flamingos, and the Clovers.

That was when race music became known as rhythm and blues or R&B. But it was all lumped together as rock and roll along with white entertainers like Pat Boone, Connie Francis, Neil Sedaka, Paul Anka, and others. Stations also played exciting records by Sun Records artists Johnny Cash, Jerry Lee Lewis, Carl Perkins, Roy Orbison, and Charlie Rich. This was the music that captivated me and inspired me to try to write songs.

Every day I was becoming more passionate about the new sounds I was hearing. I would listen to WMPS and WHBQ out of Memphis. They were mainstream pop stations that we could pick up on radio in Pontotoc, mainly in the daytime. After school in the mid-1950s I used to watch the Dewey Phillips Show on

WHBQ-TV. Dewey was a wild man disc jockey who played all the great rockabilly and R&B records. Trying to describe Dewey is like trying to describe the wind.

Dewey had a nighttime radio show, "Red, Hot and Blue," but WHBQ radio was hard to pick up at night as far away as Pontotoc. Dewey was the first person to play an Elvis Presley record, "That's All Right" written by Arthur Crudup. It created a manic response among teenagers in Memphis and north Mississippi before anyone else knew who Elvis was. Music would never be the same.

Even before my teenage years, almost every night I would lie in bed and listen to WLAC on the little plastic Emerson radio on my nightstand. It was a powerful 50,000-watt station out of Nashville that captured the imaginations of teenagers across the Mid-South. Those little radios were our smart phones.

Legendary DJs like John R, Gene Nobels, and Hoss Allen played great R&B and blues artists like Howlin' Wolf, Big Joe Turner, B.B. King, Ray Charles, and Ike Turner. They also played songs like "Rocket 88" by Jackie Brenston and his Delta Cats, considered by music historians to be the first rock and roll record in the history of the music business.

Soon, I found it wasn't enough to listen to the new music. I wanted to make my own.

The Empaladors playing at the Community House. Nanny and Daddy James are at the far left

4 ——⚬

First Guitar

I got my first guitar for Christmas when I was 12. It was a Sears and Roebuck Silvertone electric hollow body and it was beautiful with those Christmas tree lights shining on it. I was sure proud of it. I started right away trying to teach myself to play. Having already learned to play the ukulele was a big help. I got a Mel Bay guitar chord book and experimented with different finger positions, trying to learn new chords that weren't in the book. I learned to play a lot of different chords by experimenting, which eventually helped me in my songwriting.

My dad, being an electrician, made my first amplifier out of an old 1940s Philco tabletop cathedral radio. It worked pretty well but was kind of hard to carry around since the guitar cord was soldered directly to the radio speaker. I couldn't plug my guitar in and unplug it. When the next Christmas rolled around, I told my mom and dad I wanted a new amplifier. Dad told me it was too expensive. I was heartbroken. But on Christmas morning, there it was under the tree, a brand new amplifier. I was jumping for joy.

Mom and Dad never pushed me toward music but they were always supportive. Dad once drove me to Sherman, 15 miles from Pontotoc, on a slick and muddy dirt road in a hard driving rain to be in a talent contest. I never forgot that. To me it was a sign of his approval. And his love.

At 15 I found another guitar I wanted, a copper colored metallic, solid body Harmony electric. I bought it from Papa Shannon's store, which sold musical instruments by catalog. I spent hours trying to come up with unique chords. I mowed yards to pay for it. Fifty cents a yard with a hand push mower and some were big yards. My mom helped me some, but mainly I worked for it. My parents taught me at an early age that working for it was the way you got money.

My dad running at Warrior Field

5 ——✸

Football

Warrior Field, where Pontotoc's football teams have played since the 1930s, is nestled in a shallow valley in the heart of downtown. It's almost as if the businesses and buildings stand looking down on the field of battle on those special Friday nights.

I remember the tall trees surrounding the field, their leaves rustling in the late summer breeze and falling softly to the ground as the season changed to autumn. It really is one of Mississippi's unique high school football venues.

We used to call it the "dust bowl," with its large patches of red clay dirt mixed with sand where all the grass had worn away from years of hard-fought battles. When you got tackled, you'd end up spitting out a mouthful of that red sand.

In the summers before I played high school football, I would watch the men from the Pontotoc Electric Power Association work at the football field in preparation for a new season. My dad was one of those men. He and his co-workers would put in new poles, hang new lights, and replace old bulbs in time for the first game.

I started out for "Pee Wee" football in the sixth grade, and I was so excited to finally play on a real team. Coach Carl Lowery, my seventh grade coach, used to tell people I was a natural. He put me at quarterback and he put in the Split T like Coach John Vaught ran at Ole Miss. We won all seven games that year.

The next year when I was in the eighth grade, I went out for high school football in the spring. It turned out to be a very humbling experience. I was the only one on the field with an old black leather helmet from the 1930s. They still had a few of those around and I ended up with one. Everyone else had new shiny white plastic helmets. I wasn't much more than a small tackling dummy that spring.

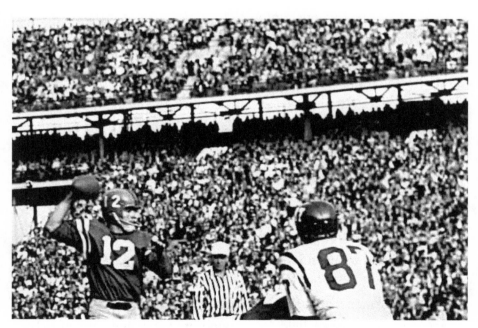

Pee wee football, 6th grade

6 ——⚬

The Fall of '57

Homecoming at Pontotoc in the fall of 1957 arrived with all the usual anticipation and high spirits. We were hosting Little Ten Conference rival, New Albany, from just up Highway 15. I was a ninth grade quarterback on the varsity that season. If I got in a game at all, it would likely be late in the game.

My head coach was Jim Butler, who played football for Pontotoc in the early 1940s with some of my family, including my dad, and then played at Ole Miss. He coached at New Albany before coming back to Pontotoc, so people on both sides of the field knew him well. He was a tough but fair disciplinarian and well liked by all of his players. I had a deep respect and affection for the man I called "Coach" until the day he died, and he had a positive influence on me that has lasted throughout my life.

That season I mainly played on the freshman team. We competed against other schools' ninth grade squads during midweek games, but I was on the sidelines with the varsity every Friday night for high school games. My dad was always there, watching every play. He would nervously pace up and down the field following the action. Sometimes he would carry the first down chains as part of the crew of officials. My mom was in the stands. My mom was always in the stands.

High school football

In a real boost to my self-esteem, I was finally wearing one of those white plastic helmets like everyone else.

We led New Albany comfortably in the fourth quarter when Coach Butler began to make substitutions, looking up and down the bench for replacements. "Jimmy, go on in." I quickly put on my helmet and raced onto the field. I weighed all of 130 pounds but I was ready to play.

After handing the ball off for a couple of plays to get used to being in the game, I rolled out to my right, looked downfield, spotted an open receiver, and released the football into the crisp autumn air. It was complete to my teammate Johnny Seals in the end zone. I had thrown the first touchdown pass of my high school career and my dad was right there on the sidelines to see it. I was excited and so was he.

We won 32-7. Dad and I talked about the game, and especially that touchdown, after we got home. He had taught me to throw a football, and watching me throw that first touchdown was a special moment for both of us.

There was more football to be played. Up next was Starkville. They were always the giant, the team that set the Little Ten Conference standard basically every season. As usual, everybody was looking forward to that one.

Wednesday of the following week seemed like a normal school day at Pontotoc High, except that it was Starkville week and that had everybody even more pumped up for football. Sometime late that morning I was called out of class to go to the principal's office. That was unusual, and I had no idea why.

Walking down the long hallway I spotted Daddy James in the doorway. He had never come to talk to me at school before. When I got closer, he immediately said, "Your dad's been in an accident."

I was stunned. The first thing out of my mouth was "Is he dead?" I don't really know why I jumped to that conclusion. He was noncommittal. "They don't know."

Daddy James and I went next door to the elementary school to break the news to my two younger sisters and to pick them up. Sherrie, my oldest sister, was in the fourth grade. She was eight, almost nine. She looked up and saw me at the door of the classroom. Daddy James was in the hallway behind me. She says she still remembers my words, "Daddy has been hurt real bad."

Elise, my youngest sister who was six, was on the playground when we went to pick her up. None of us knew what to think but we were more than concerned. We drove to Daddy James' house, about a minute away. When we got there, several people were milling around looking sad. I don't remember who it was, but I think it was my mom who told me my dad was dead.

We were in disbelief. He was just 34 years old, full of life.

In an instant on a crisp autumn Mississippi morning, Wednesday, October 17, 1957, I became the man of the house for Mom, my two younger sisters, and my little brother, who was just a year old. I was 14. My dad had been killed working on a power line north of town, not all that far from our house on Warren Street.

A few years earlier he had left Roberson's Electric Supply to go to work for the Pontotoc Electric Power Association. Daddy James simply wasn't able to pay him the kind of wage he could earn working for the power company. With a wife and four children to support, he needed the money. So he left the family business. It was a move that would haunt my granddad the rest of his life.

My dad's coworkers, a close-knit group, were devastated. When he was electrocuted, some of them tried for hours to revive him. It was no use.

Uncle Billy drove over from Baldwyn, where he lived, and took my mother to the site of the accident. After that, he drove her to the funeral home. Billy remembers Mom asking the funeral home people to check Dad's body for life one more time to make sure, that sometimes mistakes are made. They did as she requested.

I didn't go to my dad's funeral. I just couldn't. Mom said it was okay. It was the first terribly tragic thing that had ever happened in my life and it shook me to my core. I was in a state of shock and didn't know how to handle it.

My dad was so young and vibrant. I had a lot of trouble coming to terms with the fact that my world would never be the same. I was worried about my mom and my two younger sisters. But I was especially concerned about my little brother, Shan. I just kept thinking that he'd never get to know his dad. My dad had taught me how to throw a football and Shan would never have that experience.

It seemed like the whole town was in mourning. Even the rival New Albany football team made the trip to the funeral to pay respects to my dad and our family.

At the end of the school year, the football page in the 1957-58 Pontotoc Warrior yearbook was dedicated to Dad's memory, a sign of just how much people respected him. The following year a football award was named in his honor – The Ike Weatherly Memorial Sportsmanship Award, presented at each year's football banquet. I was honored to be the first recipient.

The months ahead were challenging. Mom struggled to raise four young children without a husband and without much money. She began to suffer severe bouts of depression and panic attacks. She was a strong-willed lady and we always knew where we stood with Mom, but at times it all got to be too much for her.

Our family's tragedies didn't end there. A year later, my mom's sister, Jean, would deal with a similar tragedy. Her husband, Lamar Wood, was killed in an auto accident. It was another terrible event that shook the lives of our family, but the bond between my mom and Jean grew even stronger. They turned to each other for support, and that was the case for the rest of their lives. In a situation similar to my mom's, Jean was now raising three young children alone – all boys, Tommy, Randy, and Terry.

We were always really close to Jean and her boys, who were

closer in age to Sherrie, Elise, and Shan than to me. We all became one big family. Daddy James and Nanny did all they could to help, financially and any other way they could.

Worry, stress, and even guilt from not being able to take better care of his family took its toll on my granddad's health. The summer before I entered college as a freshman in 1961, Daddy James died of a heart attack at age 60.

My mom was trying to be both mother and father now. She was 34, had two young girls and a one-year-old boy to raise – and a teenager, me. I'm sure she wondered how she was going to do it. She had never been as strict as my dad, but now she was trying to be. We had a few arguments over that.

Sometimes when Mom and I would get into an argument, I'd pick her up and sit her on top of the refrigerator and she couldn't get down. Eventually she'd start laughing and I would walk away like I was going to leave her up there. She would yell, "Get me down from here, James Dexter!" and she'd be laughing. I would start laughing, too, and the argument would soon be forgotten. And yes, I would get her down from the top of the refrigerator.

I was growing up and football was as important to me as ever. In my junior year, one of the highlights of my high school career came in a big showdown with Starkville for the conference championship. It was the biggest game any of us had ever played in.

My teammate Don Zimmerman said there had to be 5,000 people there. Both teams were undefeated. It was our last conference game. Whoever won would be Little Ten Conference champions.

Don recalls standing by Coach Butler on the sidelines when he turned to him and said, "Go get you one."

"He told me to tell Jimmy I was going to go five yards deeper than what we'd been practicing. Jimmy said, 'Got it.' Jimmy threw it and I caught that thing and nobody caught me," Don recalled.

"We beat them 20-0. It was the first time Pontotoc had beaten Starkville in almost 20 years. We were undefeated, untied, and champions of the Little Ten Conference."

My senior year we almost had another perfect season. It was Starkville, our old nemesis, that tied us.

With me starting at quarterback, we wound up with a 24-2-1 record for my three seasons of high school. It was a really special time for Pontotoc football.

I was named first-team All-Little Ten Conference both my junior and senior years in football and also in basketball and was named All-State in football my junior year and honorable mention All-State my senior year. I was also selected to play in the Mississippi High School All-Star football game in Jackson, which wrapped up my high school career. But I was happier about winning two Little Ten Conference titles in a row.

In the 1990s we had a reunion from that championship season and I got to visit with my old high school teammates. One of them came up to me and said, "Remember me?" Well, I knew his name as well as I knew my own, but it just wouldn't come to mind. I stumbled and fumbled trying to recall it when he said, "Billy Sewell. I was your center our senior year." I said, "Billy, if you'd have turned around and bent over, I'd have known exactly who you are."

Left to right: Danny Weatherly, Ray Bedingfield, Buddy Eubank, LaVaughn McGregor, Jackie Gillespie, Jerry Young, and me — The Empaladors, first band

7 ──⤳

The Empaladors

When I first started trying to write songs, I was in the sixth or seventh grade. It was something I felt compelled to do. I would try to write something like I heard on the radio. I liked writing ballads best because I didn't have to move my fingers as fast when playing my guitar. I really enjoyed being creative and being in control of what I was doing, even if the songs weren't very good. Back then I thought they were. I felt like I was accomplishing something even if no one would ever hear them. It was my own little private world. The fact that I really enjoyed it was what kept pushing me to do it. As a matter of fact, I couldn't not do it. I never imagined then that millions of people would someday hear my songs.

I was in the ninth grade when I formed my first band, not long after my dad died. I got together with my good friend Jerry Young, who had introduced me to Elvis' music, and we started jamming. He was a great self-taught rockabilly piano player. Then I talked my next-door neighbor, Buddy Eubank, into buying a used set of drums advertised in the newspaper. We found out Buddy had a timing problem, so we got Danny Weatherly (no relation) to play Buddy's drums. That didn't last too long, even though he could keep time. Shortly after that we found a talented guy named Stony Sappington. He went to school with us at Pontotoc and played snare and bass drum in the high school band. He had his own set of drums, one of those red sparkle sets. Having drums and a real drummer made us look and sound like a real band.

We soon had a five-piece band. We named ourselves Jimmy Weatherly and the Empaladors and started playing high school assemblies. Don't ask me where I got that name. It just sounded good to me. It had a musical ring to it.

Now that we had our band together, I thought it would be cool if we added some background singers. Ray Bedingfield remembers when he was one of those back-up singers.

"I was in there for just a brief period, until Jimmy learned I couldn't sing," Ray said. "We had a high school assembly performance one time and Jim told me to lean over the microphone and say something like 'da, da, da, da, dum.' So during the performance I leaned over and I forgot what to say. I think my band career ended shortly after that. I was a doo-whopper for just a short time, but I have fun with it by saying I was in Jim Weatherly's band."

I never really considered myself a great musician. I couldn't read or write music. But I compensated with imagination and a good ear. I could hear everything inside my head – sounds, harmonies, all the different instruments. That's how I could sometimes tell the musicians what to play or at least what I wanted to hear. I just had a natural ability to put it all together based on what I was hearing in my mind.

I started out playing the guitar in my first band but, like Buddy, I always felt like I had a little timing problem. I couldn't keep time like I wanted to while singing. So when we eventually got a real guitar player, I quit playing guitar when I was performing.

The Empaladors rockin' out

Ray Bedingfield and me, football teammates — peewee, high school, and college

8 —⟨⟩

Pontotoc Power Association

Living in a small town, everybody basically knew what was going on with everyone else. Sometimes her struggles were embarrassing for my mom. More than once, paying the bills was a challenge. My brother Shan remembers an employee of the Pontotoc Power Association where my dad had worked coming to the door and, in a polite and apologetic way, telling Mom the electric bill was past due, and the power would be cut off if it wasn't paid. That had to be tough for him to say and for her to hear, especially since Dad was killed working for them.

Before our junior year in high school, Ray Bedingfield and I went to work for the Pontotoc Power Association as a summer job. My mom had talked them into letting us work there. They paid us one dollar an hour each, $40 for a forty-hour work week. We didn't have a clue what we were supposed to do, but my dad's friends quickly whipped us into shape. They told us we were grunts, meaning we did whatever they told us to do.

We walked from pole to pole, laying wire on the ground so it was there when the linemen needed it. We got them whatever tools they needed. We never climbed poles or got near hot wires. They called Ray "Thunder" and I was "Lightning." Ray remembers, "Jim's dad's co-workers took really good care of us."

We had to go to Corinth one day to do some work. Corinth is about sixty miles northeast of Pontotoc. While we were there we spotted a boat store. So on a break Ray and I went in to take a look at what we couldn't afford. We found an old used motorboat without a motor. It looked like an old speedboat with a planked wooden hull. The salesman only wanted a hundred dollars for it. We thought, man, we could clean this up, repair it and paint it, buy us a used motor and have us a nice little boat for skiing or fishing. Suddenly the money we were making was burning holes in our pockets. It didn't matter that we rarely went skiing or never fished. It was the thought of ownership that mattered.

So Ray and I coughed up 50 bucks apiece and bought the boat. When we got off work we went back to Corinth to get it, towed it back to Pontotoc, and stored it in an old shed behind Ray's house. Boy, we were proud of that thing. We'd leave work every day and go directly to Ray's house and start sanding.

One night around midnight, I heard the urgent wail of the fire siren. In a small town like Pontotoc, people would get out of bed, get in their cars in their bathrobes or pajamas, and drive to see where the fire was.

I got up and went out in the yard to see if I could spot a glow in the sky. I looked over toward Ray's house, which wasn't too far from mine, and there was this reddish-yellow glow. I said, "Nah, it can't be." I went back inside and went back to bed. It wasn't too long before the telephone rang. It was Ray.

"Jimmy, you got a bucket?" he said.

"Why?" I asked.

He said, "You need to come over here and get what's left of your half of this boat."

Ray always had a great sense of humor, sometimes at the strangest times. We had left some oily rags lying around in the shed and somehow they'd caught fire and burned it down with our cherished boat inside.

We hated losing 50 dollars apiece that we had worked a whole week to earn. It had been a lot of hard work trying to salvage that boat and we were still nowhere close. Now it was gone.

The Empaladors enjoyed playing for school assemblies. There weren't any clubs for bands to play like there were later. So our first real paying job was at the Pontotoc VFW, which was off limits to anyone but military veterans and their spouses. That was before my junior year. I think Mom talked them into letting us play. It paid us 40 dollars for the group of five. That's eight dollars each for four hours with a 15-minute break every hour. That was two dollars an hour, which was a dollar an hour more than I made sweating in the hot sun for the Pontotoc Power Association. In the mind of a 17-year-old boy, this was a windfall. I got to thinking that maybe music could be a good deal financially.

We played from eight o'clock until midnight on a Saturday. It wasn't long before we were playing once or twice a month. The dancers seemed to really enjoy our music. We were a rock & rolling, rowdy, walking jukebox, even if we did sound a little bit on the ragged side. We played mostly rockabilly, ballads, and a few updated standards. We began playing community houses and high school dances in gymnasiums and at National Guard armories in different towns around Pontotoc for high school kids. We felt like we were on our way.

I was a high school senior when our band played a Friday night dance at the community house right after a home football game. Coach Butler didn't like that too much, but we won the game. I just couldn't see why it was a problem. But I was a young man in a hurry. A lot of people thought my playing in a rock and roll band was just plain crazy and would get in the way of football. Coach Butler, exasperated, finally said to me, "Why don't you hang up that guitar and do something worthwhile?"

About 30 miles south of Pontotoc down Highway 15 in Houston sits a powerful radio station. WCPC was owned and operated by brothers Ralph and Robin Mathis. Robin said it was the first 50,000-watt radio station in Mississippi. It was popular and the signal came in crystal clear throughout north Mississippi.

The station had a Sunday afternoon show called "Open House" and bands from all over north Mississippi would perform. Each band had a 15-minute segment.

My band and I drove down there a lot of Sunday afternoons when we were in high school. Robin said our band was among the most popular on the show. Because of the reach of the WCPC signal, a lot more people were beginning to know who we were and becoming fans. Sometimes after the show, Ralph would take the whole group to a local café and buy us hamburgers. I thought that was really cool. No one had ever bought me a hamburger before.

One of the updated standards we played on WCPC was a song called "Suddenly There's a Valley." It had been a pop hit for a singer named Gogi Grant in 1955 and we worked up our own version. Ralph really liked it and suggested we go into the studio after hours and record it just to play on WCPC.

Ralph and Robin both began to play it on their morning shows, and people started calling in and requesting it. They thought it was actually a record. It became so popular that it rose to number one on WCPC's hit list charts and stayed there for several weeks. We thought we'd made the big time with a number one song on WCPC. I used to get up in the morning and turn on the radio before I went to school and listen for them to play it. That was a huge thrill – me singing on the radio.

As we gained more confidence, we decided to try to get on the George Klein Show. George was a Memphis disc jockey, who had a Saturday afternoon show called "Dance Party" on WHBQ-TV that featured bands and recording artists in Memphis and surrounding areas.

Memphis was really the big time for us. People in several surrounding states throughout the Mid-South were now watching and hearing us.

We did George's show three or four times, and it was always a big deal. George and I became friends and have stayed in touch through the years. A few years ago he called me and asked if I would do an interview on his Friday afternoon show on the Elvis channel on Sirius XM radio. I've done that several times now.

George Klein is one of the longtime beloved personalities of the Memphis music scene, and he and Elvis Presley were close friends. As a matter of fact, Elvis was best man in George's wedding.

9 ———❧

Elvis

As time moved on, I continued to be more and more influenced by Elvis Presley. I was blown away by the knowledge that someone born not more than 20 minutes from my hometown could change the world and its culture with his music.

It's hard to overstate the impact he had on me. I bought all of his records and saw all of his movies. I've read almost every important book there is on Elvis, some of them twice. Even his name sounds and looks like a rock and roll name.

And the way he sang, at a time when no one else sang like that, made it a brand new, exciting kind of music. Part of his appeal was the way he moved when he sang. It was pure raw feeling and emotion mixed with a youthful innocence. It was almost like he had come from another planet. He changed our music and our culture forever. Decades after his death, his impact continues to be felt worldwide.

In 1956, when he came back to Tupelo to play at the Mississippi-

Alabama Fair and Dairy Show in his hometown, I was 13. I begged my mom and dad to take me or let me go with someone else. They said "No" and that was that. It was one of the biggest disappointments of my life.

I credit Elvis Presley as being the one person directly responsible for my career in the music business. His music had set my world on fire. My biggest regret is that he never got around to recording one of my songs.

10 —⁊⁊

College Recruiting

Meanwhile, my other love – football – was about to take over my life for a while. Unlike so many other Ole Miss players, I didn't grow up thinking about playing there. No one had ever told me that I was good enough. Coaches didn't go around hyping players about how good they were in those days, so I really had no barometer.

I just accepted it and didn't think about it – until after football season my senior year in high school. Then everything changed.

It started with an unexpected knock on our door. There, standing on our front porch, was Tom Swayze, the Ole Miss baseball coach and main football recruiter. It's pretty well documented he was the first person in the Southeastern Conference to have the role as head recruiter for a football program. That's how progressive head coach John Vaught was with his plan to develop the Ole Miss program into one of the best in the nation beginning in the late 1940s. Coach Swayze was the man who scoured the state to find the big, fast, and versatile players who made those Ole Miss teams of the 1950s and 1960s some of the best in the nation.

He sat down in our living room like he'd always lived there, smiled at Mom and me and said he wanted me to consider playing football at Ole Miss. You could have knocked me over with a feather. His visit was the first time I knew Ole Miss was even interested. It felt good to be wanted, especially by a school I had always liked.

Later on I got a call from Buster Poole, an assistant football coach with the Rebels, who wanted to take my teammate Ray Bedingfield and me to lunch. We went to a place called the Cotton Bowl in Pontotoc. While we were eating he told us Coach Vaught wanted us both to play for him at Ole Miss.

Recruiting was nothing like today's hyper publicity and ever-increasing pressure, starting as early as your freshman year in high school or even before. It was a fairly quiet process for just about everybody back then.

Ray and I immediately committed. I finally thought maybe this means I am good enough. I had gotten some letters from other universities like LSU, Tulane and Mississippi State.

Mississippi State finally offered me a scholarship, but I had already made up my mind to go to Ole Miss. Those were the only two football scholarship offers I had.

I didn't know it until later, but I apparently also had an opportunity to play college basketball. Uncle Billy was a longtime friend of Babe McCarthy, Mississippi State's head basketball coach. They had coached together at Baldwyn High in northeast Mississippi.

Coach McCarthy told Billy he was going to recruit me to play basketball for Mississippi State, which had a really good program then. Billy told him, "I think you'll be wasting your time. Jimmy says he's going to play football at Ole Miss."

He was right. There was no way I was going to turn down a chance to play quarterback for the Rebels.

I graduated from Pontotoc High in the spring of 1961. It had been almost four years since I'd lost my dad. Life hadn't always been easy for our family as we tried to cope emotionally and financially. Now I was heading off to college. But it was only 30 miles away. My mom was happy about that. And the football scholarship would help offset the costs for a family struggling to make ends meet.

Scoring two points in a high school game against West Point

Perry Lee Dunn, Coach Vaught, and me

11 ——✥

Ole Miss

"The University is buildings, trees, and people. Ole Miss is mood, emotion, and personality. One is physical, the other spiritual. One is tangible, the other intangible. The University is respected, but Ole Miss is loved...The University is geographical, but Ole Miss is universal...The University gives a diploma and regretfully terminates tenure, but one never graduates from Ole Miss."
—*Frank Everett, Ole Miss, B.A. 1932, LL.B. 1934*

I was now an Ole Miss football player. But deep down, I still wasn't at all sure if I could measure up. Even though I was good at sports and played in a rock and roll band, I'd always had a real insecure streak and needed reassurance. Sometimes not getting it got the best of me.

I got to Ole Miss in late summer for my freshman year. I checked in at Miller Hall, the athletic dorm. The fairly new red brick building was packed with new recruits introducing themselves to each other and finding roommates. Mine was halfback Raymond Morgan from Grenada, who I'd played against in high school.

After checking into our rooms, we all went over to the Student Union in the heart of the campus where the varsity players were waiting for us, clippers in hand. We knew what was about to happen. It was a ritual, a rite of passage for freshmen players.

One by one on a grassy area across the street from the Union they began to shave our heads in full view of everybody passing by. This was the tradition, and it was our turn. But they wanted more from me than hair. My musical reputation must have preceded me, because after the haircuts the varsity players all sat down together on the grass and made me sing for them.

It was a little awkward and embarrassing, but it was something I had to do or they'd put me through some kind of real torture – like maybe shining shoes or something. I think they thought I would try to get out of it, but I sang for them and after that they didn't bother me as much.

At times during my freshman year, my musical services would be required by some of the varsity players. Kenny Dill, an All-American center I played against in high school, and Whaley Hall, an All-American guard, would call me to their room at night to sing them to sleep. So would running back Billy Sumrall and lineman Bobby Robinson. If I tried to leave before they were totally asleep, they would call me back in and make me keep singing. Sometimes they would even call their girlfriends on the phone and make me sing to them. It was really no big deal and I actually didn't mind doing it. And besides, it was a way for me to get on the good side of some of the varsity players, and that was important.

NCAA rules allowed for an unlimited number of signees in those days. There must have been 40 or more players in my freshman class. And 17 of us were quarterbacks. By the second year some had left the program and some had moved to other positions, a trademark of the Vaught program – sign the best players and put them where they could help the most.

I always thought you had to be great to be an Ole Miss quarterback. I just never thought of myself that way. Besides, it was a big difference between playing for Pontotoc and playing for Ole Miss, known to sports writers at the time as "Quarterback U."

Playing for the same college team as legends like Eagle Day or Jake Gibbs or Charlie Conerly just never crossed my mind. It seemed like Ole Miss always had great quarterbacks that were All-SEC or All-American. They were celebrities and I was in awe of all of them.

Back-to-School Dance

Thursday, August 29, 1963

9:00 – 1:00

DREW YOUTH CENTER

MUSIC BY

Jim Weatherly and The Vegas

Casual $2.00 Stag or Drag

This invitation arrived at the Drew, Mississippi, home of Archie Manning and his sister, Pam, and was kept by their mother for years

A few years after I played, Archie Manning became one of those Mississippi kids who grew up to be a great Ole Miss quarterback. When he was in high school, Archie idolized Ole Miss' quarterbacks. "Those Ole Miss quarterbacks were my heroes and Jimmy Weatherly was one of them." Archie told me he remembers driving "all the way from Yazoo City to Tunica" to hear our band play.

"My memory of Jimmy Weatherly and the Vegas is if I knew he was playing, I definitely wanted to go," Archie said. "That was pretty cool to me."

The John Vaught years at Ole Miss included three national championships and six Southeastern Conference titles. Ole Miss practically always ended up in a bowl. And in those days there were only eight or ten. It seemed like no season was complete without a New Year's Day Sugar Bowl game in New Orleans, a favorite destination of Ole Miss students and fans alike.

The Ole Miss Rebels were a household name to those who followed college football. I was three years old when Coach Vaught arrived in Oxford. In those days coaches seemed to stay a lot longer at one school, especially if they were having success. Vaught was named head coach in 1947, and he finished up his coaching career in 1973 with a 38-10 win against Mississippi State.

I was in awe of Coach Vaught. The moment I first saw him when I arrived on campus, I was more than a little intimidated. I'd heard his name since I was a little kid. He was a legend in the football world of the South, as well as all across the nation.

One thing that always impressed me was that Coach Vaught always spoke very softly. I don't ever remember him raising his voice to any of his players. Yet his mere presence was so overwhelming that when I met him, it was kind of like meeting John Wayne, who I later met in Los Angeles at RCA recording studios and once in Nashville at a party.

Coach Vaught had this classic, rugged face that looked like it should be carved on the side of a mountain. He was a true gentleman and one of the greatest football minds to ever coach the game. I'm very proud to be a part of his legacy.

When we started practice that first fall, I quickly found myself in competition with a whole slew of other freshman quarterbacks. Back then freshmen had their own team. NCAA rules didn't allow them to play with the varsity. That didn't change until the early 1970s.

As the hot sweltering days of late summer two-a-day drills wore on, some of that year's quarterback crop were culled out and moved to other positions. Overnight, they became defensive backs, wide receivers, or running backs. I managed to stay at quarterback. But I was still fifth or sixth down the roster. I carefully studied my competition as they ran plays and passing drills. For the first time, I began to think to myself, "Maybe I do belong here."

There were some good quarterbacks, but I didn't see anyone that I thought was that much better than me. I began to think maybe I'd been selling myself short.

I worked really hard to get noticed, but I got the distinct feeling that Coach J.W. "Wobble" Davidson, the hard-nosed freshmen coach, just didn't like me very much.

Wobble Davidson had played for Ole Miss during the early 1940s on some of the most successful Rebel teams up until that time. He had served as a Marine in World War II and was a tough, strict, demanding coach who, I assume, didn't care much for me playing music in a rock & roll band, although he never said it. I just felt like I was being overlooked or he didn't want to give me a shot at winning the quarterback position. Or maybe he just thought I wasn't good enough. I never was really sure.

At the time, folks of his age were often suspicious of anyone and anything connected to rock and roll. But I never played with my band during any football season at Ole Miss. Never! I knew better than to do that. After the season and in the summers, at times I did. Football wasn't a year long business like it is today, at least for the players.

Our freshman team played three games that season. The first was against the LSU freshmen in Oxford. Coach Wobble kept me on the bench. He could make a guy feel real insecure. We won 13-6.

The second game was against Vanderbilt, another home game. That day was a turning point in my Ole Miss football career.

Coach Vaught and the varsity sat in the stands watching us play while waiting for buses to pick them up for a road trip.

We had been struggling and couldn't seem to mount much of an offensive attack. Vanderbilt was ahead 6-0 late in the second quarter when Coach Wobble looked at me sitting on the bench and said, "Go on in."

I hadn't been real sure he would ever play me. Without hesitation I jumped up, grabbed my helmet and ran onto the field. I figured this was my chance. "It's now or never." So I decided to try to take advantage of the situation.

I basically threw away the game plan. If I was going down, I was going down swinging. It seemed like we'd tried everything else so I started calling short, drop-back passes, not necessarily a staple of Ole Miss football. We were more of a sprint-out passing team. Left to Allen Brown, right to Billy Carl Irwin. We moved quickly down the field. We mixed in some running plays and got down to Vandy's six-yard line. I called a sprint-out pass to the left. With no receiver open, I tucked the ball under my arm and ran it in for a touchdown. After a missed extra point we were tied 6-6 at halftime, but that play had given us the momentum and the confidence we needed to start the second half.

We wound up winning 52-6.

I had another touchdown on a one-yard sneak, as well as a five-yard touchdown pass to end Kenny Smith. I had proven I could play.

And, most importantly, Coach Vaught had witnessed it.

The third and last game of our freshman season was at in-state rival Mississippi State. It was a dark, cloudy, depressing day in Starkville, and I hated to play on that kind of day. I always felt a little out of sync, like my biorhythms were off or something.

Coach Wobble told me I was going to start at quarterback. I was shocked.

I struggled to get the team moving, but I wasn't having a good day. It seemed like nothing I called worked. So I was benched. I was really disappointed because I'd had such a good game the week before. State scored three touchdowns in the first half but couldn't cross the goal line again. We finally got going and scored twice in the third quarter with someone else at quarterback. That was all we could muster. Not a very upbeat note to end the season on. (Pardon the pun.)

Freshman football players weren't allowed to have cars on campus. So when summer rolled around and I was no longer a freshman, I bought a used car, a black 1957 four-door Bel Air Chevrolet for the grand sum of $500. I called it the black bomb. It had a floor stick shift, and there was a big hole in the floorboard so wide you could see the ground. But that made it special. I'll bet not many other cars had that feature.

Me with Coach Vaught

12 —⚬⚬

Varsity Football

Coach Vaught had a practice system where the first team wore red jerseys. The second team wore blue, the third green, and the fourth orange. Before and during games he would say, "Red team offense starts," or "Blue team defense go in," etc. He had everything down to an exact science and had been having great success for years with the way he ran his program.

As we got close to the start of spring practice before my sophomore year, I still didn't know where I stood. Still nagged by my own insecurities, I thought I was probably fifth or sixth down the roster of quarterbacks, maybe about to be redshirted.

On a bulletin board in the athletic cafeteria in Miller Hall, Coach Vaught posted which players were on which teams – red, blue, green, orange. One day I walked in and looked at the bulletin board. The teams had just been posted and, much to my surprise, I was listed on the blue team at quarterback. I was moving up to second team varsity for spring practice.

That told me that my guitar playing was of no concern to Coach Vaught. He believed in me as a player and a person and was giving me a chance.

Coach Vaught had decided to move Perry Lee Dunn, a big, talented quarterback from Natchez who was a year ahead of me, to fullback for the 1962 season. With senior and co-captain Glynn Griffing at Red team quarterback, Perry Lee was just too good an athlete to sit on the bench for any length of time, and at fullback he would give us added strength along with Buck Randall, Freddie Roberts, and Frank Kinard. I would be Glynn's back-up.

"Jim could run and throw the ball well and handled the quarterback duties admirably well," said Freddie Roberts, a junior at the time. "He knew the game. He practiced hard. He was a good teammate and he wanted to win. He wasn't a prima donna type. Jimmy went about his business. Went to class. Good student."

And something else, too.

"He always had a real interest in music. We can all see why now."

13 — ❧

The Beginning of a Band

In the fall of 1961, Pat Kincade arrived at Ole Miss as a freshman from his Mississippi Delta hometown of Clarksdale. One spring day in 1962, he walked into Miller Hall looking for Wayne Harris, a friend from high school who was on the freshman football squad. Pat was not a football player. He was a guitar player.

Pat said the dorm seemed deserted. He looked for a directory. No luck. Then he started wandering the halls until he found an open door. As fate would have it, it was my room. He poked his head in and asked where to find Wayne Harris and I told him.

When he turned to leave I said, "Wait a minute, don't you play guitar?"

Pat said he did, wondering how I knew that. I asked him if he would listen to some of my songs on my reel-to-reel tape recorder.

"The guy sounded just like Elvis Presley," Pat recalls. "I went, 'Wow, this is really good.' Great voice. Songs are great.

"When I walked into his room, Jimmy stood up, stuck his

hand out and said 'Hi, I'm Jimmy Weatherly.' That impressed me. A lot of guys I met that first year of college didn't do that and subconsciously it had a negative impression. I felt at home. We sat there for a couple of hours talking and listening to music."

It was the beginning of a lifelong friendship. We just seemed to click. Over the course of the next few weeks, Pat and I got together and worked up a few songs.

Pat recalled how we "would work up the top twenty songs of that time, the top fifty, which was basically rockabilly and late '50s and early '60s rock and roll." On weekends he would go back to Clarksdale and teach the songs to his band.

"Later, I got a call from a lady who wanted to know if my band would play at her daughter's graduation party at the country club in Clarksdale," Pat said. "I said 'Sure.' Keep in mind Jimmy had never met the band before. I booked us for like a hundred dollars. Jimmy had a little old amplifier and a microphone. We set that thing in a metal chair, and we played the dance."

Then something happened.

"Girls went crazy," Pat said. "Thought we were awesome. We didn't even have a name. I'd always say 'Jimmy Weatherly and the….whatever we called ourselves in those days.' After all, he was the Ole Miss quarterback. And he was our lead singer."

Later, Pat started driving over to Pontotoc and occasionally playing guitar with my band, too.

Throughout this whole time there was a football-music debate going on among Ole Miss fans. At Pontotoc and Ole Miss, there had always been some people who felt my music got in the way of my sports.

In a June 11, 1989, story in the Jackson *Clarion Ledger*, Coach Butler, my high school coach, was quoted as saying, "I called the guitar a problem, but Jimmy and his mother didn't see it that way."

Even though Coach Butler didn't like the guitar, he was quoted in the same story saying, "Jim is a fine, All-American boy I never had any trouble from."

Pat's dad, Robert Kincade, was a big man who had played football at Ole Miss. He didn't like for Pat to play in the band, and Pat didn't even play football. Pat would have to put his guitar and amp outside his bedroom window and go out the front door, then sneak around the side of the house to get them and put them in his car.

A lot of people thought we were ruining our lives and corrupting the youth of America. Some radio stations banned rock and roll. Many older Americans, still hooked on Frank Sinatra, Perry Como and Big Band music, watched their kids twisting and bumping on the dance floor and thought rock and roll was evil. Preachers even preached against it.

Not my mom. She was always totally supportive, always behind me in whatever I did, and believed in me no matter what.

Through it all, Pat and I became almost inseparable, like brothers. It was a friendship that would take us a long way in music over the next several years.

"Jimmy and I were always together," Pat said. "I mean always. Between or after classes, you could almost always find the two of us hanging out together on the steps of the Student Union. We'd get together at night and work up some songs. I'd go with him to Pontotoc, stay at his house. He had a piano in his basement. What an ear this guy has. He can hear all these notes and fiddle around on the piano and a note would fit. We did that all through college.

"That must have been some kind of destiny thing when I found that open door."

Where the Walk of Champions begins in the Grove

14 —⁂

1962 Football

As Clarksdale native Sam Cooke told the world through song in the 1960s, "Change is gonna come."

As the 1962 season approached, Ole Miss was in the midst of its greatest era of football. The Rebels had won three Southeastern Conference championships over eight seasons, beginning with the 1954 team. In 1959 and 1960, two of the best seasons in school history, the Rebels were named national champions by at least one poll or publication. Such had become a way of life for those who followed the University of Mississippi's football fortunes and the program Coach Vaught had built.

The 1962 preseason polls had Ole Miss again ranked among the nation's top teams. Some picked the Rebels to win the SEC championship along with another national title.

Ole Miss had developed a significant national following because of radio, television, and postseason bowl games. The Rebels, with grey pants, a red, white or blue jersey with two stripes on each shoulder, and a powder blue helmet with a red stripe down the center, had become one of the country's most recognizable teams – college or pro.

There were only a handful of regular season college games televised at the time. But the major bowl games were always shown to a national audience, and the Rebels had been in eight bowls the previous ten seasons.

As football season drew close, swirling throughout Mississippi was an underlying current that change was not only coming but had already begun. In Coach Vaught's 1971 memoir *Rebel Coach* he wrote, "More than football was at stake in 1962."

Every Mississippian knew what he was referring to.

Segregation was still the law in Mississippi but the NAACP was waging a court battle to get a black student, James Meredith, admitted at Ole Miss.

As usual Coach Vaught kept in touch with our team that summer by letter, but he did not mention the rising racial tension. Instead, he did what he'd always done throughout his successful tenure of fifteen seasons as head coach. He told us to remain focused on the season ahead.

My high school and college coaches always stressed high standards of character. That has stayed with me. I always tried to live up to those standards. I was never a rebellious kid, even though some thought my playing in a rock & roll band was rebellious. I just didn't see it that way. I knew who I was and I liked who I was. I just enjoyed playing football and playing music. After all, both are religions in Dixie.

College football season back then started a few weeks later than it does now. I reported to Ole Miss for fall football practice in late August after working for the state highway department in Tupelo all summer. My band had played some dances on weekends, but when football practice started, the music stopped.

When I got to campus, I discovered that one other player and I were the only two players left without roommates. The other player was Buck Randall, a tough, hard-nosed fullback and ferocious tackler from Greenwood. We were roommates for the '62 season and became good friends.

When fall practice began I was still listed as Glynn Griffing's backup at quarterback. I had finally proven myself during my freshman season and spring practice. It boosted my self-esteem because I had worked so hard to get noticed.

We started the season in Memphis, just an hour up the road. Coach Vaught was dressed in his usual coat and tie with a hat similar to Bear Bryant's except that Vaught's wasn't houndstooth.

More than 30,000 filled up old Crump Stadium in midtown to witness a neighborhood rivalry that had always been one-sided. Memphis State, today called the University of Memphis, had never beaten Ole Miss.

We were favored again and won 21-7. Memphis State was predicted to have a good team and finished the season with an 8-1 record. We were their only loss. We more than doubled the Tigers in offensive yardage and our defense allowed them only two trips on our side of midfield. It was a good start to the season.

I didn't get to play any that night. I had ruptured a thigh muscle in preseason practice and was still getting daily treatments and hobbling around.

We played only nine regular season games in that era. So after we beat Memphis State we were feeling pretty good about things. And it was one down, eight to go.

We jumped right into Southeastern Conference action the next weekend against Kentucky.

As I was getting healthy, I began to worry about something. We were scheduled to play our first "home" game that season in Jackson, and back then we flew to games there. I'd never flown and I was really nervous. When we boarded the Southern Airways twin prop, I got even more worried.

The juniors and seniors didn't make it any easier. When we hit an air pocket and the plane bounced all over the sky, some of them would jump up and yell like something was wrong. Even today I hate flying. I felt relieved when we landed in Jackson.

Kentucky quickly became much more than just another game. It turned into a rallying stage for Governor Ross Barnett's crusade to keep Mississippi segregated.

We were in the locker room at halftime, leading the Wildcats 7-0. We had no idea what was going on outside until after the game.

Former Ole Miss political science professor Russell H. Barrett described the emotionally charged scene in his book, "Integration at Ole Miss."

"To a halftime crowd which looked like a sea of confederate flags, Governor Barnett spoke words not calculated to promote law and order: 'I love Mississippi! I love her people – her customs! And I love and respect her heritage!'"

That wasn't all he said, but it was most unusual for something like that to happen at an SEC football game.

We had a tough time against a stubborn Kentucky defense, but ended up winning 14-0. I got in for three plays and completed the first pass I threw in a varsity college football game. I was glad to get that out of the way.

Two games, two wins. Seven to go.

Feeling pretty good about ourselves, we boarded the flight back to campus. We knew the battle to integrate the university was building to a climax. But we had no idea a storm was about to strike. A storm fiercer than any Ole Miss had ever seen.

Events on campus the following day – Sunday, September 30, 1962 – became a significant chapter in the Civil Rights movement.

James Meredith would become the first African-American to gain admittance to the University of Mississippi, but not without much turmoil, bloodshed, and even death.

We knew things could be coming to a head concerning the integration of Ole Miss. We'd been keeping up with what was going on while trying to stay focused on school and football.

Late that Sunday afternoon I was standing off to the right side of the Circle, a grove of trees in front of the Lyceum administration building in the center of campus. People had been gathering all day. You could feel rising tension in the air.

I was close to Fulton Chapel, watching from a distance. Federal marshals had been called in to protect Meredith and they were holed up in the Lyceum, trying to hold back what was fast becoming a hostile mob. Around twilight, I heard an explosion and saw smoke. The feds had set off the first tear gas canister to try to disperse the crowd. A full-fledged riot now raged.

I turned around, walked back to Miller Hall, picked up my guitar and began to strum. I knew things were bad outside, not all that far from our dorm. Playing guitar was the best way to keep my mind off the turmoil. I stayed inside the rest of the night. Miller Hall was a fortress for our football team.

Glynn Griffing remembers that night. "Coach Wobble came down the hall and collected everybody's guns and took them up to his place in the dorm." It turned out to be a small arsenal. As Glynn pointed out, "Mississippi is a hunting state and everybody had a shotgun or rifle in those days."

The coaches made sure no football player could even be suspected of doing anything with a gun.

The next morning when I went outside, clouds of tear gas still hovered over the campus. Burned-out remains of automobiles smoldered in the street close to the Student Union. Two people had been killed and around three hundred injured. National Guardsmen and federal troops patrolled the streets with rifles, bayonets fixed and ready. The riot was over, but the place was in utter chaos.

During the week that followed thousands more troops converged on the campus. They pitched tents on the baseball field, just west of the football stadium. The U.S. Army had taken over Vaught's Valley, our practice field. It was cluttered with helicopters, tents, and soldiers.

Coach Vaught moved practice into Hemingway Stadium. Probably 2,000 military people were sitting in the stands watching us run plays. Finally Vaught gave Don Estes, one of the equipment managers, the job of telling the soldiers to get their helicopters off his practice field.

"I don't think Coach Vaught ever knew my name," Estes said. "He always called me 'manager.' He said, 'Manager, go out there and clear the practice field.' I said, 'Yes sir.'"

So Don went out to the practice field to look for somebody with some rank. He told someone, "Y'all have got to clear the field."

And the guy says, "What are you talking about? Who are you?"

Estes said, "Coach Vaught wants to practice."

The guy says, "Oh, Coach Vaught wants to practice, huh?"

Don says, "Yeah, y'all have got to clear the field."

It's been told many times that it may well have been the fastest the 101st Airborne ever left the premises without a round of fire to cover their retreat. They immediately cleared the field. Such was the power of an order from Coach John Vaught.

Meanwhile, tensions were running high throughout Mississippi. Unbeknownst to us, political pressure was building to shut down the university.

In his memoir *Rebel Coach*, Vaught wrote: "Ole Miss faced six crucial days after that Sunday night riot. The life of the University was at stake. Mississippians were divided on the question, but I felt the vast majority shuddered at the idea of closing (the university)."

I didn't know Governor Barnett was seriously considering closing Ole Miss down. I was too busy concentrating on football and schoolwork and staying away from all of the distractions. I just kept myself removed from it all like Coach Vaught told us to do.

As it turned out, the next game was in jeopardy and maybe the whole football season. With all the angry talk about closing the school, Coach Vaught and some of the alumni felt it was imperative that the team play its next football game, which was against the University of Houston and was scheduled to be played on the Ole Miss campus. They felt it might help to calm things down and be the catalyst to keep the school open.

Team co-captain Louis Guy remembers it well.

"There was rumor they were not going to let us finish the football schedule. They finally said we would have to go to Houston to play the game. But we ended up not knowing until Friday that we would play Houston in Jackson."

In the game against Houston, which was indeed moved to Jackson, I saw playing time again as Glynn Griffing's backup. I was four of six passing for 49 yards, including a touchdown pass of 27 yards to future All-American Allen Brown. Allen grabbed three of the receptions, while the other pass was caught by wingback Larry Johnson. We rolled up an impressive 451 yards on offense. The Cougars were no match for us. We won 40-7.

I can't overemphasize what an important win that was for us. It had been a very difficult week for everybody. The victory helped ease some of the tension hovering over the campus and the rest of Mississippi just like Coach Vaught suspected. And it was proof the team had stayed united and kept its focus.

Three down, six to go.

After a much-needed open date, we went back to Jackson on October 20 and beat Tulane 21-0. The Green Wave was still in the SEC at the time. In fact, it was a charter member of the conference and we played them every year. They left not long after my playing days.

The campus had calmed down some and it seemed like things were getting back to normal. The Tulane game had already been scheduled for Jackson before the season. A rainy night welcomed players, coaches, and fans to Mississippi Memorial Stadium. I got more snaps in this game. Veteran sportswriter Carl Walters of the Jackson *Clarion Ledger* took note:

"Coach Vaught was complimentary of his sophomore quarterback, who rushed three times for forty-three yards and was two for three passing for thirty yards, including a touchdown pass of fifteen yards to Billy Carl Irwin. 'He looked real good. He's coming along fine and is going to make us a good quarterback,' Vaught said of Jim."

Four down, five to go.

The next week we were back at Crump Stadium in Memphis against another outmanned SEC opponent, Vanderbilt. We defeated the Commodores 35-0. For one of the five scores, I hit Woody Dabbs on a 10-yard pass. That play came just before halftime and helped give us a 28-0 lead. I passed to Allen Brown for 11 yards, to Reed Davis for 19, and after a six-yard keeper, threw the touchdown pass to Dabbs. On the first play of the fourth quarter I scored from the two-yard line on a quarterback keeper.

Five down, four to go.

I was becoming more confident with every game. Now we headed into an important stretch in November. Could we keep the unbeaten streak going? Next up was the biggest game we played every year. We were going to Baton Rouge to play LSU. We flew again. I still wasn't any more at ease than when we flew to Jackson to play Kentucky early in the season.

When Ole Miss and LSU play football, it is a special weekend. This was my first time to play a varsity game against the Tigers, but I knew what it meant. I'd followed this game since I was a kid. It was like no other all season.

The rivalry between the two programs, especially the past decade or so, had become a national headliner. Everybody who followed college football knew about Ole Miss-LSU.

Playing in Tiger Stadium – "Death Valley" as they call it – was always tough, and back then we played there a lot. During my three varsity seasons we played LSU in Baton Rouge every year.

They had a caged tiger on the sideline and as we ran onto the field, they would poke the tiger and he would roar. Their fans could get so loud you couldn't hear yourself think. The game was a sellout and you couldn't find a ticket at any price. It was reported that one fan made an offer – in an advertisement – to swap a case of Scotch liquor (12 fifths) for a pair of tickets.

Before the game, the *Clarion Ledger's* Carl Walters sized up the two teams.

"Both have size, speed and depth. Mississippi should have a better aerial attack with Glynn Griffing and Jim Weatherly doing the throwing."

He was prophetic. We beat LSU 15-7 in a really hard-fought game to continue our undefeated season. We were the better team and proved it. But it wasn't easy.

Six down, three to go.

We hosted Chattanooga in Oxford the following week and won easily, 52-7. It was our first campus game since the turmoil of September. All was calm. We finished that one off quickly and were still undefeated.

Seven down, two to go.

Tennessee was next. We headed to Knoxville knowing we were two wins away from an undefeated season. If we could win the last two we would become the first undefeated and untied team in Ole Miss history. Fans may find it hard to believe, but we didn't dwell on that. The coaches made sure. It was one game at a time.

During that game a fight broke out. Players from both teams threw punches and swung helmets. Some rowdy fan from the Tennessee end zone stands actually jumped over the fence swinging an umbrella at the Ole Miss players. I saw Glynn walk over and stand behind Coach Vaught on the sidelines. I went right over and stood behind Glynn. We quarterbacks weren't about to get involved in the skirmish.

The altercation soon got resolved and we were ahead in a tight game when Louis Guy, our senior cornerback and one of our team captains, abruptly ended a late Tennessee threat when he intercepted a pass in our end zone and ran it back 103 yards for a touchdown. It was a beautiful thing to watch and has always been a highlight from that season. The Ole Miss fans went crazy. We won 19-6 and got out of Knoxville.

Eight down, one to go.

Up next, the annual Battle for the Golden Egg. A few years after I played, the press started calling the Ole Miss-Mississippi State game the Egg Bowl. We always just called it the State game.

The only team that stood in the way of the first perfect regular season in Ole Miss football history was our in-state rival. Most people expected us to win. I know everybody on our team did.

The last time Mississippi State had beaten Ole Miss, the players on both teams were little kids. That was in 1946, the year before Coach Vaught became the head coach. There were a couple of ties in there, but State hadn't beaten us under Coach Vaught's tenure.

The game was on December 1. The turmoil on campus earlier in the season and all that surrounded it had been put on hold each Saturday. Everybody in Mississippi was paying attention to see if we could "win 'em all." State was better than its 3-5 record, but the Bulldogs were still a three-touchdown underdog.

MSU scored in the first quarter on a two-yard run by Ode Burrell. Freddie Roberts blocked the extra point attempt by Sammy Dantone, and it was 6-0. Louis Guy scored a touchdown from a yard out to tie the game in the second quarter. Billy Carl Irwin's extra point kick gave us a fragile 7-6 lead.

That's the way things stood at halftime, and that's the way things remained at the end of the third quarter. It was anybody's ballgame.

We started a fourth-quarter drive in our own territory, trying to keep the football, run the clock down, and maybe score a late touchdown. We moved it to State's 43-yard line when Coach

Vaught motioned for me to go in. He never had any reservations about swapping quarterbacks at any point during a game. That gave me a lot of confidence. But in this game, the undefeated season was at stake. He told me to run a play called "35 Trap."

I took the snap and stepped back, then rolled around to hand the ball off to David Jennings. But he wasn't there. I'd missed the handoff.

David said he was glad I did. Otherwise, "the play might have lost yards because I was tackled right there at the line of scrimmage," he said.

Apparently just about everyone in Hemingway Stadium, including both teams, thought David actually had the football.

"Jimmy called one play and ran another," said left guard Sam Owen. "We were all in the wrong place except for Jimmy. The rest of the team ran to the left and he ran to the right. The defense went our way. It sure was a good fake."

All season long we had run that play with the right guard pulling to his left to trap the defensive lineman in the five hole on the left side of the line. The right halfback would take one step over to his left and then cut up behind the pulling guard into the five-hole. I would reverse out deep and give the football to the halfback on the inside as I rolled around.

For the Mississippi State game Coach Vaught changed the play. He had the right tackle pull to his left instead of the right guard. The right halfback, instead of taking one step over to his left and then cutting up, would now take one step forward, then cut to his left following the tackle into the five hole. I was supposed to reverse out more shallow than deep and give the ball to the halfback on the inside as he stepped up and over behind the tackle.

When I reversed out, I ran it the old way and stepped too deep. When I turned to give David the ball, he had already passed me and I couldn't reach him. I looked up and saw State's left defensive end crashing to his inside following our tackle who was pulling to his left. He never even looked at me. Never saw me. State's outside linebacker saw their defensive end crash and he moved to his inside as well. The safety followed suit by moving to his inside. None of them noticed me.

David had carried out such a great fake that the whole State team converged on the left side of the line at the five-hole where the ball should have been. There was not one Mississippi State player on the right side of the field. So I hid the ball on my hip and ran around right end, trying my best to be invisible, to the end zone. By the time a State player saw me, it was too late to catch me. I sailed 43 yards untouched and almost unnoticed.

When I ran off the field, our long-time trainer "Doc" Knight was the first to come running on the field to greet me. I was laughing and said, "Doc, I missed the handoff." Doc said, "Well don't tell anybody, don't tell anybody." We were both giddy with laughter.

No one was more surprised than I was. I had fully expected to hand the ball off to David. For a split second it was like "Oh no, what now?" Everything seemed to be in slow motion. Then I just took off running.

The extra point was no good, and we led 13-6. State could still have tied us or beaten us, because there was some time left on the clock. But now they couldn't beat us with a field goal. They had to have a touchdown and a two point conversion. But our defense got stubborn and shut them down.

Glynn Griffing said he knew I missed the handoff. "Maybe," he said, "we should have put that play in more often. That sealed the game. That gave us our undefeated season."

"The Goof that Laid the Golden Egg" read the headline in the

Memphis *Commercial Appeal* the next morning. Over the years I can't tell you how many people have come up to me and said, "I was in the stands when you made that touchdown run against Mississippi State."

Louis Guy likes to say there were three significant plays that season.

"One was at LSU when A.J. Holloway caught a pass and backed his way into the end zone right before the half, then my interception against Tennessee (for a touchdown). Then Jimmy missing the handoff for a touchdown against Mississippi State."

Nine down, none to go.

SEC champs. On to the Sugar Bowl.

We still had to beat Arkansas in the Sugar Bowl at Tulane Stadium in New Orleans to complete the perfect season. The Razorbacks at the time were members of the Southwest Conference. Coach Frank Broyles had built a powerhouse program in Fayetteville.

We knew we had to get to 10-0 for the season to be as special as we wanted, one that would be remembered down through the years like no other, especially with all the adversity we'd encountered since September.

So we did what we'd done all season. We won.

Final score: 17-13

Ten down, zero to go.

The perfect season was now in the record books, and the Rebel faithful could breathe a long-awaited sigh of relief. The national nightmare of a campus and a state in turmoil had momentarily slipped to yesterday's news, and a new storyline had emerged.

The 1962 Ole Miss Rebels were undefeated and untied

Throwing a pass in the Sugar Bowl on January 1, 1963, against Arkansas to complete the perfect season of '62

Southeastern Conference champions, Sugar Bowl champions, and national champions by vote of the Football Writers Association of America (FWAA). It was the fifth SEC title for the Rebels in 16 seasons.

Apparently, we picked up a new fan that year, a very famous one. Years later fullback Freddie Roberts had coffee with James Meredith in a Kroger store on the north side of Jackson where he lives.

"James told me, 'All I wanted to do was come down there and watch y'all play a game. But the (federal marshals) wouldn't let me do it. They said it would create too much of a commotion with that big of a crowd,'" Freddie said.

Coach Vaught in his memoir *Rebel Coach* summed up the season this way.

"The '62 team had courage. I have never seen another bunch of boys respond so well to my requests. They kept their emotions in check. They conducted themselves as gentlemen. In squad meetings they pledged themselves to keeping things going. I am convinced that successful football team kept Ole Miss from closing its doors that year. The 1962 Ole Miss football team did much more than just win all 10 of its games. Their accomplishments rate a chapter in the history of collegiate football."

On game days at Ole Miss, the beautiful 10-acre Grove, with its towering majestic oaks, comes to life as an unsurpassed scene of wall-to-wall people, one of college football's most entertaining tailgate atmospheres. One of the most anticipated moments of the day is when the Rebels walk through the Grove on their way to Vaught-Hemingway Stadium. The ritual is called the "Walk of Champions."

The name of every player on our '62 team appears on the archway

1962 Football Team Roster

Bo Aldridge	Whaley Hall	Joe Pettey
Ray Bedingfield	James Harvey	George Randall
Allen Brown	Jimmy Heidel	Jerry Rayborn
Bobby Boyd	Andrew Holloway	Fred Roberts
Billy Champion	Billy Carl Irwin	Jim Roberts
John Champion	David Jennings	Bobby Robinson
William Crosby	Larry Johnson	Richard Ross
Woody Dabbs	Fred Kimbrell	Kenny Smith
Reed Davis	Frank Kinard	Larry Smith
Joe Dean	Frank Lambert	Wesley Sullivan
Donald Dickson	Lewis Lanter	Billy Sumrall
Kenny Dill	Tommy Lucas	James Terrell
Jim Dunaway	John Maddox	Douglas Tillery
Perry Lee Dunn	Richard Mascagni	George Tupman
David Finley	Rodney Mattina	Robert Upchurch
Cecil Ford	Donald McIntyre	Jim Weatherly
Glynn Griffing	Charles Morris	Joe Wilkins
Louis Guy	Sam Owen	Don Windham

This plaque is on the Walk of Champions arch in the Grove at Ole Miss

at the starting point of the walk, a tribute to that Ole Miss team when I was a sophomore quarterback. We remain the only perfect football team in the history of the program.

I was so caught up in football and school, I didn't realize how much anxiety and depression my Mom was battling. I learned later that she would sometimes have panic attacks traveling to our games.

It had been five years since my Dad's death, but it was still fresh on my Mom's mind. She had three children at home and I was in Oxford. Those were very difficult times for her. I didn't realize just how difficult. She had been having panic attacks for some time that were a direct result of the stress of raising the kids alone, with constant money worries to boot.

My Uncle Billy remembers when he would pick Mom up and head to Oxford to watch me play.

"Sometimes," he said, "we'd get part of the way there, and Edith would ask me to turn the car around. But I'd say 'Edith, we're going to see Jimmy play.' I would tell her that sometimes sternly, because I knew she would be fine once we got there. And by the time we got to campus, she would be in a completely different mindset and back to her normal, dominant personality.

"'I'm Jimmy Weatherly's mother and we want to park in here,' she'd tell the parking attendants near the field house and stadium. Sometimes another car or two might follow us over there. She would say, 'And those other cars back there. They're with us, too.'

"I remember after Ole Miss and Memphis State played a night game at Crump Stadium in Memphis to open the '63 season, I was driving home with a car full of sleeping family members in a Chevrolet station wagon," Billy said. "I was the only one awake. When we drove through Holly Springs, a policeman pulled us over sometime after midnight. Edith woke up startled, looked up at the cop and yelled, 'You scared the hell out of me!' And I think she must have scared him too, because at that point he shined his light in the car and saw a bunch of sleeping kids and let us go on our way."

My brother, Shan, and Uncle Billy used to come by the field house after games on campus to wait for me to shower and dress. Sometimes I would come out holding a jersey or a chinstrap to give to Shan, who was about seven or eight.

Shan told me about one time when the other players and I were signing autographs. "An Ole Miss cheerleader came up to me and said, 'Little boy would you like to come over here and get Jimmy Weatherly's autograph?' I looked up at her and said, 'Why would I want to do that? He's my brother.'"

15 —⅛

1963 Football

The band played some high school dances in the spring of 1963. When summer rolled around Buck Randall and I drove to Jacksonville, Florida, to work for Ryder Trucking Company along with some other teammates. After the back-breaking work of loading freight for half the summer from 4 a.m. to 2 p.m. each day, Buck and I decided to drive back to Oxford and go to summer school. We'd had enough.

When the fall semester started, Buck and I were roommates once again and we were suitemates with running back Mike Dennis and guard Stan Hindman.

For the '63 season, Coach Vaught moved Perry Lee Dunn from fullback back to quarterback. So we pretty much split playing time, even though he was listed on the Red team and I was on the Blue team.

We started the season with a huge disappointment and an unusual final score, tying Memphis State 0-0 in Crump Stadium in a real defensive struggle. We had been picked to beat them, so that was certainly not the way anybody thought we'd start a new season. There were no overtimes in those days.

It was a rocky start, especially offensively, but the next week we bounced back and beat Kentucky 31-7 in Lexington. So we were 1-0-1 overall and more importantly 1-0 in the SEC.

Then we went to Houston to play the Cougars.

"In that game," Mike Dennis recalled, "Jimmy hit me on a couple of passes out in the flat. On one play I broke a couple of tackles and got it in the end zone. We beat Houston that third game of the year 20-6.

"Jimmy threw the easiest pass to catch of any quarterback I ever played with," Mike continued. "That includes Roman Gabriel (of the Los Angeles Rams) and some other guys. He threw a good spiral. It was soft, especially on the little swing passes when you're so close. He had a touch. If you were 12 yards, he'd put a little more on it. He and I teamed up for a bunch of touchdowns."

After Houston, we took on Tulane in New Orleans and beat the Green Wave 21-0. Then we played Vanderbilt in Oxford and won 27-7. So heading into the annual war with LSU, we were sitting pretty in our usual place, except for the tie with Memphis State. At that point we were 4-0-1 overall and 3-0 in SEC play.

The Tigers were 5-1 and had a halfback named Joe Labruzzo who was crowned by many as the fastest back in the Southeastern Conference. We always expected a really hard-fought game when we played LSU. Not this time. We beat them 37-3.

Probably the most memorable play that day was Stan Hindman running down a wide open Labruzzo and catching him from behind just short of the goal line on a 60-yard run. People have talked about that play for years. Then the Ole Miss defense dug in and held the Tigers for four straight downs. When we took over on downs at the five, it took all the air out of the Tigers, who were already down 23-3.

Wayne Thompson, sports editor of the Jackson *Clarion Ledger*, recapped the game in a way that showed just how dominant we were:

"...The Rebels, looking better than they have at any other time this campaign, completely dominated all phases of play...Perry Lee Dunn had 47 (yards) in 11 rushing attempts; and Weatherly 44 in eight to pace the attack that netted 233 ground yards against only 78 for the opposition. In the air Weatherly completed a rather outstanding seven-for-seven for 105 yards and Dunn one for five for five yards. Ole Miss wound up with a net offense for the day of 343 yards against only 144 for LSU – and the Rebs led the SEC in both departments and are first nationally on defense."

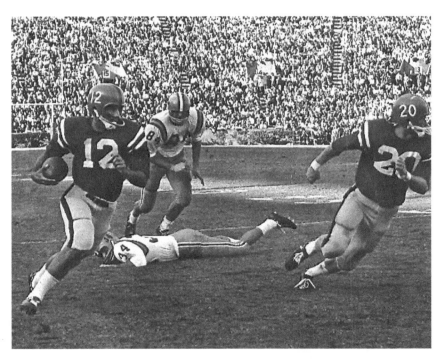

We beat LSU in '63 for the second year in a row

We got back from Baton Rouge feeling pretty good about how things were going. Next we beat an outmanned University of Tampa team 41-0 at Oxford. I had another good day, completing eight of nine passes for 73 yards including two touchdowns to receiver David Wells. I also had one rushing touchdown.

The next week we played Tennessee in a familiar place – Crump Stadium in Memphis. Even though we were in Tennessee, Memphis always felt like a home game no matter who we played there. We usually had as many fans as Memphis State or Tennessee. We were a football program with three hometowns – Oxford, Jackson, and Memphis.

Freddie Roberts recalled how an injury to Perry Lee Dunn forced a change at starting quarterback.

"Late in the year in Memphis, Jimmy started against Tennessee and we beat them 20-0. Frank Kinard scored a touchdown. I scored a touchdown. Jimmy was a big-time player that game. He threw the ball well, and we scored three touchdowns. And we had a great defense," he said.

I completed 14 of 23 passes, which gave us a big edge in passing, 160 yards to the Volunteers' 92. Our first touchdown came on what *Jackson Daily News* sports writer Lee Baker called "A lightning strike to wingback Larry Smith covering 33 yards."

We shut Tennessee out and moved on to the Battle for the Golden Egg, this time in Starkville. It would be my first trip there in two years, since that gray overcast day when I was with the freshman team in the fall of '61. I was hoping for a better day this time around.

The week before the Mississippi State game we had an open date.

On the afternoon of Friday, November 22, 1963, I was walking out of the old gym from a class, headed toward the Student

Union. I was about to cross the street in front of the gym when our equipment manager, Jack Townes from Grenada, came around the curve in his car and yelled, "Kennedy's been shot."

I yelled back, "What?"

"Kennedy's been shot," he said again. "They think he may be dead."

I remember getting a sick feeling in my stomach, stunned to hear those words about an American President. It was a surreal experience and I really don't remember much after that. I was glad we had a week off to try and digest what had happened before we headed to State to try to finish up another unbeaten season.

"When in doubt, kick," were the first words in Lee Baker's *Jackson Daily News* story the day after we played State.

That's what Coach Vaught decided to do late in the game facing fourth down at the MSU three-yard line. State led by three, 10-7. Those were an important three points. A win or a tie meant we'd be SEC champions for the second year in a row and the sixth time ever, the most of any school in the league at that point. It also meant another trip to the Sugar Bowl. It was a dramatic moment. Then, with just over three minutes remaining, Vaught made his decision. "Go kick it."

Billy Carl Irwin trotted onto Scott Field to try to tie the game with a field goal. There was still time for State to drive down the field and score. Or maybe for us to hold the Bulldogs on their next possession, get the ball back, and score ourselves. We'd trailed almost the whole second half.

Billy Carl kicked the football through the uprights, and the game eventually ended in a 10-10 tie.

Coach Vaught caught a lot of flack over the years from fans who thought he was too conservative. But I agreed with his decision to kick. We all wanted to win, but it was far more important to win the SEC. We had sputtered offensively most of the game, and we couldn't take a chance of not making it on fourth down, trailing by three points.

Wayne Thompson of the *Clarion Ledger* agreed.

"Vaught really had no choice but to tie the game and hope for the best from his championship team, even if some fans had expressed their displeasure with settling."

But, he pointed out, those same fans "would have been far, far more disturbed had Vaught gone for the touchdown and failed."

The Sugar Bowl decided to match us up against Alabama in a showdown between two SEC powerhouses who had not met each other that year. We had accomplished Coach Vaught's fourth unbeaten regular season in his 17 years. Ole Miss had another SEC Championship notch in its belt. We were 7-0-2 overall and 5-0-1 in the SEC. We had tied the season opener and the finale.

On January 1, 1964, we played Alabama in Tulane Stadium. The Crimson Tide quarterback, the great Joe Namath, had been suspended by Coach Paul "Bear" Bryant. His backup, Steve Sloan, replaced Namath at quarterback.

Ironically, Sloan would become the head coach at Ole Miss prior to the 1978 season, one of the last major decisions Coach Vaught made as athletic director after his coaching days were over.

I was excited about playing against Namath and equally disappointed when I heard he wasn't going to play. Even though I played for Ole Miss, I was a huge Namath fan.

An Associated Press story talked about Coach Vaught's quarterbacks and how he was always able to have them ready to play.

"A top-notch quarterback year after year is one of Vaught's trademarks. Another Vaught tradition is to have one or more outstanding reserve quarterbacks waiting in the wings. This year's Ole Miss team is no exception. Dunn's understudy is Jim Weatherly, a junior who backed up Glynn Griffing in Mississippi's 17-13 victory over Arkansas in the 1963 Sugar Bowl…Weatherly connected on 52 of 96 passes during the season for 676 yards and seven touchdowns."

Significant snowfalls are rare as far south as New Orleans. But that holiday season the city had gotten a big blast of wintry weather. Snow was piled up two to three feet high all around the Tulane Stadium field. It was freezing cold. I could hardly feel my hands.

Playing football in those conditions was difficult for both teams. There were a combined 17 fumbles. We had 11 and lost six. Alabama had six and lost three.

On one not-so-memorable play I took the snap, sprinted out to my right to throw, and the ball popped right out of my hand as I launched my arm forward. It was really a strange feeling. Unfortunately Alabama recovered the fumble. It was that kind of day.

Alabama's Tim Davis kicked four field goals for a 12-0 lead. We had yet to cross into Crimson Tide territory at that point, but we still had time to win it if we could just execute offensively.

In the fourth quarter, a 42-yard pass from Perry Lee Dunn to David Wells got us down to the Alabama five-yard line. Perry Lee then threw to Larry Smith for a touchdown, and Billy Carl Irwin's extra point made it 12-7. We had a chance to win, but we weren't able to score again.

It was a major disappointment. It was our first loss in two years. Not since the 1961 team lost the Cotton Bowl to Texas on January 1, 1962, by an identical 12-7 score had Ole Miss lost a football game.

As Marty Mule' of the New Orleans *Times-Picayune* put it, "It was difficult to believe that a game with 17 fumbles, 11 by Ole Miss, both all-time bowl records, could be so exciting at the finish."

It wasn't all that exciting for us since we lost. But it was competitive and close. I just didn't have one of my better games. I had three interceptions and couldn't get the team moving. I was trying too hard to make something happen. That caused me to make some bad decisions. Sometimes I put way too much pressure on myself.

Perry Lee had a much better game and was elected second team All-SEC.

But...we were still SEC champions, and nobody could take that away from us.

I continued to write songs all through college, but I was still learning and enjoying it more and more. When I'd go back to Pontotoc on weekends after football season, I'd play what I'd written for my sisters, Sherrie and Elise. I did that throughout my songwriting career. They said they loved everything they heard and I appreciated their ego-boosting comments. I needed positive feedback.

"We would sit down on the bed and he would say, 'I want to play something for you.' Later on when we would hear it on a record, it was always fun to know we were the first to hear it," Sherrie said.

Elise said it was "a really special time" for her, too. "In the quietest moment, he would gather us together and would want us to just listen. Nine times out of ten, I would end up crying. Every song he wrote was so meaningful. When our kids got married, we used his music in their weddings. That was like a gift he was giving them through his songs."

We had needed a name for our band while we were in college. Pat Kincade remembered when we named it.

"Jimmy said, 'Call it The Vegas.' I asked him why. He said, 'Because it's the brightest star in the summer.' So that's what we called ourselves."

During football season Pat and the others played gigs without me. Along the way, Pat found new members for the band. He found J.D. Lobue and asked him to play the piano for us. He spotted a good drummer, Dulin Lancaster, playing drums at the Sigma Chi house, Pat's fraternity. He joined us a year or so later.

Pat was also looking for a bass player. He heard that Leland Russell from Greenwood was a pretty good bass player. Pat went to hear him play with another band and noticed something right away.

"One thing I noticed was he played loud," Pat said. "He had a Fender bass, he had a nice amp, and he had a car. That's all positive stuff."

Pat was interested, and so was Leland.

"I looked like a Beatle," Leland said, "and I owned a big amplifier. I was still a freshman in college, but I got with the band. There were four of us. We were Jimmy Weatherly and the Vegas, and we were on our way."

Pat had done some great scouting. It helped that he and I trusted each other's judgment.

As Pat puts it, "Jimmy and I never had an argument or even a discussion over anything. When it came to business, I'd say, 'We're going to do it this way.' And Jimmy would say, 'OK.' And when it came to music Jimmy would say, 'We're going to do it this way.' And I would say, 'OK.' That was all there was to it."

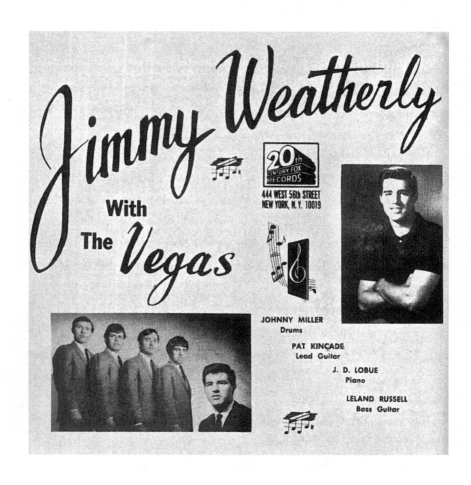

16 ——⚜

The Singing Quarterback

College football in the 1960s was a sport, a game. It wasn't a science or big business like it is today. It wasn't nearly as sophisticated or complicated. And it wasn't a year-round commitment for the players like it is today.

We were just what the name implies – student-athletes. We had a lot of free time as long as we kept in shape. We didn't have any private coaches or trainers who specialized in working with quarterbacks on passing drills, throwing motion, footwork and accuracy like some have today. We didn't have a full-time weight program like high schools and colleges today. Some of us didn't work all that hard at gaining weight and becoming bigger and stronger. I was six feet tall and played at 183 pounds throughout my college years. I couldn't put on weight. That size quarterback has a hard time playing college football in today's world of huge players.

Fiesta Club marquee in Biloxi

Most of my teammates worked during the summer because none of us had any money. Some went to summer school. Besides paying for our education, the school could only give us fifteen dollars a month, which was called laundry money. We were sure glad to get it. Fifteen dollars stretched a little farther back then.

The summer of 1964 before my senior season, the Vegas decided it would be fun to drive down to the Mississippi Gulf Coast to try to find work playing music. Our plan was to stay two or three weeks and then drive back to Oxford and play some weekend dances and go to summer school. We auditioned for Jake and John Mladinich, who owned a popular place called the Fiesta Club on the beach in Biloxi. They liked what they heard and hired us on the spot.

The response from people was so good that we spent the whole summer playing music there until a few days before I had to leave to report to football practice in August.

I had asked Coach Vaught about my playing music on the coast that summer and he gave me his blessing. I continued to run and work out, and I was also making some money, which I needed to do. I think he understood my family situation.

The audience at the Fiesta Club knew I was the quarterback for Ole Miss. They advertised me in the local papers as "The Singing Quarterback." That didn't sit too well with me. I wanted to keep football and music separate in people's minds. It turned out to be an impossible task. Sportswriters all across the South started calling me "The Singing Quarterback."

The Fiesta Club was an upscale nightclub right on the beach. It was decorated like a south sea island hut. The roof had an artificial thatched look. A big neon sign hanging outside advertised who was playing.

Inside there was a large bar and two bandstands at either end of the club. One stage was for easy listening or jazz and the other stage was for rock.

Our group consisted of Pat on guitar, Leland on bass, J.D. Lobue from Hammond, Louisiana, on organ, and myself. We had picked up Jeff Mitchell to play drums for us for that gig. Seems like drummers were the hardest guys to keep in the band, so we were always changing drummers.

The crowds at the Fiesta Club grew as soon as word got around that the Vegas with "The Singing Quarterback" were playing there. The place was generally packed. It was not a rough and rowdy crowd by any means. Some came to dance and some were curious to see if an Ole Miss quarterback really could sing. Two Alabama football players even came in to hear us – Jackie Sherrill, who years later would be the head coach at Mississippi State, and fullback Steve Bowman.

When the Ole Miss faithful found out I was playing in a

nightclub in Biloxi the summer before my senior year of football, it was a pretty unanimous disapproval. I really didn't see anything wrong with it, so I never thought about it being a problem. But it seemed to be for a lot of other people. If football had been the all-consuming, year-round business it is today, I would have never gone to the coast to play music. As a matter of fact, I might have never had the opportunity to get into the music business. To us, football was a game, an important game, yes, but still a game. And playing music at the Fiesta Club was just a summer job like any other. And it sure beat loading freight.

I know people weren't accustomed to that kind of thing. Rock and roll was still somewhat in its late infancy and the Beatles were on their way to America.

A lot of rumors were swirling around and got back to me that some so-called Ole Miss fans (or maybe Mississippi State fans) were saying that I was on the Gulf Coast getting drunk and carousing and partying all the time. Nothing could be further from the truth. I wasn't a party person. I was having fun, but I was always a responsible kid. I never took one drink of anything alcoholic or smoked a cigarette or – pick a name for it – grass, pot, weed, marijuana, which I'd never even heard of at the time. Not even to this day. The strongest drinks I had were Cokes with a cherry in them. I even learned to tie a cherry stem in a knot with my tongue. I've never taken any kind of illegal drugs, ever. I don't relish the thought of being out of control, and I don't want to have to apologize to anyone for my behavior. Every song I've ever written I wrote stone sober.

While playing the Fiesta Club, I met someone who would become a life-long best friend. Marty Gamblin, who was my age, had been booking bands in his hometown of Philadelphia,

The Vegas – J.D. Lobue, me, Johnny Miller, Leland Russell, and Pat Kincade

Mississippi, and had come to the coast to see us play and see about booking us for some dances. Marty would later have his own long and successful career in the music business in California and Nashville before returning home to Philadelphia. He eventually became executive director of the Mississippi Arts and Entertainment Experience in Meridian. When he came down to the coast, he was just getting started. And he liked what he heard.

"What I saw in Jimmy Weatherly and the Vegas was – the music, the name, the mystique." Marty said. "I thought, wow, this is big time. So I tracked down Mr. Russell (Leland's dad and the band's manager) and he wanted something like $250 to $400 a night guaranteed. I was still going to junior college. I said to him, 'What if I don't make that?' He said for me to do the best I could and to make every effort to make it a success. And it was.

"I started booking shows for them," Marty said. "The first time I booked Jim's band was at the National Guard Armory in Philadelphia."

Marty wasn't what you would call a "professional" booker at the time, but he was one of the hardest working, most honorable guys I'd ever met. And probably the most loyal person I've ever known. There was nothing I couldn't trust him with. He's also one of the funniest people on the planet. We share the same goofy sense of humor. We remain the best of friends to this day even if we don't get to see each other much.

Marty once told me a story about one of his cousins. It's our kind of Mississippi humor.

"Neshoba Central High School was trying to decide if they should build a new band hall or add on to the existing one," Marty said. "They had a community meeting. The band director got up and said, 'You can tell by the number of people here, and our band is even larger, that when we all get in here you can imagine how cramped it is. And besides, the acoustics in this building are terrible.'

"My cousin stood up and said diplomatically and seriously, 'I've been sitting here listening to everything and I have done carpentry work most of my life. It makes far more sense to me to add to the existing facility rather than build a new one. And as far as those acoustics are concerned, I will personally call Orkin in the morning and have them come out here and get rid of those things.'"

I still laugh every time I think about that.

After playing music on the coast all summer, it was time to go back to Ole Miss and report for fall football practice. Somehow

Pat had booked a high school dance for us that night, on the same day the team was supposed to report at Miller Hall. Back then we had a 10 o'clock curfew. That was bed-check time. So I had a real dilemma.

Nervously I went to see Coach Vaught. I was used to talking to him because during each season we had weekly quarterback meetings to discuss strategy for the upcoming game. But this was different. This was more sensitive.

I explained my situation. To my surprise he didn't flinch or change expression. Very calmly he said, "Well, we just won't start bed check until tomorrow night." End of story.

I couldn't believe what he had just said, but I was certainly relieved.

Coach Vaught never said an unkind word to me about playing music. As a matter of fact, he was very supportive. He was a very wise man and he was interested in every facet of his players' lives, not just football. It was a privilege to play for him. I don't think many, if any, other coaches would have reacted the way he did.

Years later Coach Vaught was asked by *Clarion Ledger* reporter, Butch John, what he thought about me playing music in the off-season, into the late hours of the night in clubs. His response:

"I couldn't have cared less if he played the tuba at 2 a.m."

That probably caught the naysayers off guard. Even my high school football coach, Coach Butler, later admitted he had been wrong about the guitar and Coach Vaught had been right.

On April 16, 1964, Coach Vaught sent a letter to attorney Jack Doty in Pontotoc concerning the '64 season, discussing my music, and protecting my eligibility status. There was an important season ahead, and he didn't want anything to disrupt the team. Strangely enough, he apparently was also looking out for me – and, unknown to me at the time, my future in music.

Dear Mr. Doty:

Jim Weatherly has been in touch with me for some time with regard to exploiting his talents as a musician. I have heard Jim perform and think he has outstanding talent and is worthy of national recognition. However, there is some conflict in receiving remuneration from employment while on SEC scholarship. Also, in view of the fact that Jim is very talented as a football player, we thought it might be well to tie his musical talent in with his football talent, and try to exploit both of these talents at the same time, namely around the first of the year 1965.

Jim has been approached by several people who desire to record his songs. I am very anxious that he have the best contact possible and with people who can do something toward getting this before the people nationally. Jim needs your help and advice. We are thinking about making the recordings during the summer and holding them for release around December 15.

I expect Jim to have an outstanding year in football. He is All American talent. If our team does well, I feel Jim will have a fine chance of making an All American player. Then, too, our game with State, which is December 5, will be nationally televised. They are always looking to me for unusual talents in some players. I believe at this time I might have an opportunity to put before our broadcasters the fact that Jim is talented musically. Also, I am in hopes of getting him on the Look All American football team, which is presented nationally on the Ed Sullivan Show. It will be known that Jim has this musical talent, and I feel sure they would like to have him demonstrate such on this type show. They are always looking for players to demonstrate any type talent, and I feel that we might be able to tie this in well with the release of Jim's recordings.

Jim is aware of this letter and is anxious to come by to see you for advice. I shall appreciate anything you might suggest that would help Jim.

Sincerely yours,
John H. Vaught
Head Football Coach

REBEL FOOTBALL GUIDE `64

UNIVERSITY OF
MISSISSIPPI

17 ——⚘

No. 1 in '64

In late summer of 1964 Ole Miss, like practically all public institutions of higher learning in the South, was in transition to a more inclusive culture. College football was changing as well. The game was moving away from its long-standing, one-platoon system – where players played both offense and defense – to a two-platoon. There was a great deal of debate about it nationally, and Ole Miss sports information even put out a statement in a press release:

"Vaught believes in 2-Way Player. No Platoon Switching for Ole Miss. Unlike most of his Southeastern Conference colleagues, Mississippi's Johnny Vaught isn't tagging along with two-platoon football. Vaught's 1964 squad isn't headed for platoon warfare – not just yet."

It was my turn as the starting quarterback for the Ole Miss Rebels. We were picked preseason No. 1 in the nation by several publications and polls including *Playboy* magazine and the

Associated Press. That kind of preseason publicity can be the kiss of death. You become each opponent's number one target. We had lost some good players to graduation, but we still had some outstanding returning lettermen.

Our first game was against a strong Memphis State team that had tied us 0-0 the year before. The Tigers were supposed to have their best team in years, and they were coming to Oxford. There was a ton of publicity surrounding the game, especially in the Memphis *Commercial Appeal*. Sports writer James K. Cazalas made note of my music when he wrote that "Mississippi and its singing quarterback, Jim Weatherly, open the 1964 campaign against Memphis State University."

Memphis State thought this was their year to beat us. Tigers head coach Billy "Spook" Murphy, a graduate of Mississippi State, was a friend of Coach Vaught and they sometimes played golf together. But once a year they set aside their friendship to battle on the gridiron.

Dan Jenkins of *Sports Illustrated* was in Oxford for the game. Afterward he wrote about the buildup, the game, and the aftermath.

Jenkins, in the September 28 issue, used a quote from Murphy that the Rebels saw prior to the game.

"If we don't (beat Ole Miss), there ain't a cotton picker in Mississippi."

Memphis State was on a 17-game winning streak and walking the walk. The only game they hadn't won during that stretch was the 0-0 tie with us the year before. We were also the last team to beat the Tigers, a 21-7 win for us to open the perfect '62 season. The media rated the '64 game as pretty much a toss-up. We figured we were in for a battle but like every other game, we felt we'd win it. We were in pursuit of another perfect season and another national championship. The game didn't unfold the way anyone predicted.

Dan Jenkins of *Sports Illustrated* continues:

"Like most of the enthusiasts, the pros believed they were going to see an epic contest between two teams loaded with prospects… Most of the prospects the pros saw turned out to be from Ole Miss. Quarterback Weatherly, for one. Weatherly sprinted the Memphis State ends with ease and completed 14 of 22 passes. The players regarded last year's tie as an insult, and in an effort to atone for it they practiced in strict privacy. Reporters, photographers, students – all were banned from Mississippi's workouts.

"After unknown Memphis State tied powerful Ole Miss last year it was no longer true that the most exciting activity around Memphis was watching the ducks float in the marble fountain with the artificial gladiolas on top in the lobby of the Hotel Peabody. The thing to do was to whoop it up for Memphis State and to believe Coach Spook Murphy when he said his Tigers would beat Mississippi this year. When the game was over, Ole Miss had won by the nightmarish score of 30-0 and Spook's friends headed home to watch the ducks."

Wayne Thompson of the *Clarion Ledger* couldn't resist the music metaphor. He reported that "quarterback Jim Weatherly showing complete versatility abandoned his own singing and turned to choir directing – he had the thousands of Rebel fans swinging with a victory march and a host of Tiger hopefuls moaning the blues."

I didn't come out of the lopsided victory unscathed. Sometime late in the first half, I got tackled hard and the tackler rolled over and twisted my right foot, injuring my big toe. The pain was tremendous but I wasn't about to come out of the game. I continued to play but was feeling the pain. I couldn't push off on my right foot very well to sprint out to the left, and sprint out passes were Ole Miss' bread and butter.

For about three weeks after the game I was getting daily treatments on the toe, but it just wouldn't respond. Coach Vaught was aware of my lingering injury and could have replaced me at any time. But he chose not to and I was really glad. It was my senior year and I wanted to play. The injury hampered me, but not enough to where I felt like I couldn't play.

The next week Kentucky came to Jackson for one of our "home away from home" games. It was a really hot late summer Mississippi afternoon.

College football was becoming more specialized and individualized, and more schools were adopting the two-platoon system. Kentucky was moving in that direction.

We were the consensus No. 1 team in the nation at kickoff. A few hours later we had lost 27-21. We were stunned.

It sent shock waves throughout the college football world. The No. 1 football team had lost to a school better known for basketball.

Stats showed the game wasn't as close as the score, although we still could have won it. Kentucky had 22 first downs to our 10. Offensively we had 187 yards and they had 415.

"I don't ever remember seeing something like that," Coach Vaught said of the defensive numbers in an Associated Press story after the game. That's because there hadn't been.

According to the AP story, 415 were the most yards an Ole Miss team had ever allowed under Coach Vaught, who was then in his 18th season as head coach.

Kentucky head coach Charlie Bradshaw called his well-conditioned Wildcats "a four-quarter football team. We practice for four quarters and get ready to play that way."

Mike Dennis, a two-way player for us, remembers how tough it was.

"I never came out of the game," Mike said. "We were still playing both ways. It was 90-something degrees. I lost 12 pounds that day. I played tailback and outside linebacker and played some cornerback. And I never came off the field. We should have won. They connected on some crazy plays, took some chances and gambled, and pulled it out. We did get tired playing both ways in the sun that day."

As for me, my right big toe was still very painful. It changed the way I ran because I was constantly favoring it. When I would drop back to throw, I would plant my right foot and the pain would cause me to relax it to take the pressure off. My concentration and focus were hindered as well, because the injury took my attention away from the way I was supposed to play.

After days of treatment and with my toe still not responding, "Doc" Knight sent me to our team physician, Dr. Gerre Hopkins. He did some blood work, and the test results showed that I had gout. Gout? I also had what they now call turf toe. In today's world it probably would have required surgery and I'd have missed most or all of the season. I began to take medication for gout, but it continued to be a problem, hardly getting better as the season wore on.

We bounced back the next week and beat Houston 31-9 on Homecoming Day in Oxford. But then we had four straight road games.

We went to Gainesville and faced a good Florida team quarterbacked by a future Heisman Trophy winner – later one of the SEC's winningest head coaches – Steve Spurrier. Florida beat us 30-14. That was the only game where we really got whipped.

I just couldn't do anything right that day and Charlie Myers replaced me for much of the game.

We were nowhere near the top of the rankings anymore. We were 2-2 on the season and 0-2 in SEC play. Nobody involved with Ole Miss football was used to this. The two losses were already more in a single season than any Rebel team since 1958 and that was six seasons earlier.

A run at Vanderbilt in 1964

We struggled but won at Tulane 14-9 the next week. Even with the win, none of us left New Orleans feeling a whole lot better. We just weren't playing well.

Then we went to Nashville and tied Vanderbilt 7-7. Late in the fourth quarter I threw a long pass to David Wells for a 50-yard touchdown that saved us from losing. I got hit just as I let the ball go and was knocked to the ground. I couldn't see David, so I didn't know if the ball got to him or not. Then I heard a big roar, but I couldn't tell if it was coming from Ole Miss fans or Vanderbilt fans. I got up off the ground and realized David had caught it and scored. I never saw it. Years later I asked David where the pass hit him. He said, "Right over my shoulder and into my arms."

Tying Vandy was like a loss to us. We had been picked to win by a wide margin.

We were 3-2-1 overall and 1-2-1 in SEC play. The polls had long since dropped us from the elite. Of course, the whole country had questions about us, especially folks at home.

NASHVILLE, Tenn. – So what is wrong with Ole Miss?

That was the first sentence of a Sunday morning column by *Jackson Daily News* sports editor Lee Baker. He didn't stop there:

"That continues as the question of the hour in Mississippi, gaining in volume after such failure by the once-terrifying Rebels to intimidate their opposition though by now after echoing over the hills, through the Delta, and down into the pine tree country, it's getting to be just a shade repetitive. Losing to Kentucky and Florida was one thing. Barely beating Tulane and then having to come pounding from behind to snake out a tie with Vanderbilt is something else again. But the question isn't "Is there something wrong?" – but rather "What's wrong?""

A lot of people tried to blame it on dissension among the players. If there was any, I never saw it. I never heard any arguments or disagreements. Sure, we were all frustrated, but we were a tight-knit group and above all we were friends. We never blamed each other. There were also unending rumblings about my music, but that honestly had nothing to do with anything except in some people's minds.

We had a chance for redemption at LSU. Tiger Stadium had its usual roar as we came calling. LSU fans sensed they could beat us following two straight losses in '62 by a 15-7 margin and '63 by a 37-3 final score.

After LSU's Doug Moreau kicked a 33-yard field goal, I scored on a three-yard keeper. Billy Carl Irwin made the extra point and we were up 7-3 in the first quarter. Billy Carl added a 28-yard field goal early in the fourth quarter to give us a little comfort at

10-3. LSU scored late after recovering a fumble on an Ole Miss punt return, went for two and made it. They beat us 11-10. Again, bitter disappointment.

Typical of our frustration was what happened on that LSU punt late in the game with Ole Miss sitting on that seven-point lead. To make sure we fielded the ball, Coach Vaught had both Doug Cunningham and Mike Dennis back to receive.

"Doug and I ran into each other trying to field the punt," Mike recalled. "The ball hit Doug on the shoulder, and LSU recovered.

"That game was typical of that season. We'd played our guts out. That 11-10 loss was horrific. A real heartbreaker. That was a blood battle. The hardest licks of any game I ever played in. There was blood on everybody."

On the winning drive, LSU quarterback Billy Ezell lofted the ball to Billy Masters for the touchdown. After Tiger head coach Charlie McClendon decided to go for two to win it, Ezell rolled out to the right and Moreau beat our defender on a slant pass to the outside. Our defensive back, Tommy Luke, Tom and Matt's dad, tipped the ball and almost knocked it away. But Moreau grabbed it and scored. Our nightmare season continued.

The following week we beat Tampa 36-0 in Oxford. I didn't play and neither did most of the other starters. The team was pretty banged up after LSU, and Coach Vaught gave us a breather. Then it was on to Knoxville and a game with Tennessee.

"Guitar-Picking QB Guides Rebel Attack" was the headline in the *Knoxville News Sentinel* on Friday November 13, 1964.

Marvin West of the *Knoxville News Sentinel*:

"For the purposes of comparison, (UT) Coach Doug Dickey thinks Weatherly is the nearest thing to Joe Namath that he has seen. He has warned the Vols that they can expect their most difficult defensive assignment of the season."

Lee Baker, *Jackson Daily News*:

"The sky was clear, the sun was shining and a Tennessee Homecoming crowd of 46,000 basked in the 70 degree weather this lovely mid-November Saturday afternoon. Then Ole Miss clouded up and rained all over the Vols, 30-0."

Finally we had put it all together. I was 11-for-16 for 126 yards passing and rushed for another 43 yards and a touchdown on eight carries. I'd had a good day. So did the entire team. We left Knoxville feeling better about ourselves and the upcoming game with Mississippi State which would be played in Oxford. NBC was televising it nationally, and we were looking forward to redeeming ourselves from what had happened over the past three months.

Buck Randall had played his last year of football in '63. My new roommate was my old friend, Ray Bedingfield. I would often strum my guitar, not only for enjoyment, but also to relax and relieve some stress and tension. The night before the game with Mississippi State, that's what I was doing in my room at Miller Hall – relaxing and strumming my guitar, but I was thinking about the game.

Coach "Bruiser" Kinard was checking rooms. Ray recalls warning me a couple of times to put the guitar down. Sure enough Coach Kinard opened the door as I was strumming.

"He kind of stared at Weatherly," Ray recalls. "I could see his color change. He sees that Jim's got his guitar out. There probably never has been a door shut with such force in Miller Hall. Wham! Coach Kinard didn't say a word. But his face said it all."

What Coach Kinard didn't understand was that playing my guitar was a way for me to relax. I was always nervous before games and noodling on my guitar was like playing checkers or going to a movie. My mind was always on the game, but music kept me from being too stressed out.

In today's world, music is a huge part of any football program. Every time I've been inside the Manning Center at Ole Miss to watch practice they've had hip hop and rap blaring through big

Handing off to Mike Dennis at a game in Hemingway Stadium

speakers. And you always see players getting off buses or even during warm-ups before games with their headsets on listening to music. All I was trying to do was get ready mentally, and my way was strumming my guitar. Maybe I was ahead of my time.

We woke up the next morning ready for another Battle for the Golden Egg. We were 5-3-1 overall and 2-3-1 in the SEC, not the kind of record Ole Miss was used to. On the same field where we would face our instate rival we had been ranked No. 1 in the country in the season opener three months earlier.

Mississippi State had a pretty good team despite its 3-6 record. The prognosticators favored us by a touchdown and a half. NBC was nationally televising the game, and there still weren't many of those during the regular college football season. Ole Miss hadn't lost to State since 1946. Why would this day be any different? Carl Walters, Jackson *Clarion Ledger*, the day after:

"There will be no classes at Mississippi State University, tomorrow, Monday, Dec. 7, 1964. Instead, State students, faculty members and all others connected with the school will have a special holiday – granted by President D.W. Colvard.

"For many of the Mississippi State students this will be their first celebration of a win over Ole Miss in their lifetime, as it had been 18 long years since the Bulldogs had triumphed over the Rebs."

We lost 20-17. I was devastated. We all were.

I had battled the toe injury since the season opener. Against Mississippi State I got hurt again.

Late in the second quarter I got tackled on the sidelines and landed on my back in front of the Ole Miss bench. Then a State player came flying in on a late hit and speared me in the ribs with his helmet while I was on the ground out of bounds. That hit drove me under one of the Ole Miss benches and I couldn't get up.

I was in terrible pain and could hardly breathe. With some help from teammates, Doc Knight quickly got me up and into the dressing room for X-rays. Doc said the X-rays didn't show a break or a crack, so they taped me up real good. But I didn't return to the game until late in the third quarter with painfully bruised ribs. This was in the days before most quarterbacks wore rib protectors. I was seriously hampered because of the pain. Trying to throw the ball was especially painful. I've still got a big knot on my rib cage from that hit.

Nobody wanted to be on the first Ole Miss team to have a mediocre season after so many years of great seasons. And no Ole Miss quarterback wanted to be the first to lose to Mississippi State after all those years of winning. Maybe it sounds silly, but I have carried that burden all of my life.

We all knew we'd been close to having another good season. We lost to Kentucky by six, to LSU by one, and to Mississippi State by three. And we'd tied Vanderbilt. We were so close to an 8-2 or 7-3 season. So close yet so far.

We were 5-4-1 and got invited to a bowl game when there still weren't that many of them. I'm sure Ole Miss' national reputation for winning helped the program get to an eighth-straight bowl. We were set to play Tulsa in the Bluebonnet Bowl at Rice Stadium in Houston.

Tulsa had a lot of talent. Their quarterback was the much-heralded All-American Jerry Rhome, who finished second in the Heisman Trophy race that year to John Huarte of Notre Dame.

One of Tulsa's wide receivers was the sure-handed Howard Twilley, who finished second in the Heisman race the following year. Tulsa also had a huge, aggressive, defensive tackle named Willie Townes from Mississippi, an African-American player who from all accounts I've heard was the first Ole Miss had ever played against.

We lost again, this time 14-7.

I scored our only touchdown on a quarterback sneak, but I also threw two interceptions. My toe and my ribs hadn't healed so I was still in pain. No excuses, just facts. Again, I was trying too hard to make something happen instead of just playing football. I always felt if we won a game it was a team win. But if we lost it was my fault.

We ended up ranked No. 20 in the nation but with a 5-5-1 record. I know there were people who felt justified in thinking that my playing music in a nightclub with my band the summer before the season was the reason for our mediocre year. But it had nothing to do with playing music in Biloxi or strumming my guitar in the athletic dorm, or Coach Vaught would have never let me do it. We just lost some close games we should have won. Except for the Florida game, the others were close enough that we could have won them. We just fell short.

Teammate Mike Dennis came to my defense.

"Some people tried to find things to blame the '64 season on, and we had a less than productive year as a team than was anticipated, but it certainly wasn't because of any of Jimmy's doings," he said. "Jimmy hasn't gotten the credit he deserves because of that year we had in 1964. He focused on football as much as any quarterback I played with. Jimmy wasn't a guy to go out there and shake you up on the field or raise his voice. But he was very much in charge."

Still, for years I carried the feeling that whole season was my fault. I just couldn't shake it off. Maybe somewhere deep inside I was reacting to the things that some of the fans had said about me. Maybe I felt guilty. I felt like I had let the team down, not to mention Coach Vaught and the rest of the coaches. A lot of the fans felt that way too as well as some in the media. If we'd had the Internet in those days, I would have been torched.

Roommate Ray Bedingfield also had some strong opinions about all the talk of my music getting in the way of football:

"In high school, absolutely not, and in college, absolutely not. Jim always stayed in shape physically. Any money I'm sure he made he shared with his family, which was needed. I think he might have been used as a scapegoat, by some to direct blame in an unfair way just because of not having a perfect season in 1964. The guy with the guitar has to be target number one."

Even though our season was less than spectacular, I was named second-team All-Southeastern Conference quarterback by the Associated Press and United Press International. Joe Namath of Alabama was first-team. I was also honorable mention All-American. According to the Sports Reference website, I completed 91 of 170 passes to lead the SEC in passing percentage with 53.5. I had 1,034 passing yards, which was second behind Rick Norton of Kentucky. I had five passing touchdowns which was third in the conference behind Rick Norton with nine and Florida's Spurrier with six.

I led the SEC in throwing interceptions with 14. That one hurt. I was second in passing efficiency with 97.9 behind Rick Norton and was sixth in rushing touchdowns with five. I was second in total yards with 1,296 and second in total touchdowns with 10.

My three-year varsity college stats for 29 games reads like this:

Passing: 158 completed out of 291 attempts. Percentage - 54.3. 1,890 yards, 15 touchdowns, 22 interceptions, 110.7 quarterback rating. Rushing: 175 for 694 yards and 11 touchdowns for a 4.0 yards average per carry. Total: 26 career touchdowns and 2,584 yards.

That's less than one season's stats in today's world of high-octane football. We didn't have the kind of wide open aerial fireworks you see in college football today. It was "three yards and a cloud of dust." Coach Vaught's theory was if you gain 3 and 1/2 yards on each play, you had a first down. That worked out well for him for a quarter century.

18 —⚬

Moving On

Jeanette Noe, the *Birmingham News*, Sunday January 24, 1965:

"It's been a toss-up so far in deciding what career, singer or pro football player, to pursue, but now it looks like Ole Miss' singing quarterback, Jimmy Weatherly, is headed toward the goal line of the musical world."

I was drafted by the Boston Patriots of the old American Football League, who later became the New England Patriots of the NFL. The Dallas Cowboys talked to me about signing with them as a free agent when I wasn't drafted in the NFL. Boston offered me $12,000, which was the median salary at the time, and a $1,000 bonus. Joe Namath signed with the New York Jets of the AFL that year for $400,000, which was the start of paying professional football players high salaries.

I really wasn't interested in playing pro football at any price – well, almost any price. I had really enjoyed playing college football and that was enough. I just had no desire to go to the next level.

Besides, my toe was still giving me a lot of trouble and I wasn't sure that I could even play pro football. At times it hurt like crazy, and I didn't want to go into a rookie season with an injury. So I decided to keep playing music with my band. I wanted to see where that would take me.

A lot of people thought I was crazy. They just couldn't get a grip on an Ole Miss quarterback playing music in a rock and roll band and writing songs and not wanting to play pro football.

I joined my band for the spring semester in 1965. We were still called "Jimmy Weatherly and the Vegas." The band still consisted of Pat Kincade on guitar, Leland Russell on bass, and J.D. Lobue on organ. Once again Pat had gone looking for a new drummer to replace Jeff Mitchell. He found a good one in Johnny Miller, an Ole Miss law student. And Pat continued to help us with his marketing skills. He knew exactly who to target.

"I started compiling a letter to every class president in every high school in Mississippi," Pat recalled. "I put in there I was with Jimmy Weatherly and the Vegas from Ole Miss. In the spring, I mailed them out to every high school in the state. I looked on a map. I'd see a town. I'd send the letter to that high school; attention class president. It worked. We played a lot of graduation parties. In fact, we had to turn some down because we were too booked.

"We played probably at least one night a week in a sorority house in a mixer or open house. And we played every single Friday and Saturday night. We were booked every weekend. There were even people changing their parties so we could play for them. We were always on the road."

We were now playing less Elvis and rockabilly and more contemporary rock songs that were coming over from England. All of us really loved the Beatles. We also added more R&B songs from artists like Bo Diddley, James Brown, and Ray Charles. At fraternity and sorority dances, the students loved hearing and dancing to R&B music.

It was great fun. We had built a strong reputation as a really good reliable band. But we quickly learned that a musician's life isn't always easy.

Pat had booked a graduation dance and costume party on the Gulf Coast in the spring of 1965. The school had rented a big auditorium, expecting 200 people who were dressing up in Indian costumes. But Leland didn't want to use his car, which we had almost worn out pulling our equipment trailer.

I told him we'd use the black bomb, my old '57 Chevy. Pat said it would never make it, but I overruled him. In retrospect, it wasn't such a good move.

Pat and a friend of Leland's named Ricky took off early and the rest of us were supposed to follow later on.

"We hadn't gone too far," Pat recalled, "and it got a little hilly and that old car was falling apart. So I pulled into this big gravel parking lot on the right that had a country store and a honky-tonk bar and a few houses around it."

Pat reasoned that the car "wasn't too far off the highway so it would be visible to the other guys passing by. We went into the bar, knowing that they were an hour or so back. We had a beer and waited awhile, me thinking they would see the car and trailer parked there for sure. After a while, I told Ricky to go stand out by the highway and watch for them coming just to be sure. Then I had another beer.

"About twenty minutes later Ricky came back in the bar, sat down and ordered a beer. Didn't say a word. So I looked at him a couple minutes and then I told him to go back out there and look for the other car. Then he told me, 'Oh, they already went by.'

"I couldn't believe it. He didn't even try to flag them down, just watched them roar by. So Ricky and I hopped in the black bomb and took off again."

Pat said five miles down the road "that old car started smoking and shaking and then it just died. I barely got it to the side of the road. And there we sat with a dead car and that blue trailer that I had someone paint this big 'V' on the front.

"We hitchhiked back to the store and called Leland's dad, our band's manager, who promised to send a U-Haul. It took forever to get there and when it did, we discovered it had a governor on it that limited the speed to 50 miles per hour," Pat said. "We limped into Biloxi at 11. The dance was from 8 to 12.

"We changed into our shark skin suits we got from Gene Ware's Clothing Store on the Gulf Coast and went to work. I remember standing there looking out at this huge auditorium from that big stage and there were like maybe 15 people there. I remember seeing this one girl who was dressed like Pocahontas with war paint on her cheeks just standing there looking at us. They had this big costume party planned and we played maybe five or six songs and then the few who were there just drifted away. So we just stood there. And then we started breaking everything down."

They actually tried to pay us but Pat refused the money. He wasn't going to let them pay for something that was our fault.

On the drive back home, Pat recalled, "we stopped at Jimmy's car on the side of the road. He didn't want it anymore and I sure didn't want anything to do with it. So we just left it."

A few days later, Pat said he went back to look for his trailer and it wasn't there with the black bomb. A cop showed up and led him to it, "sitting on the side of this backwoods gravel road with the lock broken off. We hooked it up and brought it back to Ole Miss.

"We never saw Jimmy's old car again. It died right there. That was the very last time that Jimmy offered any input on travel arrangements. He left all of that up to me right up to the very last day."

The Vegas – Pat Kincade, me, J.D. Lobue, Johnny Miller, Leland Russell (lying down)

The Vegas performed in the New Orleans area of the World's Fair in New York in 1965

19 —⚮

The World's Fair

At the end of the school year in 1965, the band decided to drive to New York to play the World's Fair for the summer. We didn't even have a booking. We just thought we'd go see what we could stir up, kind of like we did when we went to the gulf coast the summer before.

When we got there we were told there was a central stage where bands could audition. So we set up our equipment and played for whoever would listen.

As Pat recalled it, "There was a girl in the audience who liked us. Her dad had a restaurant in the New Orleans area of the Fair and was looking for a band. So we went to talk to him at the New Orleans Pavilion. It was like Bourbon Street in there. We set up in this restaurant on stage and played for him. He liked us and he hired us right then. We had a lot of fun playing there but we really weren't making any inroads in getting a record deal."

Leland knew I never touched alcohol. Not even a taste. So while we were playing the Fair he decided to play a prank on me.

"I'm at the German beer garden and talking to the waitresses," Leland recounted. "I told one of them, 'I've got a friend and I'd like to play a little joke on him. He will order a German Pepsi, but bring him a dark beer.' Those look just like a Pepsi. I told Jimmy that German Pepsis were really good and he should try one. She brings it. He takes a big swig. And he spits it all over the place. That was Jimmy. We all got a good laugh out of that."

While in New York we scouted around for an agent who could help us get in to see some record executives or at least book us in some New York clubs. We found one that booked us in a dump in New Jersey. It was horrible, really rundown, no crowds, a very depressing place. It looked like an old dilapidated lodge of some sort. We didn't play there very long.

I also checked out some New York music publishers to see if I could drum up some interest in my songs, but I didn't have any luck. Finally, we went to see someone at the Creative Arts Agency. A guy there said he could book us at a club in Erie, Pa., called the Village Hotel. He said they would pay us more money than we were making at the World's Fair so we decided to leave New York and drive to Erie.

When we arrived we took one look and said, "Oh no, not another one of these." It was a really rundown looking joint, but not as bad as the one we had played in New Jersey. And it was more like a motel than a hotel. The first night we played there only two guys were at the bar and they looked like they were drunk. We thought, "It's going to be a long rest of the summer."

Then word began to spread that there was a pretty good band playing at the Village Hotel. Crowds began to pick up, especially young people. Soon the place was packed every night and stayed that way until we left at the end of the summer. We made friends with a lot of the people that came to dance to our music. They turned out to be a really friendly bunch and loved us.

With September approaching, the band drove back to Mississippi to enroll in the fall semester of 1965 at Ole Miss. I still didn't have my degree. But with football behind me I was free to play with the band during the season.

I was in my fifth year and I was supposed to help coach freshman football with Coach Wobble. When Wobble saw me he said, "You're not going to coach freshman football with me until you cut your hair." He could be really intimidating.

My hair wasn't real long at all, especially by today's standards. But it was to Coach Wobble and he made it an issue. I went to talk to Coach Vaught. When I told him what Coach Wobble had said, he responded, "Well, just go on and go to school and don't worry about coaching the freshmen," which is what I did.

It seemed to confirm my suspicion that Coach Wobble didn't like me very much. I wasn't a troublemaker and never had been, so it must have been the fact that I played guitar and sang in a rock band.

I had really wanted to coach freshman football. My major was physical education and I would have learned a lot working with Coach Wobble. The experience would have helped me get a coaching job after graduation. I really felt he was being unfair but I refused to let him bully me. So I went on to school and worked on getting my degree.

Meanwhile, the band was booked almost constantly on weekends at sorority and fraternity parties and high school dances around Mississippi and Memphis. I was still "the singing quarterback." We were having fun making money making music. So I guess in the long run, Wobble did me a favor.

In October of 1965, I flew to Los Angeles to appear on "Shindig," a popular nationally televised contemporary music show. It was aimed strictly at the teen market. Mary Ann Mobley, who attended Ole Miss and was crowned Miss America in 1959, was an actress and knew the producer. She got me on the show. It aired on October 14, 1965.

They wanted me to sing "I'm a Happy Man," a song made famous by The Jive Five. I really didn't want to sing that song. It just wasn't me, but I sang it anyway.

By coincidence, Delaney Bramlett was a member of the Shindogs, the regular house band on the show. Delaney was from Randolph, in my home county of Pontotoc. We played basketball against each other in high school when he was a senior and I was a freshman. We also competed in a talent contest at the Joy Theatre when I was in the eighth grade. He had a three-piece rockabilly band, and I just stood there with my guitar and sang. Both of us wound up in the top five, which meant we got to go to Memphis to appear on the "Pride of the Southland" TV show.

Later on, Delaney became part of the 1970s iconic rock duo Bonnie and Delaney and Friends. Among the "friends" who played in his band were George Harrison of the Beatles and Eric Clapton.

That trip to do "Shindig" was the first time I'd ever been to L.A. Right away I knew that's where the band should be if we wanted to have any chance at success in the music business. It really crackled with great music of all kinds.

We didn't make plans to go to California right away. Instead we headed to Nashville on Christmas break. Mr. Russell had set up a recording session for us there through a friend we had met while playing the Fiesta Club. His name was "Prof" Carpenter. He was a former band director at a Biloxi High School and he really liked the group and wanted to help us. He had some friends in the music business in Nashville and he contacted them to set up the session.

We recorded three songs at the historic Studio B at RCA where many of the country hits of that time were recorded including "Heartbreak Hotel" and several others by Elvis. Prof even hired the Jordanaires, Elvis' backup singers, to back me up vocally.

We recorded two songs that I wrote – "When You Get What You Want (You Don't Want It Anymore)" and "Wise Men Never Speak." J.D. and Leland wrote the other one, called "I'm Gonna Make It."

We took an extra guitar player with us. Freddie Hester was from Tupelo and he had occasionally played with us since high school. He was an outstanding guitar player who really added to the tracks we cut.

That was the closest we'd been to the real music business.

Our manager, Julian Russell, sent our tapes to A&R (Artists and Repertoire) man Bernie Wayne at 20th Century Fox Records in New York. Mr. Wayne liked them and said he wanted to sign us to a recording contract. We were beside ourselves.

We were thinking, "Wow, this could be the break we'd been hoping for." We signed the papers before he could change his mind. Then we waited excitedly for our record to come out.

Mr. Wayne wanted me to fly to New York to hear the newly mastered songs before they were released. Pat and I flew with Mr. Russell and his pilot from Jackson to Flushing, New York, in a six-seat Cessna. Julian had also hired a photographer to go with us. A Jackson DJ, Ron Grantham, also went. I was still nervous about flying and the bumpy ride over the Appalachian Mountains in a small plane didn't change my mind.

We got to New York and drove immediately to the record company offices at 20th Century Fox. We excitedly sat down in Mr. Wayne's office ready to hear our record. The first single was going to be "Wise Men Never Speak." I sang the lead vocal. When he played it for us, Pat and I just looked at each other.

We couldn't believe it. They had recorded a soft delay of the entire song directly behind the original track trying to be creative. But instead they had totally ruined our record. I was heartbroken and mad. Pat was just mad. We couldn't believe that professionals would do something so stupid. Over time, I would learn that it's really not all that uncommon.

We flew back to Jackson in a blue funk. Seems like there was always a stumbling block in our way, from people ignoring my songs to people screwing up our records. We were learning fast that some things in the music business just don't work out the way you want them to.

The "B" side of the record was the song J.D. and Leland wrote called "I'm Gonna Make It." I thought it was really the stronger cut and a great rocker. If we'd had some national promotion, I think it could have been a hit. I sang lead on that one as well.

Both songs got some airplay on radio stations across Mississippi and the South as well as on Memphis station WMPS. There was a disc jockey there named Jack Grady who really liked "Wise Men Never Speak." He constantly played it on his call-in show.

We could pick the station up at Ole Miss, and I listened for it every night. Our song on Memphis radio, now that was really something to brag about. It never got near any of the record charts, however it did get enough call-in votes to make number one on Jack's show several nights in a row.

Twentieth Century Fox just didn't seem to have the wherewithal to do a very good job of promoting it. At least we got some good bookings in the South because of those records.

After the first record fizzled, Fox released "When You Get What You Want." We backed it with "Unchained Melody," which we recorded in Memphis at Pepper-Tanner Studios. It was one of my favorite songs, and I wanted to sing it even if I didn't write it. Same thing happened. Some airplay in the South and that's about it. Back to the drawing board.

Years later, I would discover that one of those songs had a much bigger impact than I realized.

Marty Stuart, a Mississippi native and country music star, would credit it with jump-starting his career in music.

"I will forever be grateful to Jim Weatherly for writing and recording a song entitled 'When You Get What You Want (You Don't Want It Anymore).' I heard it on radio as a kid. It moved me and helped light a fire in my heart that has led to a lifelong love affair with music," he said.

In the mid '60s Marty Gamblin was working for our manager, Julian Russell. Julian was also managing a black female trio from Mississippi called The Poppies. Dorothy Moore, later of "Misty Blue" fame, was their lead singer.

In the 1970s Dorothy wound up recording eight of my songs, including "He Knows Where to Touch Me."

"I love that song," Dorothy said. "I love all of Jim's songs. He just has the gift. Jim is one of the greatest writers. And I'm glad he's a Mississippian, too, and my friend."

The Gordian Knot – J.D. Lobue, me, Dulin Lancaster, Pat Kincade, and Leland Russell.

20 ——⚬

The Gordian Knot

At the end of the spring semester of 1966, I hadn't done my practice teaching so I still couldn't graduate. For the summer of '66, the band decided to go back to Erie and play the Village Hotel again. We'd had such a good time the summer before that we wanted to go back and see our friends. We packed the place night after night.

Dulin Lancaster of Jackson had joined the band as our drummer. And he was a good one. We played half the summer in Erie and then, on a whim, decided to drive out to L.A. looking for a record company that might like us enough to let us make an album.

My plan was still to go back to Ole Miss in the fall of '66 and do my practice teaching, get my degree and become a football coach. Success in the music business, at that point, seemed like a wild and distant dream, something unattainable.

She never said it, but my Mom probably didn't want me to go that far from home anyway. Knowing I would be back in time to enroll at Ole Miss in the fall must have given her some comfort.

On our way to Los Angeles, we decided Jimmy Weatherly and the Vegas wasn't the right name for the band anymore. It was fine in Mississippi and the South where I was known, but we needed a more contemporary name to compete with L.A. bands.

We kicked around some names and finally came up with The Gordian Knot. We thought it had a classy ring to it and sounded more like the names of bands making records at the time, yet it was still different. It just sounded good to us. It sounded contemporary, and it looked good in print. It also represented something that could not be undone, and we were a close, tight-knit group.

Headed for L.A., Dulin was taking his turn driving the truck through Colorado. The rest of us were in back in the camper asleep. When we woke up and looked out, there were mountains all around us, close enough to touch. We wondered where in the world we were.

Several miles back Dulin had seen a sign that said Rocky Mountains. He said he'd never seen the Rocky Mountains so he thought he'd go take a look. Typical Dulin. He turned off the freeway and now he was lost. He tried to find his way out, but every road led him deeper into the mountains.

Dulin was a free spirit and it was no big deal to him. He just shrugged it off. We couldn't help but laugh. It seemed like we were in those mountains for two days and didn't have a clue which direction to go. Finally, we found our way back to the freeway. After that, one of us always rode in the cab with Dulin. And stayed awake.

At that point, Leland remarked, "We had traveled around the Mid-South, up the East Coast to play at the World's Fair, then to Erie, Pa. Then we followed Horace Greeley's advice, 'Go West, young man, Go West.' We ended up settling in the Promised Land and performing together for the rest of the 1960s. We arrived in California at the birth of flower power, psychedelic music. It was a 'trip.'"

A road weary group pulled into the Sunset Palms Motel on the Sunset Strip in Hollywood near La Brea Avenue in mid-summer of 1966 with wide eyes, big dreams and a new name.

The Gordian Knot, along with our equipment manager Jerry Hadley, who we'd met in Erie, all stayed in one room for at least two weeks. We didn't have enough money for separate rooms. It was really cramped quarters, but we had been together as a group long enough to know how to put up with each other.

Amazingly, we never argued. Pat was our banker. He kept what little money we had so we wouldn't spend it all. He doled out three dollars a day to each of us. That's all we had to eat on and whatever else we wanted to do.

Leland remembers.

"We would go across the street to Tiny Naylor's. It was a drive-in where carhops rolled out food on roller skates, a forerunner to today's Sonic. It was a popular place often frequented by unemployed actors, out of work dancers and hungry musicians. We'd go over there and eat. They liked us so they would give us extra food and pie," he said.

We began immediately the task of calling Hollywood agencies. Finally, we found one that said they could get us some bookings. We became friendly with a young agent there named John Babcock. He was part Hollywood and part average guy. He became our new manager.

I began looking on the backs of album covers and in trade magazines, and I'd call on the producers whose names I saw. Most of the time we couldn't get through the front door. And when we did we still couldn't get in to see anybody. At least it was an exciting time, despite the rejection.

There was talk from time to time of packing up and heading back to Ole Miss. Spirits were running low and we were just about to run out of money when Babcock finally got us our first gig, a one-nighter at a club on Hollywood Boulevard called The Mystery House. They were going to pay $100 for the night and that was for the whole band. But it gave us enough money to stay out there a little longer.

After a while we began to get bookings at clubs like P.J.'s, The Rag Doll, The Pink Carousel, and It's Boss, all top L.A. clubs that bands wanted to play. Trini Lopez, who later cut two of my songs in Spanish, got a record deal and became a star by playing at P.J.'s. As a bonus we got to watch the acts in the showroom while we were on break. We watched comedian Richard Pryor several times and later the popular group The Fifth Dimension. Meanwhile, we were building a reputation as a good, dependable band.

Our camper was the only transportation we had. We couldn't use it to go anywhere unless everybody went or if the other members agreed they didn't need it. Nobody had a car. We were finally making a little money. Things were going so well we decided to postpone going back to Ole Miss for the fall semester. We didn't know where we were headed, but we were having fun getting there.

One of the first people we met in L.A. was Teri Brown. Teri's dad was Warren Brown, head of publishing for MCA. Her uncle,

Les Brown, was the leader of his own orchestra, the famous "Les Brown and his Band of Renown," one of the popular big bands during the war years. We all became friends and in 1967 Teri was appointed head of A&R (artists and repertoire) for Decca Records. One of her jobs was to scout clubs for new talent. She saw us playing in P.J.'s and wanted to sign us to Decca Records.

"I liked the guys, and they were really good," Teri said. "They always had original songs that were good. For some reason it didn't work out (with Decca). Maybe they got a better deal. They wanted some new equipment for the band, and they had to justify why they were asking that kind of money."

As Teri remembered it, "The L.A. scene was changing, mainly because of significant cultural shifts throughout the country. The music scene itself was changing because there were so many rebellious people. They were having riots down on the Sunset Strip protesting the Vietnam War.

"The (music) groups that made it were just lucky to have made it. If you got a hit then you could sustain because you had money coming in and lots of money. But if you don't get a hit the first time out of the box, particularly in that time period, it was pretty hard to think you could go two or three albums deep," she said.

I think Decca didn't offer the kind of upfront money we needed. Or maybe they wanted to own our publishing. I don't remember. I do know I was adamant about not signing away our publishing rights to anybody.

L.A. is a networking kind of town. It was my good fortune to run into a young agent named Mickey Freiberg while we were playing at P.J.'s. We became friends and he thought I might be good for television commercials.

One day Mickey told me the Pepsi Cola Company was shooting

a commercial on the beach and looking for someone who could throw a football. He asked if I was interested.

I thought, "Why not?" It would bring in some cash and get me a Screen Actors Guild card. So I jumped at the chance. Mickey told me where to go for the audition. He told me to wear a swimsuit. I joined all these guys and girls in their swimsuits at a huge house in Beverly Hills with a big swimming pool.

After I'd been there for a while, one of the people casting the commercial handed me a football and said, "Throw it." I started passing the ball to different people and I was hired on the spot.

When the day came to shoot the commercial, all the actors were loaded on a big bus in Hollywood and driven to the beach just north of Santa Monica. It was sunny and warm, a perfect day. We played football on the beach while the cameraman shot whenever, wherever, and whatever he wanted. That was the only national commercial I did, and the residuals kept me afloat while I struggled to make something happen with the band and my songs.

Years later, my Ole Miss teammate Sam Owen told me he was watching TV one day and the Pepsi commercial came on. He said, "Judy (his wife), come here. Look at this. It's Jimmy Weatherly."

I continued to write songs and tried hard to find a publishing deal or someone to pitch my songs to. I saw the names Charlie Greene and Brian Stone on some record label or in *Billboard* magazine and decided to call them. They managed Sonny and Cher. They were also record producers. I actually got in to see them.

They were about to produce a record for a guy named Magnificent Malouchi. They told me it was an R&B act, so I took them an R&B song called "Mama, Your Daddy's Come Home." It was a really funky little song that I'd written, and I wasn't even sure if it was any good. But they seemed to like it and they cut it on

Magnificent Malouchi. It was released as a single but never made a dent at radio. That was usually the case, but at least I had my name as a writer on a record label. That was the first song I'd ever had recorded by someone outside the band.

All dressed up and wondering where we're going

The Gordian Knot in motion

21 —⚬

Beverly Hills Party Circuit

Meanwhile the Gordian Knot kept playing L.A. clubs. Later that summer of '66, as luck would have it, we ran into another fellow Mississippian named Carl Brent, who introduced us to the celebrity party circuit.

Carl seemed to be friends with everyone in Hollywood. He was from Shannon, 20 miles or so from Pontotoc and just south of Tupelo. Common ground. He was full of energy and sharp as a tack with Southern charm and a Hollywood demeanor. You would have thought he knew everyone's phone number in Hollywood by heart. At one time Carl had been Judy Garland's road manager.

He became our new manager and Babcock went to work for him. Carl had real clout. We were at his house in Benedict Canyon one day when he called Eddie Fisher, one of my favorite singers growing up. Eddie was throwing a party that night at his home.

Carl said, "I have a new band that I want to play your party tonight." Eddie told him he already had a band. Carl said, "Cancel them. I've got a better band and I'll pay half the cost." Eddie canceled the other band and hired us.

That afternoon we went over to Eddie's house to set up. He seemed to be a very lighthearted guy, and he hung around talking to us while we were setting up our equipment.

Connie Stevens, who starred in the TV series "77 Sunset Strip" and movies such as *Parrish* and *Palm Springs Weekend* and who was also the future Mrs. Eddie Fisher, was at the party that night. So were Stuart Whitman, Richard Harris, Dinah Shore, and Sal Mineo, as well as some of the other Hollywood elite.

We were having the time of our lives rubbing shoulders with people we'd grown up watching in movies and on TV. We played on a stage by the pool until 4 a.m., packed up and went home.

That was just the beginning.

The band went on to play parties at the homes of Joan Collins, Robert Mitchum, and Natalie Wood, among others. Our reputation was spreading fast. It wasn't long after the Eddie Fisher party that the Gordian Knot was asked to play a party outside at Richard Harris' house. He had just finished the movie "Camelot" and he had a big home in Bel Air.

"Joan Collins was there, who later became a big fan of our band. Tony Curtis and Richard Chamberlain were there. We must have played until three or four in the morning. Then all of a sudden everybody was gone. So we went inside and started looking for food in the kitchen," Leland recalled.

When we started to pack our equipment to leave, we couldn't find Babcock. We were really tired so we all found places somewhere in the house to sleep. Pat crashed in the kitchen with the beef stroganoff, and I slept on a couch in the living room. I don't know where the others slept. At daylight we were all still there.

Suddenly, Richard Harris came strolling down the big staircase in his robe. He said, "'Ello, mates," as if finding people asleep in his living room and his kitchen was something that happened all the time. It was about then that Babcock, disheveled and still sleepy, stumbled in from the patio. He had fallen asleep out there. We didn't want to overstay our welcome, so we packed our instruments and said goodbye. Richard Harris was a very warm and gracious host. Not to mention understanding.

Next, Carl found us work playing in a club in Riverside, 70 miles east of Los Angeles. One day I drove by a used car lot and something caught my eye. It was a 1950 XK120 Jaguar convertible. It was only about 16 years old and I thought it was beautiful. They wanted $1,800 for it. I couldn't afford it so I borrowed the money from a bank in Pontotoc. They wired the cash, I got behind the wheel of my "new to me" car and started driving back to L.A.

About 10 or 15 miles up the freeway it went dead. Somehow, I don't remember, I got it fixed and drove it home. I drove that little car around L.A. for four years, then sold it to Pat for the hefty sum of one dollar with the provision that he would sell it back to me for one dollar whenever I wanted it. That was because I didn't want to have to keep paying the insurance on it.

Then I bought a used Ford Mustang, like the one Steve McQueen drove in a movie called *Bullitt*. Later, I bought the Jag back from Pat and kept it until the 1990s when I was living in Nashville. Then I sold it. It was tough to part with. Growing up in Pontotoc, I never thought I'd drive a Jag at any price.

After playing in Riverside for a couple of weeks, Carl got the band a gig playing for a party at Natalie Wood's home.

Our stage was 30 yards from the house, next to the fence by the pool. We quickly got a lesson in the Hollywood pecking order.

"On a break we went inside to eat," Pat said. "Natalie's maid told us in no uncertain terms that we had to eat in the kitchen. When Carl Brent came rushing in and saw us sitting there, he stopped and stared then turned around and walked out. You could tell he was pissed. His face was beet red. Dean Martin's wife, Jeannie, knew we were eating in the kitchen, so she got a plate and ate in the kitchen with us. She was one sweet lady."

On another break, the band stayed outside because it didn't seem like we were wanted in the house. Peter Lawford, one of Frank Sinatra's Rat Pack, was out there. He started talking to us and before long Natalie Wood came out and told us we couldn't mingle with the guests. To her we were just the hired help and she treated us like hired help.

We were playing parties and clubs while still looking for our big break. We had gained some notoriety but were no closer to a record deal. Still, we were having a good time.

Leland had met Robert Mitchum's daughter, Trina, at the Richard Harris party. He ran into her again at a club on the Sunset Strip called It's Boss. We happened to be playing there and she had come to see us. They became friends and she invited Leland over to the Mitchum home in Beverly Hills on the Saturday afternoon after Thanksgiving, 1966, to eat. Leland asked Pat and me to go with him. I had been a big Robert Mitchum fan for years and so had my dad. I thought it was pretty cool to be going to his house. He was one of those bigger than life guys for that era of moviegoers. One of my favorite movies he starred in was *Blood on The Moon* made in the 1940s.

When we got there, Trina took us around to the backyard patio area by the pool. We stayed out there talking for a couple of hours when Mrs. Mitchum came out with a tray of uncooked steaks.

"She was rather brisk. Not a Mississippi welcome," Pat recalled.

"Of course her under-aged daughter was out by the pool with three strange guys. So I guess under the circumstances, it was nice of her not to run us off."

They brought out side dishes and spices for the steaks and then left us alone. So Pat, being the chef of the group, put together a sauce, seasoned the steaks and tended them on the grill. Suddenly, the side gate opened from the front yard and in came Robert Mitchum and his son, Jim.

"We froze." Pat said. "I was thinking he was going to tell us to leave and his son was going to make sure we did. Mr. Mitchum walked right up to within six inches of my face, looked at the steaks, then looked back at me. He looked at me for several seconds and then said, 'Son, would you keep those coals going for me? I might want to put a steak on later.' I said, 'Yes sir, I sure will!' Then he and his son just turned and walked away."

Pat recalled, "We ate steaks out there with Trina until it started getting dark and cold. Then Mrs. Mitchum's maid invited us in and took us to the study where Mr. Mitchum was sitting in a big leather chair. We sat there talking to him until 4:30 in the morning. The man we thought would throw us out turned out to be the most genuine, nicest, most caring and most interesting man I had ever met. He told us all sorts of stories about his movies, including the special booze cart he had while making the movie *Home From The Hill* in Oxford (Mississippi) in the late 1950s."

Then, Pat said, "He told us a story about when he was in Tanganyika making a movie and he went out drinking one early afternoon and stumbled back to his hotel at 10 p.m. and passed out across his bed. He woke up and looked at his watch and it said 12:00 and he jumped up and showered and dressed real quick, because he was supposed to be on the movie set at 12:00.

"He went down to the desk and nobody was around so he asked

the desk clerk where everyone was. The clerk told him it was just after midnight. He'd slept two hours and thought he'd slept 14. He blamed his watch and took it off and gave it to the desk clerk. Said he couldn't trust that watch. He was a funny guy." He told us he had won that watch in a poker game.

Even though he played a tough guy in many of his films, he was just the nicest guy in the world. He had lived "a lot of life." After meeting Mr. Mitchum, much to the band's surprise, we were asked to play a party at the Mitchum's home.

In fact, he threw that party "so we could have a payday," Pat said. "Leland had told Mitchum's daughter, Trina, in passing, that we didn't have much money. She told her dad and he decided to throw the party so we could make some. We were told later that he didn't even like parties and never went to them."

For a man who didn't like parties, he spared no expense.

"The whole yard was transformed," Pat said. "The pool was covered and they had laid sod over it. They had a bandstand and a whole bunch of tables and chairs and lanterns, and a buffet. It was the first time I ever saw a pig with an apple in its mouth. Mr. Mitchum and his wife were greeting all of the guests. His wife was all over the place, tending to everything and everybody. Mr. Mitchum just stood there in his black tux saying hello and welcome."

As we got ready to play, Mr. Mitchum asked Pat if everything was OK. When he said yes, Mr. Mitchum nodded and went in the house. We never saw him again that night.

Pat recalled the food.

"There was a huge inverted seafood tower of ice that was cone shaped. Never saw anything like that. Must have been eight feet tall. After our first set, I made my way over there to eat some shrimp and crab. I looked around and Henry Fonda was standing next to me. He asked, 'What do you see in here that's good?' I told him it all looked good, especially the shrimp that were as big as your fist.

"Nobody danced during our first set, and on our first break as I was making my way to the seafood tower I passed Steve McQueen's chair," Pat said. "He stopped me to request a song. He said, 'You guys are really good,' and asked why no one was dancing. I told him that as soon as the first couple got up to dance, everyone else would, too. When we started the second set, about 30 seconds into it Steve McQueen and his wife started dancing. A few seconds later another couple followed and then more started getting up. I looked over at Mr. McQueen and he looked at me and nodded, and then he and his wife walked back to their table. He got it started for us. The two of them didn't dance another time.

"The cream of the Hollywood crop was there that night, so many legends. Dean Martin was there. Donna Reed was there. Lee Marvin was there. Things started winding down late into the night. Only two people were still on the dance floor. Lee Marvin and Steve McQueen were dancing with each other," Pat continued. "They looked like they both might be a little inebriated. Marvin was beat and sat down in a chair, leaning over with his elbow on a knee, white hair and face as red as could be."

Mr. Mitchum had given that party for us. That's the kind of man he was. He was a tough man with a kind heart. At one time in his younger life, he had been a hobo, riding trains from town to town. I'm sure he remembered what it was like not to have any money.

"We had arrived in L.A. in August of 1966 on Sunset and La Brea wondering, 'O.K., now what do we do?' And before the end of the year," Pat said, "we were playing at Robert Mitchum's house."

22 —⊷

"Get Your Helmets, Boys"

In February of 1967 we were asked to go with Nancy Sinatra and Jimmy Boyd on a 17-day USO tour of Vietnam to entertain the troops. Nancy, of course, is the legendary Frank Sinatra's daughter, best known for her big hit "These Boots Are Made for Walking." Jimmy was a singer/comedian who recorded "I Saw Mommy Kissing Santa Claus" when he was just a little boy. The song became a timeless hit and is still heard today at Christmas. Jimmy Boyd was born in south Mississippi, so we had a natural bond.

Nancy had heard us play at a party and thought we might be a good band to back her on her tour. Her music director was a guitar player named Billy Strange who came up with the guitar lick that became the song "Limbo Rock," but for some reason he couldn't go on the USO tour. We were playing a club called the Rag Doll in North Hollywood and one afternoon Billy and Nancy came to the club to work with us on some of Nancy's songs for the show.

They liked what they heard.

Carl Brent came over to us after our audition and said, "Get your helmets, boys. You're going to Vietnam."

A few days later we were flying out on a commercial flight from L.A. to San Francisco. They announced that Nancy Sinatra was on board with her band headed for Vietnam to play for the soldiers. Everyone applauded. When we got to San Francisco, we got on a commercial plane packed with military guys. We were the only civilians. We refueled in Tokyo and flew on to Saigon. When we got there we met Captain Frank Livolsi, our escort officer, who babysat us during our time in Vietnam.

The war had left Americans bitterly divided. Everyone seemed to have strong opinions about it. On her website "Nancy Sinatra, California Girl," Nancy expresses some of her own deeply-held feelings about that Vietnam tour:

"All of the people of my generation were involved in one way or another in the Vietnam War. They were enlisting, drafted, escaping to another country or a marriage and children they didn't really want. I knew I had to do something so I called the USO and volunteered to go and entertain the troops.

"The USO was happy to have me. I joined forces with singer Jimmy Boyd and a group called the Gordian Knot, led by Jim Weatherly, and planned a 1967 tour. We did big shows (it seems as if 250,000 people saw us in Cam Ranh Bay) and little shows for as few as 50.

"Each outfit put us up wherever they could – sometimes a building, sometimes a tent – with shells going off over our heads. We spent one night on the aircraft carrier Kitty Hawk. My God I was terrified. But once you are committed to something like that, you move past the fear. I cannot talk about the sights, sounds or smells of war. I have only feelings – no words. But I do run into guys all the time who say 'Thank You.'

Nancy Sinatra, me, and Pat Kincade

"The combination of the pinup pictures in Stars and Stripes and my hit song 'Boots' brought me thousands of letters from G.I.s, along with several pairs of army boots. Many troops adopted 'These Boots Are Made for Walking' as their marching song.

"When you are in a war zone the people around you become your brothers and sisters. They were then, are now and always will be a huge part of my life."

We were always surrounded by lots of soldiers. Still, we were in a war zone. Occasionally, we were reminded of that.

Pat recalled that Nancy was determined to make the most of every second in Vietnam.

"The first morning we were in Saigon, we had the day off. Our first show was to be in Saigon that evening. Nancy said, 'Well, we're not going to waste the morning.' So she took us to visit a hospital. There were some chairs set up outside the hospital in Saigon and a lot of soldiers were looking out the windows. We set up our equipment and did a full-blown show right there outside the hospital. Then we went and visited some of the wounded soldiers," Pat said.

The first night the band played in Saigon, Pat said he noticed these big guys standing behind us in uniform.

"There was normally no one on stage but the band. We found out the military had intercepted a transmission that the Viet Cong knew Nancy Sinatra was going to play in Saigon on that stage that night and all the generals and high-ranking officers were going to be there. They (the Viet Cong) had planned an attack and were going to bomb the place. One of the soldiers said that if they got the word that was happening, he was supposed to physically pick me up and take me down and put me in a shuttle. There was one of these soldiers for every member of the band as well as Nancy and Jimmy Boyd."

After the first week of traveling to different camps by helicopters, the band was set to have a day of rest. But that wasn't the plan for Nancy, who had come to Vietnam to make a difference.

"Nancy told us 'We didn't come here to rest,'" Pat said. "So she got on the phone with one of the generals. They told her there was no activity planned for that day. So she got in touch with the people in charge of the USO. Soon we were on a small prop plane where the seats were all facing backwards, flying out to the USS Kitty Hawk in the Gulf of Tonkin. Flew in, did two shows. Spent the night and flew out the next day. Then we went to our next destination to do a noon show. And we played one that night."

Leland has always been energetic and impulsive. He was always ready to take on any challenge.

"The admiral in charge of the fleet was sitting in his admiral's seat in the control room and Nancy and I were sitting across from him. I asked him if I could drive this boat. He said, 'Son, this is not a boat. It's a ship.' But he said I could at 0230 in the morning. That was when they were making the turn back. They were going up and down the coast. So at 0230 I went in there, took the wheel, and made the turn. It took 45 minutes," Leland said.

On the tour, Jimmy Boyd would open each show and mostly tell some jokes. After his comedy act we would play our set. Then Nancy would come out and do her show. We did this for 17 days with no days off, sometimes two or three shows a day. We traveled by Jeep, Hueys, and other helicopters. The soldiers seemed to really enjoy our performances. Especially Nancy's.

"These guys would go crazy over Nancy," Pat said. "Some of the soldiers tried to jump up there on stage and grab her, want to hug her and kiss her. The MPs would have to come up on stage and stop them and make them leave her alone.

"When we went to Da Nang in the northern part of Vietnam, we were housed in a villa outfitted with military cots and mosquito nets," Pat remembered.

"While there, we heard gunfire. Way off in the distance you could see tracer bullets. One night I couldn't sleep and went out into the central room at like 3 o'clock in the morning. Nancy came in and said she couldn't sleep either. She came in there and I played the guitar and we talked until the sun came up.

"When we got back to Saigon (after our tour was over) a special dinner had been arranged for Nancy and the rest of us before we flew out the next day. The dinner was to be at General English's house, a top general under General Westmoreland. Some dignitaries and high-ranking officers, as well as General English, were there to greet us. The table was set for a formal dinner, with

Performing with Nancy Sinatra in Vietnam

a beautiful tablecloth, china, silverware, and crystal glasses. As we were eating, there was a lot of conversation about what we had just experienced for two weeks. We were all so tired — exhausted may be a better word – the drinks were flowing endlessly and we were getting giddy with laughter and blowing off some steam. It should be noted that Jimmy drank way too much Pepsi. It was a memorable night," Pat said.

"The time to leave the dinner arrived. We didn't see J.D. anywhere, but Leland and I found him sleeping on the General's couch. We got him up, said our goodbyes with laughter, handshakes, and hugs and got into the vans for the ride back to the hotel."

The next day, General English himself saw us off.

"He walked up to us, shook everyone's hand, thanked us and told us that he hadn't had so much fun in a very long time. He wished us a safe trip and told us if we ever had to come back to Vietnam in a different capacity, to contact him and he would take care of us," Pat said.

On every flight on the Vietnam trip, Leland recalled, "Nancy would sit next to me and have me hold her hand while we took off and landed. When we landed in San Francisco on the way home, Nancy called her dad. He calls a general of the air base, who sends in this private plane to pick us up to fly us from San Francisco to L.A. So we're on Frank Sinatra's private plane. Nancy gave us a tour of the plane. I didn't have to hold her hand on her dad's plane. She said, 'I know the pilot. I'm fine now.'"

When it was all over, the band breathed a collective sigh of relief. We were worn out from the heavy schedule and the tensions of war. And we were glad to be back in the good ole USA.

Soon after the USO tour Pat and I received our draft notices to take our physicals. Pat's eyes were so bad that he was legally blind. That kept him out. I took my physical in downtown Los Angeles. I had letters from two doctors back in Mississippi saying they had been treating me for gout and I had to take medication for it. The Army physician looked at the huge knot on the joint of my big toe on my right foot. He didn't say anything so I went on and finished my physical.

All of the potential draftees then went into a waiting room where we would receive our draft cards. It was really nerve-wracking. When I finally got mine it didn't say 4-F, which was "not qualified for any military service." But it didn't say 1-A either, which was "available for military service." It said 1-Y, which meant they would only take me in case of some national emergency. It was a relief to get that behind me. I could now move on and concentrate on music.

The Gordian Knot, Nancy Sinatra, and Jimmy Boyd (bottom right)

Back in L.A. we resumed our search for some company that would give us a record deal. We caught a break when we were asked to appear in a Blake Edwards movie for Paramount Pictures called *Gunn*. Blake, one of the premier filmmakers of the era, wanted us to come over to Paramount Studios and meet with him. We were going to audition for the part of a band in a nightclub, so we had all our equipment set up there. We were waiting in this big room when Blake walked in with Ron Joy, a photographer friend we had met through Carl Brent. Ron was dating Nancy Sinatra.

"Then Henry Mancini came in," Pat said. "He was doing the score for the movie. He wanted to hear the song we were going to sing so we played it. He must have liked it because after we had finished he said 'good' and got up and walked out. Blake said a few words to us and then he said, 'See you on the set,' and that was it. We had the job."

In the movie, Pat recalled, we sang a song I had written with the rest of the group called "If Only I Could Fly."

"We spent many, many hours in the studio recording that song with as much precision as we could muster," Pat said. "The day of our shoot we went to the soundstage and set up all our equipment in this nightclub set and were ready to lip-sync the song. Blake was a loose and fun guy. He said 'Action' and the music started over the speakers and we pretended to play. Blake said 'Cut' and then asked if our equipment was in working order. Jimmy said, 'Yes sir, it's all here.'

"Then Blake told us that the music on the recording was too slow so he wanted us to play it live and speed it up a little. So that's what we did. Turned on the amps, turned on the mics, J.D. counted it off and we played it live. Got it on the first take. We had spent a month in the studio working on every little detail and ended up spending three minutes playing it live for the movie."

In July of 1968 the band was asked to play the wedding reception for Dean Martin's daughter at his home in Beverly Hills. It seemed like all of Hollywood was there. It was another one of those moments that, looking back, is hard to believe happened so fast for us out there.

Pat's mother couldn't believe it either. He took her to the reception. "She felt somewhat intimidated," Pat said. "So Jimmy gave her a guitar pick and told her if anyone asked, she could just say she was with the band."

The Gordian Knot, all Southern boys, had been in Los Angeles less than two years. We weren't used to seeing movie stars and celebrities just being themselves. It was still somewhat of a culture shock to us. And now we were playing parties at their homes. We still couldn't believe how quickly it had happened. Sometimes, it was difficult to believe it had happened at all.

We were having a blast and had made some good friends and a few inroads into the business.

As Leland put it so well, "We were famous among the famous."

23 ——⸙

Life Changing Moment

I was still writing songs, but I felt like I was writing just to be writing instead of writing with a purpose. I wrote for the group but I was trying to write other kinds of songs as well. I was struggling to find out who I was as a songwriter and the kind of songs I really wanted to write.

One day I got to pitch some songs to Johnny Rivers. Johnny grew up in Baton Rouge. He was discovered at the Whisky a Go Go nightclub on the Sunset Strip and went on to have a ton of hits including "Poor Side of Town," "Memphis," "Swayin' to the Music," "Mountain of Love," "Secret Agent Man," and a lot of others. I knew he had an office on Sunset Boulevard close to a club called Gazzarri's, so I looked up the phone number and called his office.

I was surprised to get right in to see him. Johnny was affable and down to earth. He listened to my songs and seemed to be impressed. He invited me to come back anytime. And this was long before I had written any of the songs that became big hits. Johnny was very encouraging and said he liked some of my songs, but he never got around to recording one himself.

While I was in his office one day, something happened that I will never forget. A young songwriter Johnny had just signed to his publishing company walked in. Johnny introduced me to Jimmy Webb.

He was maybe 20 years old and had moved to L.A. from Oklahoma when he was in his teens. When I met him I think he'd only had a few cuts at that point. One of those was on Johnny's *Changes* album called "By the Time I Get to Phoenix." I fell in love with the way Jimmy Webb wrote songs.

As fate would have it, Johnny invited me up to his house in the Hollywood Hills one night for an informal get-together. Jimmy was there. It was just the three of us. After we talked for a while, Jimmy went over to the piano, sat down and played "Galveston," "Didn't We," "The Sidewalk Song," "Rosecrans Boulevard," and more incredible songs. I was speechless. I'd never heard songs written like that before, with that level of sensitivity and reality.

Some 40 years later, I spoke with Jimmy about that night at a music industry function. He didn't remember it. I doubt if Johnny would either. But the important thing is – I remembered it.

And it changed my life forever.

Hearing Jimmy Webb songs was the inspiration I needed to find my own way as a songwriter. His songs were beautiful, heartfelt, emotionally honest, and real. They connected immediately to my Southern soul. I knew right then and there those were the kinds of songs I wanted to write, and I began to try to write the way he wrote.

I studied his songs. I knew I could never write like him, but I tried to write with the elements of poetry, melody, truth, sensitivity and honesty that I heard in his songs. Above all, I tried to keep it real.

Jimmy Webb went on to write "MacArthur Park" for Richard Harris as well as many other great songs. Several became huge hits for Glen Campbell – "Wichita Lineman" and "Galveston" for example. Jimmy became the toast of the L.A. music scene. I was in awe of him.

Around this same time, Johnny Rivers was preparing to record a new act he'd signed to his new label, Soul City Records. The act was called The Fifth Dimension. Johnny invited me to their recording session at Western Studios on the Sunset Strip.

Jimmy had written several of the songs they were going to record and was also conducting the orchestra. At that session The Fifth Dimension recorded one of their biggest hits, a song written by Jimmy called "Up, Up and Away."

A guy I had seen often on television was also at the session. Lee Majors was an actor best known at the time for the role of Heath Barkley in "The Big Valley" TV series. Later he would star as "The Six Million Dollar Man" in the 1970s TV series.

Lee and I began to talk and discovered we had some mutual friends, and we'd both played college football in the South. It was an easy conversation. As everyone was packing up to go home, Lee handed me a piece of paper with his phone number on it. He said, "Call me sometime and we'll hang out."

I really had no idea at the time, but that was one of the most important nights of my life. I was just enjoying the moment, rubbing elbows with some amazing musicians, a session group called The Wrecking Crew, an incredible songwriter, Jimmy Webb, some great recording artists, Johnny Rivers and The Fifth Dimension and also someone who would become one of my really good friends, Lee Majors.

One day I pulled out the piece of paper Lee had given me and called his number. He invited me out to his house in Malibu to shoot some pool. It was a large ranch house, very rustic and comfortable with a lot of western influences. Out back he had a large fenced-in area where he kept his horses. We hung out, shot pool, and talked for a while. Later on we began to go to a few movies together.

Lee had been playing flag football with a group of guys for some time, and he invited me to play with them at Van Nuys High School one Saturday. I had been battling some depression, and I knew that exercise helped keep it at bay. So I jumped at the chance. I began to play regularly on weekends with them. They were really good players and good guys to boot, and I became friends with some of them.

I played some of my songs for Lee one day and he really liked them. He said he'd like to introduce me to Jim Nabors, another southerner who was a friend of his, and let him hear some of them.

Jim Nabors was a well-known TV personality who played Gomer Pyle in "The Andy Griffith Show" and then had his own show – "Gomer Pyle, U.S.M.C." – which was a spinoff from the Griffith TV series.

Jim was a talented singer and by this time had his own variety show on CBS – "The Jim Nabors Hour." Lee set up the meeting with Jim, and I played some of my songs. Jim really liked them and told me if I ever needed a job writing songs to call him. He gave me his phone number. At the time I didn't think about it too much because I was still trying to make the Gordian Knot a success. But I kept the offer in the back of my mind. And I kept his phone number.

The band, still playing clubs in and around Hollywood, was having fun making money making music. One night while we were playing P.J.s, Lee came up to me and told me boxer Joe Frazier was in the club. He asked me to introduce him from the stage as the next heavyweight champion of the world. I did and he was.

Our friend Teri Brown brought Dave Clark and some of his band members into P.J.s to see us play one night. The Dave Clark Five had arrived in America from England shortly after the Beatles, and they had several hit records in the mid-1960s. They soon became fans of The Gordian Knot.

Dave asked us to open for them at a show they were about to do in Bakersfield, California, on June 24, 1967. We jumped at the chance. We flew up with them in their chartered plane and on that trip we became friends. It was great fun to be associated with a group of true stars in the world of rock music as well as some really nice guys.

Pat, J.D., Leland, Jerry Hadley, and I were living in Hermosa Beach by now. You could step out the back door, walk a few steps, cross a sidewalk, and you'd be on the beach. We were playing at a club in Manhattan Beach called Cisco's. We asked The Dave Clark Five to come spend a day at our beach house sometime. They said they needed some relaxation and were looking forward to it. They came to the house and we hung out on the beach all day.

We were still chasing that elusive record deal with no success. We were already a hit, at least among fans and others who heard our music. But one critical group hadn't gotten on board just yet. Everyone loved us, it seemed, but the record companies.

One evening with night closing in, we were getting ready to leave the house and drive the 20 miles up the 405 Freeway to go to work. We were back for another run at P.J.s and were supposed to start playing at nine o'clock. Our equipment manager, Jerry Hadley, had gone to pick up Dulin, who was living with his family in a house nearby.

Jerry had been gone just a few minutes when he came back in the side door. He had his hands up and had this weird look on his face. Out from behind him stepped a man with a shotgun pointed directly at me. Then two more men with guns drawn came into the house through the same door. From across the living room some more men with shotguns came in through the door that led to the beach. I was sitting on the couch and I stood straight up and yelled, "What's going on?"

The man with the shotgun pointed at me said, "Sit down and shut up." I sat back down, scared to death. I thought we were about to be permanently eliminated. Pat was in the living room with me. We were frozen stiff. Leland and J. D. were in their rooms getting dressed.

"We're FBI," one of the men said. "Get everyone in here now."

At that point I relaxed a little because I knew we hadn't done anything wrong, and there were no drugs or anything illegal in the house. Still, there was just that small matter of six or seven men with guns pointed at us. Leland and J. D. walked into the living room to see what all the commotion was about. They saw guns and froze.

The FBI agents finally told us they had gotten a tip that someone they were chasing had been spotted in Santa Monica, which was about 10 miles north of Hermosa Beach. It just so happened that this person was a friend of mine from high school. They thought that he might possibly try to get in touch with me, maybe even be in our house. That was the reason they busted in on us. I told them I hadn't heard from him and explained that there was nobody but the band members in the house and they could search if they wanted to.

After looking through the house, they seemed satisfied that we were telling the truth. They said if I heard from him to call the FBI immediately. Then they left. We breathed a sigh of relief but were all shook up by what had just taken place. We really didn't know what to make of it. All of a sudden Pat, with a straight face that was still a little white from fear, said, dead seriously, "Hell, I thought they were shotgun salesmen."

That broke us all up and relieved some of the tension. We got dressed and drove to work, still somewhat in a state of shock.

Clowning around inside the Factory

24 —❧

The Factory

Carl Brent had gotten us signed to an entertainment company called Mother's Inc., owned by the likes of Paul Newman, Anthony Newley, whose wife was Joan Collins, and Peter Lawford, as well as a few businessmen and attorneys. They were opening a new nightclub that catered only to the Hollywood elite. You had to be a member to get in the exclusive club.

It was called The Factory, located in West Hollywood on Robertson Boulevard. Originally it had been an old factory. They gutted it and rebuilt the inside. The outside still looked like a factory with its original tin siding. It was a place where movie stars and celebrities could go and have fun and dance without being bothered by paparazzi. Also it meant they didn't have to throw parties at their homes if they didn't want to. We were the first band to play The Factory, and we became their house band. We opened there in August of '67 and played until sometime around April of '68.

Pat, Leland, and I got to work early one night. We didn't have to start playing until 9 p.m. and had some time to kill. There was a room called the Directors' Room off to the side in a separate area of the club where the owners held their meetings. It had large, comfortable couches against the walls all around the room, and a TV was hung from the ceiling at one end.

Since we were early and no members were there yet, Pat talked Leland and me into going into the Directors' Room to lie down on the couches and watch TV. Leland and I weren't quite sure we should do that. What if we got caught?

The movie we were watching just happened to be *Hud* with Paul Newman. After we'd been lying there for a few minutes, there was a knock. The door opened slowly and someone stuck his head in and said, "Newman here. Can I use the phone?" We kinda gulped and said, "Yeah, come on in." It was Paul Newman himself.

The phone was on a little table at the same end of the room as the TV. Paul sat down and while he was dialing he looked up at the TV a little surprised and said, "Hey, that's me." So he hung up the phone and laid down on one of the other couches, and we all watched *Hud* together until it was time for Leland, Pat, and me to go to work.

I thought, "Only in Hollywood."

It was crazy that it happened, but it was the kind of world we were living in. But with Paul Newman in the room hanging out with us and watching a movie with him in it, it seemed to take things to another level.

Eventually we had to go to work, so we got up and left the room. Paul never said a word to us about being in the Directors' Room. He seemed real easy-going.

It was a fun run at The Factory. Sammy Davis Jr. got up and sang with us one night. Rosey Grier of the Los Angeles Rams got on stage and sang with us once. Joan Collins became a big fan of the group.

During a break one night Jerry Hadley and I went into the game room where people were shooting pool. Steve McQueen was sitting by himself watching, so Jerry went over and started talking to him. Soon I followed. He was a really nice guy, real easy to talk to, no pretenses that I could tell.

"Joan Collins adored us," Pat recalled. "What an absolute sweetheart. She really took care of us and protected us. She even took us to Hollywood Costume to get us Sgt. Pepper outfits to wear at a Halloween party she was giving at her house. This time we were guests. Not playing music."

Later on, in November of 1967, Joan asked us to play a party at her home.

"She was giving the party in honor of Rudolf Nureyev and his dance partner Dame Margot Fonteyn, both regarded as the greatest classical ballet dancers in the world at the time," Pat said. "And the two of them — the best in the world — were out there dancing to OUR music. I was totally starstruck. I actually sat down at their table to eat with them. Nureyev couldn't speak English but Fonteyn could and said a couple of nice things to me while sitting there. Wow. What a memory."

While we were on stage one night at The Factory, we noticed Fred Astaire, the legendary dancer of movies and TV fame, standing off to the side of the dance floor watching us. When we were on a break, someone came over to us and said Mr. Astaire would like to talk to us. He was very gracious and asked if we would perform with him on his upcoming TV special. He barely got the words out of his mouth before we said, "Yes."

He wanted us to do a song he was famous for dancing to, so

The Gordian Knot with Fred Astaire

he gave us a version of "Top Hat" and told us to come up with a rock version. He showed us the tempo and gave us some sheet music that noted all the spots where he wanted the drums to hit to emphasize his dance moves. No easy task, but the band did it with J.D. doing the heavy lifting. We had to pre-record the song for the special and Mr. Astaire was with us in the studio. He really liked what we did with it.

A Mississippi band of young guys called the Gordian Knot and the incomparable Fred Astaire. You can't make this stuff up.

The special aired February 7, 1968, on NBC and today is in the Library of Congress. Among other guests on the show that night were legendary singers Paul Simon and Art Garfunkel along with a popular band of the era, Sergio Mendes and Brazil '66.

In 1968 we got a job in another movie, this time at MGM, called *The Young Runaways*. We sang "Ophelia's Dream." We also did a song called "Couldn't We" but that one was cut out of the picture. No speaking lines, no acting. Just music.

That same year the band was booked on "The Steve Allen Show." Allen had been on TV practically since TV had been around and was the original host of NBC's "The Tonight Show."

We wore these colorful Nehru jackets, the 'hip' thing at the time. Back then everyone thought it was real cool. But looking at pictures I still have from the show, we look real '60s, which was a decade all to itself as far as fashion.

Every once in a while I'd allow myself to think how far we'd come in such a short time since those days when we played high school graduation dances in Mississippi or were trying to break through in New York or in the club we'd played back in Erie. We never knew what was around the next corner. We were just enjoying the journey.

After many months of struggling to find a record deal with many disappointing rejections, Verve Records came to our rescue and signed us to a recording contract. We were finally going to make an album. We were gonna be in the real music business.

We had been talking to different producers and it came down to Bones Howe and Clark Burroughs. Bones was a great recording engineer, one of the best in the business. He had worked with Johnny Rivers and the Mamas and the Papas. Clark had been a member of the '50s singing group The Hi-Los. He had arranged the vocals on records for The Association, a highly successful group in that era.

We decided on Clark because we wanted him to arrange our vocals as well. The only drawback was Clark wanted to use studio musicians instead of letting us play our own instruments. That was a big disappointment, because we wanted to create our own sound so we could reproduce it when we performed live. But to keep things moving, we went along with him.

Looking back, I'm not sure it was the right decision. It just wasn't us. We were singing Clark's vocal arrangements, which were beautiful. But we sounded like The Association. We wanted our own sound.

We had a hard time establishing our own musical identity and playing other artists' songs all those years hadn't helped. I think the fact that we hadn't established our own identity confused the record labels. They didn't know who we were or how to categorize us.

We went into the studio on January 2, 1968, and recorded two songs I wrote: "Strong Wind Blowin'" and "Carnival Lights Again." We couldn't complain about the quality of musicians Clark hired: the legendary Hal Blaine on drums, Ray Pohlman and Joe Osborn on bass, Al Casey and Mike Deasy on guitars, Larry Knechtal and Don Randi on keyboards. All were "A" list players who were musically responsible for most of the hit songs that came out of L.A. during the '60s, often called the "Wrecking Crew." Joe Sidore was our recording engineer. We went in for our final session on May 7 and the album was released in June.

The title of the album was *Tones*. We wondered how they came up with that title, since it wasn't our idea. We found out that on the 24-track box, our recording engineer had written the word "Tones" above the list of song tracks. But what he meant by that was that the tones were an electronic signal on the front end of the 24-track tape for setting the meter levels for the record. So it was totally by accident that the album was named *Tones*.

It was actually a pretty good album. We set out on a short promotional tour in West Coast cities like San Francisco and Seattle and then in Dallas. But the album didn't sell well and Verve dropped us.

That was our only album.

25 ⟶⋙

A World Turned Upside Down

June 5, 1968, appeared to be another normal day in the lives of the Gordian Knot. We were playing our regular night job at P.J.'s when the crowd began to murmur. People who had been swaying to the music turned grim and distant.

On a break we asked what was going on. We found out that presidential candidate Robert F. Kennedy had been shot and killed by a single gunman at the Ambassador Hotel in downtown Los Angeles. It wasn't all that far from where we were playing. We were in a state of shock. It was the second time in our young lives a Kennedy had been assassinated.

We had played at one of RFK's campaign events in L.A. a few weeks earlier. Kennedy noticed us as we played.

Leland Russell does a good RFK imitation when he describes how "he even came over to us and shook our hands and then spoke to the crowd in his New England accent. 'I would, ah, like to thank the, ah, Gordian Knot for playing. They are my kind of people. But

I, ah, had to cut my hair for the campaign.'"

His mention of the Gordian Knot wound up in some of the Hollywood columns and trade magazines. He even invited us to play at the White House when he won. He never had a chance to fulfill his promise.

The '60s were a turbulent time for Americans, and we had front row seats – on the Vietnam trip and with the Kennedy assassinations. Back in our home turf, Dr. Martin Luther King, Jr., was assassinated in Memphis on April 4, 1968.

That same year, I heard NBC was holding open auditions for dancers. I wasn't a dancer, but they said, "All you gotta do is move like Elvis." So I got Pat, Leland, and J.D. to go with me, and we all went over to NBC studios. The large room was full of Elvis wannabes doing their best moves. When it came my time, the choreographer said, "OK, make some Elvis moves." So I made some Elvis moves, which I'd been doing for years anyway. The guy said, "You're hired." Pat and J.D. were hired as well, but Leland didn't make the cut because of his height – too short to be Elvis.

"The choreographer told everybody on the count of four to make an Elvis pose and then on every fourth beat to go to another pose until the song ended," Pat recalled.

"We could do whatever pose we wanted, just change it on every four count. We were all dressed in black and holding toy guitars. They hired about fifty or so of us."

We were going to be in the opening song sequence of the '68 Elvis Comeback Special. They had built this huge scaffold to stand on while we held our guitars. The lighting they used made us silhouettes up there behind Elvis as he sang the opening song

"Trouble/Guitar Man." It was similar to the famous dance scene from *Jailhouse Rock*.

Yeah, I was one of those guys. It was some kind of fun watching Elvis perform from the scaffold. Even if I was just a shadow.

The Gordian Knot had been giving it "the ole college try" for quite a while. We'd been in L.A. for three years and were heading into our late 20s, still searching for stability, success and our own identity. Finally it all began to take a toll on us.

We were a well-known Southern California band, but we still hadn't cracked the record business. So we weren't well known across the nation except maybe in the South. Despite our local success in L.A., I couldn't help but wonder if our time had passed. We began to lose the spark that made us a top club band. We were on a downhill slide, although no one wanted to admit it.

One gig we played in November and December of 1968 was back in the South, down in Mobile, Alabama, at some funky club. I don't even remember the name. We just weren't very good anymore and didn't seem to care. Somehow we'd lost our drive to be the best.

J.D. had to go back home to Louisiana for a while for personal reasons and that made things even worse. J.D. was such an integral part of the group with both his playing and singing that without him we sounded worse than terrible.

During a break one night, weary from all the stress, I sat down on the edge of the stage to rest. A girl I didn't know came over and started talking to me. We were engaged in polite conversation when out of nowhere this guy appeared. He grabbed her with his left arm and said very forcefully, "You're supposed to be with me!" Then he came across with a right hook and BAM! He sucker punched me right in the face. Then he ran away.

I saw stars and the force caused me to slide back on the stage a couple of feet. He didn't knock me out but it surely stunned me. When I gathered my senses, which took just a few seconds, I got up and started to look for him. I found him just in time to see him run out the door. Hit and run, the coward's way. There was blood on my shirt, and my mouth was bleeding pretty badly. The owner of the club or one of his employees took me to find a doctor and he stitched me up inside my mouth. Then I went back to the club. I couldn't sing but I was up there with my band. I never saw the guy or the girl again. In all my years of playing music, it was the only altercation I'd ever had.

I think that gig might have been the beginning of the end for the group. We were wearing down. We had gotten a new bass player to free Leland up to sing more. We had to eventually replace our drummer, Dulin, who wanted to go back to Mississippi with his family. Then Leland found another musician he wanted to add to the band. At that point discontent was brewing among the original members. There were just too many chefs trying to stir the soup. We had lost the camaraderie of five guys from Mississippi that people responded to when we first got to L.A.

Things started to fall apart. We began to self-destruct.

Meanwhile I kept on pitching my songs.

I met a young, independent record producer named Eddie Garner who was going to cut some songs on movie star/singer Ann-Margret. He wanted to record her singing one of my songs called "Shine." It was never released, but he gave me a copy. I've still got it.

Garner was associated with the Dino, Desi, and Billy group of that era and had set up an audition for our band with Columbia Records. Terry Melcher, a friend of Garner, was on the staff at Columbia Records and expressed interest in signing us.

Later someone told us that Melcher had been the actual target for Charles Manson's notorious and gruesome murders of actress Sharon Tate and four others in August, 1969. Terry had met Manson at Melcher's home some months before. Dennis Wilson of the Beach Boys had introduced them. Manson wanted Melcher to produce records of his music. Terry turned him down and Manson wanted revenge. Fortunately for Melcher and his then girlfriend, Candice Bergen, he had moved out of the house where he had met Manson. That's the home where his cult carried out their infamous "helter skelter" attack.

Since Columbia Records had expressed interest, we went down to their studios in Hollywood and set up our equipment. We played a set for their executives and, according to Pat, "blew them away." Columbia offered us a contract.

I was excited to think this just might be the break that had eluded us for so long. The contract was dated January 30, 1970.

Unfortunately, some members of the group, including at least one of the new guys, talked to a lawyer who thought we shouldn't sign the contract. There were now six guys instead of five, as well as two and sometimes three new members. There was too much dissension and it just wasn't worth it anymore. It had become too much of a headache. So, reluctantly for Pat and me, the band passed on the record deal with Columbia that we had worked so hard to get.

It's strange to think we had come all this way and worked so hard for something that now seemed to be within our reach just to blow it off. It just goes to show how discombobulated we'd become as a group.

The Gordian Knot broke up in February of 1970. Pat remembers the split.

"There wasn't any arguing or any pleading or anything," he said. "Jimmy called me up and said, 'I guess we're breaking up.' It all just ended, like having a sharp knife and cutting the rope in half. I couldn't believe it. I cannot remember us ever having an argument. Ever. We never argued when it was just the five of us. We just did our thing, but we finally sort of just ran out of air."

So the original band members, all of us good friends for years, decided to part ways. Pat and J.D. stayed in L.A. Leland went back home to Mississippi. Dulin had already gone back. I decided to stay in L.A. for a while longer and try to find someone who liked my songs.

26 ——⚮

On My Own

I'd always had the members of the band to lean on. We'd been together daily for more than four years since we left Ole Miss. We were like brothers. I don't think I would have ever gone to California if I hadn't been a member of the Gordian Knot. So when we split up I was on my own, trying to figure out what to do next.

I felt alone and frustrated. But I still couldn't let go of my desire to try and make it as a songwriter, a good one. I seemed to have no choice. The desire to write songs was like an ache deep in my soul that wouldn't let go.

But without my support group, I was lost. My world looked and felt different. A lot different. Empty. For a long time the band members didn't keep in touch. We were all just trying to get our lives together and move on.

There was one silver lining that I discovered later on. I didn't have to get the approval of four other guys to write what I wanted to write or record what I wanted to record – if I ever got the chance. I had been a team player for so long, both in football and in music that it came as somewhat of a relief to be able to make creative decisions for myself, without anyone else's input.

I had very little money saved up, but I had enough to get an apartment at 1764 North Sycamore, just off Hollywood Boulevard. It was just a small, furnished single on the first floor with a stove, a refrigerator, and a tiny bathroom. It cost me $125 a month. I rented an upright piano and sat my reel-to-reel tape recorder on top of it. I would sit there all alone in my room, get in my zone and write. I worked at it constantly.

I also used my guitar to write. It was an old Martin, not a real big one, and I felt comfortable writing with it. I'd bought it from one of the guys I played weekend sports with, Jay Laskey, for $125. At the big round end it had a colorful eagle with wings spread. I used that guitar when I wrote the songs that became my biggest hits.

I had never been a part of the so-called party scene. It wasn't in my upbringing or a part of my early adulthood. I just didn't have time for it. I wasn't interested in it. That was just who I was – maybe better put, who I wasn't. It had been true for both football and music. Tobacco was the only vice many of my family members ever indulged in. I always thought it was stupid to suck smoke into your lungs and blow it out. I just figured it couldn't be good for you.

Alcohol and illegal drugs were never a part of my life. I have never been drunk or stoned. It was just something I never even thought about doing, which might be considered unusual since I was around it in L.A. I was never tempted, thank the Lord. It was the same way with marijuana. I never touched any of that stuff.

I had loved playing football, and I loved writing songs, and the fact that I was getting better at it kept me going. I had a good upbringing and came from a wonderful, close-knit family. There was no alcohol in our home when I was growing up and that might have had something to do with my aversion to it.

My friend, Charlie Monk, has always told me that I'm the most boring man he's ever known. I take that as a compliment.

Performing in my home state capital of Jackson

27 ——❦

One Last Option

I continued to pound the pavement pitching my songs only to see them rejected. I kept hearing, "You write such sad songs. Write something up-tempo and positive, and then come back to see us." Or sometimes simply, "We're not interested."

A month or two after The Gordian Knot split up, I came to this conclusion. I had a decision to make. I didn't want to become one of those sad Hollywood stories where you park cars or pump gas or wait tables until you wake up one morning and come face to face with the fact that you're old and a failure and have wasted your life. I liked myself too much to let that happen.

Before I headed back to Ole Miss, I figured I had one last option. I pulled out the scrap of paper with Jim Nabors' phone number. I called Jim and asked if he was serious about signing me to his publishing company as a songwriter. He enthusiastically said, "Yes." He wanted me to call Dick Link, his manager, and set up a meeting to make the deal.

I really didn't want to give up the publishing rights to my songs, but time was running out and I really needed some money. I felt if I could get enough to live on, maybe I should take the deal.

Richard Link was one of the most powerful men in Hollywood. He was Andy Griffith's manager, and he was the producer of "The Andy Griffith Show," "Gomer Pyle, U.S.M.C.," "the Jim Nabors Hour," and "Mayberry R.F.D." Pretty intimidating.

I had to sit across from this industry giant and negotiate a publishing deal. I was not a businessman and I didn't have an attorney. I couldn't afford one.

When I walked into Mr. Link's office and sat down, he got right to the point. "I hear Jim wants to make a deal with you for your songs. What do you want?" Well, I knew unknown songwriters at that time got about $25 to $50 a week from publishers for their songs. I also knew there was no way that I could live on that.

All of a sudden, I heard myself blurt out, "I want $300 a week because I need it and I'm worth it."

I actually surprised myself. I don't know where I got the nerve to say it. But I was that confident in myself and in my songs. I figured the worst he could do was say "No way. That's a ridiculous amount." And laugh me out of his office.

But he didn't bat an eye. He simply said, "OK, I'll have the papers drawn up." Negotiation over. For that kind of money I was willing to part with my copyrights.

I was finally going to have a publishing deal with a major entertainer, and I was going to be paid real money for it. And it came just when I needed it.

A miracle.

Right away I started saving as much as I could for the next rainy day. I knew I wasn't always going to be with Jim's company because

My writing guitar — used to write my biggest hits

they pitched songs to older acts that didn't get mainstream radio airplay. I wanted to write for hit acts that got airplay on Top 40 radio. But this gave me an opportunity to work at my songwriting without the stress of wondering where my next meal was coming from.

As a bonus, Jim would sometimes hire me to work as an extra on his TV variety show. I did skits with Roy Rogers, my childhood cowboy hero, and Vicki Carr, a popular singer. That gave me a little extra money. Sometimes I would drive down to CBS studios just to watch rehearsals.

While under contract to Jim Nabors' publishing company, he recorded three of my songs, "It's My Life," "If I Never Laugh Again," and "Louisiana Lady," all produced by Joe Guercio, who became Elvis Presley's orchestra conductor in Las Vegas for several years.

Things were starting to happen for me. I had an album cut by Peggy Lee, a true music icon, called "He Used Me." I also had a cut by John Raitt, a well-known Broadway star and Bonnie Raitt's father. That song was called "My Love for All Seasons." It certainly boosted my self-esteem.

I was proud of those cuts because they represented progress, but I knew they weren't the kind of records radio would play. Still, they were on albums and my name was on them as writer. And it was a relief to have money coming in.

After a little more than two years of writing for Jim's company that next rainy day appeared. Jim called me and said his variety show was being cancelled and he didn't need a songwriter anymore. He said, "I'm going to have to let you go." I understood and thanked him for the great opportunity he had given me. We parted as friends and it was once again time for me to start a new chapter.

I had saved $7,000 of the money Jim's company had paid me. That gave me a little breathing room. Back in those days $7,000 could go a long way if you were resourceful and didn't spend it foolishly. I was still back at square one, looking for someone who could help me get my songs cut. This was in 1971, five years after I had arrived in L.A.

I quickly got busy writing new songs since Jim owned the copyrights to the old ones. I knocked on doors and made phone call after phone call. I got more and more frustrated and depressed. I was running out of positive energy, running out of people to see. Running out of confidence. I didn't know where my life was headed, and I was beginning to doubt that I'd ever find success as a songwriter.

To make matters worse, I was in a relationship that was draining me.

The self-doubts were crippling. At my worst moments, I tried to tell myself something positive – that if I failed, I could always go back to Mississippi to coach high school football. That notion was beginning to take root.

Night after night, I lay in bed staring at the TV and feeling so bad I could hardly stand it. I was depressed, in a state of nervous panic. I felt like the world was beginning to cave in on me. I'd get up most mornings and try to keep on keeping on, though some days I'd just stay in bed and sleep. It was a really discouraging time. I prayed a lot for guidance and direction about what I should do. I was always left with the feeling that I shouldn't give up just yet.

The medications they have now to correct the chemical imbalances, which cause depression, were in the early stages of discovery back then and I wasn't taking any. Looking for any port in a storm, I read books like *How to Stop Worrying and Start Living* by Dale Carnegie and *The Power of Positive Thinking* by Norman

Vincent Peale. They helped me begin to see things a little clearer. I read more books like *The Magic of Believing* by Claude M. Bristol. The fog gradually began to lift.

Again, it was decision time. I had to face facts.

I decided that when the $7,000 I'd saved was almost gone, if I hadn't made any progress in my songwriting career, I was going to take what was left of my money – and my songs – go back to Mississippi, get my teaching degree and become a high school football coach. It wasn't my nature to give up, but it seemed like I might not have a choice. Making that decision at least gave me some peace of mind.

I kept writing songs, wondering if anyone would ever hear them. I was trying to figure out how to find what I was looking for in the music business, while also struggling to conquer my self-doubts.

That's when I found myself sitting on the bed in my little apartment, trying to stay afloat in a flood of sorrows. Full of raw emotion, I picked up my guitar and softly began to play. Without any conscious thought, I started to sing:

> *It's sad to think we're not gonna make it*
> *And it's gotten to the point where we just can't fake it*
> *But for some ungodly reason we just won't let it die*

And then came those fateful words:

> *I guess neither one of us wants to be the first to say goodbye.*

I knew then I had my title. I felt like I was on to something honest and real. It sounded like something people could relate to even if it was sad. I was amazed how easily it came together.

It was an otherworldly experience. The song more or less came through me. It was out there somewhere, and it just happened to come through me.

I sang the whole first verse of "Neither One of Us" like it was someone else's song that had already been written. It just all came pouring out. I wrote that first verse down very quickly. Didn't take me anytime. The second verse came almost as fast. The bridge followed immediately. It was almost as if the song was writing itself.

Then I wrapped it up with one last verse and wasted no time putting it down on my reel-to-reel recorder. My first thought was that it was a really special song, and that lifted my spirits.

It was all there, as if it was fate or destiny or the hand of God … but would anyone else like it? I put down my guitar and closed my songwriting book. Then I said something out loud to myself.

"Well, there's another sad song nobody will ever want to hear."

NEITHER ONE OF US
(WANTS TO BE THE FIRST TO SAY GOODBYE)

It's sad to think we're not gonna make it
And it's gotten to the point where we just can't fake it
But for some ungodly reason we just won't let it die
I guess neither one of us wants to be the first to say goodbye

I keep wondering what I'll do without you
And I guess you must be wondering the same thing too
So we go on together living a lie
Because neither one of us wants to be the first to say goodbye

Every time I find the nerve to say I'm leaving
Old memories get in my way
Lord knows it's only me I keep deceiving
But when it comes to saying goodbye
That's a word I just can't say

There can be no way this can have a happy ending
So we just go on hurting and pretending
And convincing ourselves to give it just one more try
Because neither one of us wants to be the first to say goodbye

28 —⁂

The Phone Call

Sometime in 1971, I made a call to Lee Majors that would change the course of my life. Lee was dating a newcomer to the Hollywood scene named Farrah Fawcett. Farrah was from Texas and was one of the new golden girls in Hollywood. She and Lee had started dating pretty soon after she arrived in Los Angeles. One of their first dates was to a club called Arthur to hear my band, the Gordian Knot.

When I called Lee's house in the Hollywood Hills, Farrah answered. She said Lee wasn't at home. She mentioned she was packing some clothes and was going to take the midnight plane to Houston to visit her family. When we hung up I immediately picked up my guitar and started to write. That phrase had hit me like a ton of bricks when she said it, and I thought it sounded like a song title – "Midnight Plane to Houston."

The words and music began to flow and once again, it just all came together. When I was writing it, I thought it sounded like it might be a good song for Glen Campbell, who had had a lot of success with Jimmy Webb songs like "By the Time I Get to Phoenix," "Galveston," and "Wichita Lineman."

It was another one of those stream of consciousness things. The song flowed like magic. I could even picture Lee and Farrah as the couple I was writing about. I didn't know where the song was going, but I kept on writing. When it came time to write the chorus I simply said:

> *She's leaving on the midnight plane to Houston*
> *Goin' back to a simpler place and time*

And then the natural place to go with the song became personal. Up until then, it had been a story song in third person, and I just assumed it would be like that throughout. Then the singer became involved and it became first person:

> *I'll be with her on that midnight plane to Houston.*
> *I'd rather live in her world than live without her in mine.*

I thought the last line, especially, wrapped the song up in a real nice package. I thought it was a great song and I was really proud of it. It took me about 30 minutes, maybe 45, to write it. Then I went to my tape recorder and put it down.

Not long after I wrote that song, I made another phone call and got a meeting with Stan Schneider, who was Glen Campbell's manager. I played him "Midnight Plane to Houston" and "Neither One of Us" as well as some other songs. I was hoping he would sign me to Glen's publishing company. I asked for $200 a week and was turned down flat.

Eventually I got a meeting at Four Star Music publishing. The guy there listened to my songs and offered me a contract. He said he would pay me $10,000 to sign with Four Star for six months with options.

You'd think I'd be jumping for joy, turning backflips, but something just didn't feel right. It didn't sound like much of a commitment to me. It didn't sound like they were interested in building a long-term career, and that's what I really wanted.

Signing with Four Star meant I would have some much-needed money in my pocket. But I needed more from someone who was going to own my songs. I wanted a real commitment. I needed a real commitment.

Ten thousand dollars was a lot of money in those days. But I would have to give up all the songs I had written to that point, which included some that would become my biggest hits. But if they didn't get any of my songs recorded after six months, what if they dropped me? I'd be back on the streets starting over again. And they would own the songs I had played for them as well as songs I would write for six months while under contract to them. And if they didn't pick up the option, I would then have to write all new songs to play for other publishers, and who knew if they would be as good as what I had? I just didn't know if I had it in me to do that.

The songs I was writing were more valuable to me than $10,000 with no real commitment. I thanked him but told him I couldn't take the offer. It was a risk and I knew it, but in my mind the bigger risk was signing with Four Star.

So I went back to square one. But at least I still owned my songs. Meanwhile the money was dwindling. That meant I was getting closer to going back to Ole Miss. I had reached the point where if I didn't find the kind of deal I was looking for, I would just head back south and take my songs with me.

I knew it was a long shot but I continued to look for that one person or that one publishing company that would give me what I was looking for – a future writing songs. I just couldn't stop looking for that commitment. I didn't want to be just one of a stable of writers. I knew what I was looking for would take a miracle to find. But something kept pushing me.

29 —⟐

The Tide Begins to Turn

I always looked forward to the weekends because that's when I played sports, even though at times my old football toe injury still gave me some real discomfort. At least I was able to get my mind off my troubles for a little while.

One Saturday morning I drove over to Studio City Park in the San Fernando Valley for our weekend football game. While we were warming up, a guy named Gary that I'd played with for three years mentioned that he was bringing a music buddy out the following weekend. I asked him who it was, and he told me H.B. Barnum, a well-known record producer, songwriter, and arranger.

I looked at Gary inquisitively and asked him "Are you in the music business?" He said he was. I asked, "What's your last name?" He said, "Usher. Gary Usher."

Well, I knew who Gary Usher was, but I didn't know I had been playing football with him all this time.

Another miracle.

Gary Usher was one of the pioneers of the surf music movement in southern California in the 1960s and had co-written the hit song "In My Room" with Brian Wilson of the Beach Boys. He had also played in a couple of surf bands like The Hondells and produced records for The Byrds.

Right away I asked him if he would listen to some of my songs after explaining that I was a songwriter and needed help finding someone, a record producer or publisher that might be interested in my songs.

"Sure. Come on up to my house and play them for me," he said.

I drove up to Gary's house in Topanga Canyon and played some songs that I'd recorded on my reel-to-reel tape recorder with just my guitar and vocals. The same ones I'd played at Four Star. He seemed to like them. Gary told me there was a guy he wanted me to go see. His name was Larry Gordon. Gary said he had worked with Larry and he gave me his number. So I called Larry and set up a meeting.

Larry Gordon was an independent music publisher whose silent partner was internationally-known entertainer Danny Thomas, the founder of St. Jude Children's Research Hospital in Memphis. Larry was married to Danny's daughter, Teri. Larry had worked as a manager and as a publicist with the likes of iconic songwriter/artists Paul Williams and Harry Nilsson. He had recently started his own publishing company, Rip-Keca Music, and he'd been looking for a writer the caliber of Nilsson and Williams that he could put all of his efforts behind.

Larry's office was in a small, two-story brick building on Sunset Boulevard close to La Brea Avenue, not far from the Sunset Palms Motel where the Gordian Knot stayed when we first arrived in L.A.

It was a small, unpretentious little office. There were only two rooms. No receptionist. Larry was on the phone in the back room. The door to his office was open. He saw me standing there and motioned for me to come on back and sit down. So I sat down and waited until he got off the phone. Then I introduced myself and told him that Gary Usher had heard some of my songs and suggested that I meet with him.

Larry was very pleasant but very intense. He said, "Let me hear what you've got." I gave him my tape and he put it on, leaned back in his chair and closed his eyes. He listened to about three songs.

In the middle of the third song, he stopped the tape abruptly and leaned forward like he was trying to make sure he had my attention. He said very intently, "I want you to meet me at my attorney's office at nine o'clock in the morning. I'm going to sign you to a publishing contract." He followed with, "I'm not going to pay you any money except what's required by law," which was about $6,000 a year at that time. Then he said the magic words.

"But I promise you, I will push your songs through the sky."

That definitely got my attention. Bells went off in my head. Those were the words I had been waiting to hear. And most importantly, I believed him. It was the commitment I had been looking for.

There was sincerity, honesty, and excitement in Larry's voice, something I hadn't experienced with anybody else who had listened to my songs. Maybe I was naïve, or even foolish to make that judgment so quickly. I knew it could all blow up in my face. But intuition told me, and sometimes you just have to go with your gut instincts, that my search was over. And just in time.

Another miracle.

I had $3,000 left of my $7,000 when I met with Larry.

Years later in an interview, Larry said he knew he was going to sign me "two seconds" into the tape. "The way he puts words to the music, and the music is great, I thought he was probably as good as any songwriter I'd heard in my whole life, based on that tape," Larry said. "And that was just a guitar and vocal, a very simple tape. I could just tell it was something special."

The next morning I was at the office of Larry's attorney in Beverly Hills at 9 o'clock sharp. The attorney was Owen Sloane, well respected in the music world. The papers were already drawn up.

I didn't have an attorney and I didn't read the contract. Larry's attorney went over it with me in layman's terms, which I still didn't understand. But I had no qualms about signing with Larry. I believed him 100 percent. Don't ask me why. Probably because he convinced me that he believed in my songs 100 percent.

I don't advise anyone else to sign a contract without an attorney's advice. But in this case it worked for me.

Signing a publishing deal with Larry Gordon was the best decision I'd ever made. I knew if we had any success at all, I would be making more than the $6,000 a year he mentioned. And Larry was confident we'd have success. I'd never met anyone with his kind of confidence. I believed in him so much that I signed a management contract with him as well.

"Prior to Jimmy, I was in the public relations business," Larry said. "I built the firm to about 80 clients from about 20, so I was a pretty good salesman. I had recognized the talents of Paul Williams and Harry Nilsson and had signed them. I sold my end of the PR business to manage them. So I thought I had a pretty good ear for music.

"By the time I got to Jimmy, there was never a doubt in my mind that we wouldn't have major success, not from the first minute. I only managed Jim because I didn't want interference, and I managed him because I felt like his career in my hands would be better than anywhere else. But I was mainly a publisher and looked at myself as a publisher. I managed more because I felt like I could make better deals than anybody else, because I basically managed out of fear that some other manager would screw up what I was trying to build, and that is the mystique of the songwriter."

Larry's belief in me gave me a renewed confidence, and really good songs came bursting forth because finally someone believed in what I was writing. He constantly encouraged me, and he made me believe I was really a great songwriter.

Larry never took a management commission out of my royalties. Because he owned 100 percent of my publishing and those royalties were split 50-50 between us, I told him I thought it would be unfair for him to take another 20 percent of my 50 percent. He agreed and that was that. I don't remember Larry and I ever having a major disagreement or confrontation about anything. Our relationship was based on fairness, friendship, and trust, somewhat unusual in the music business.

So many other music people and publishers had listened to my songs (when I could get them to listen) and seen the small picture. Larry listened and saw the big picture. He saw my songs as an extension of who I was as a person and, as a writer, what I had to offer. Other publishers listened only to the songs. Larry listened to the songwriter. Other publishers listened with their ears. Larry listened with his heart.

He immediately went to work making things happen. He had an intuitive nature just like I did. I told Larry I had written for Jim Nabors' company for two years and Jim owned the copyrights to about 80 of my songs in his publishing catalog. Larry said he wanted to buy the songs back. So he called Jim to set up a meeting. We drove up to Jim's house in Bel Air.

Jim was glad to see me, and we spent some time making small talk before Larry went to work. Larry asked Jim what it would take to buy back my songs.

Without hesitation, Jim said, "You can have 'em."

Larry's jaw dropped. My jaw dropped. Jim said he didn't need them anymore, so he would just give them to us.

After paying me good money for two and a half years, he was just giving them to us?

Another miracle.

Larry had expected a pretty intense negotiation. We were both shocked by Jim's generosity. That kind of thing is truly rare in the cutthroat music business. Neither of us expected him to be so gracious. We thanked him profusely and drove away still in disbelief at what had just happened.

Larry and I became great friends. I trusted him completely with my songs and my career. He took me under his wing and became my mentor, my advisor, my manager, and my publisher. And he kept me fed. He always paid for our meals. That impressed me.

The first thing Larry did was to go to ASCAP, the American Society of Composers, Authors, and Publishers, and talk them into giving me an advance on royalties. That's how much he believed in my songs and what he could do with them. He made ASCAP believe as well.

The ASCAP advance was substantial and relieved the financial woes that had been weighing me down.

The next thing Larry did was to take me to meet with Stan Schneider, Glen Campbell's business manager, who became my business manager and has kept me solvent ever since. Ironically, he was the same guy who turned down my songs for Glen's company.

Stan is a soft-spoken, affable guy who has become a very trusted and valued friend. Stan has other clients in the entertainment business as well. Besides the late Glen Campbell, he also had Gene Autry and took over management of the Autry estate when Gene died.

Another one of the first things Larry did was to find someone to record a whole album of my songs. Since Danny Thomas was a partner in Larry's publishing company, Larry thought he was the perfect guy to go to.

A year before, I couldn't get a song cut. Now Danny Thomas was recording a whole album of my songs.

"Danny came into my office one day, and now he was a fan of Jimmy's," Larry remembered. "And his wedding anniversary was coming up. He said, 'Would you have Jimmy write a song for my wife for our anniversary?' So Jimmy wrote 'You're the Best Thing That Ever Happened to Me' and he delivered it to the office. I said, 'This is really good.' That's how that song came about."

Danny was the first person to record one of my biggest hits, "You're the Best Thing That Ever Happened to Me." At the end of the song he sang, "Rosey, you're the best thing that ever happened to me." Rosey was Danny's wife and he dedicated the song to her.

I tell my wife, Cynthia, that I wrote the song for her. It's just that the song showed up before she did.

"You're the Best Thing That Ever Happened to Me" became an iconic song for singers from Gladys Knight and the Pips to country singer Ray Price, to Dean Martin, to Andy Williams and many more, including the Reverend James Cleveland, who recorded it as a spiritual song paying homage to Jesus Christ.

That led to more cuts in the Gospel genre. Today it has become a Gospel classic as well as a Pop and R&B classic and is sung in churches across the nation. It has become one of my best known and most recorded songs, as well as one of my biggest sellers.

BEST THING THAT EVER HAPPENED TO ME

I've had my share of life's ups and downs
But fate's been kind; the downs have been few
I guess you could say I've been lucky
And I guess you could say it's all because of you

If anyone should ever write my life story
For whatever reason there might be
You'd be there between each line of pain and glory
'Cause you're the best thing that ever happened to me
You're the best thing that ever happened to me

Lord there have been times when times were hard
But always somehow I made it through
'Cause for every moment I've spent hurting
There was a moment that I spent just loving you

If anyone should ever write my life story
For whatever reason there might be
You'd be there between each line of pain and glory
'Cause you're the best thing that ever happened to me
You're the best thing that ever happened to me

The Danny Thomas album gave me a newly found credibility as a writer and it didn't hurt my ego any either, even if Danny wasn't the kind of artist who would get Top 40 radio exposure. He had a huge following from his TV show "Make Room for Daddy" as well as his nightclub act.

Larry was fearless in his approach to getting my songs recorded because he was convinced the world needed to hear them. Using every contact he had, he worked tirelessly to get me a record deal. He even got on a plane once and shuttled back and forth between two record executives from different companies trying to make a deal for me, playing one against the other. And he hates to fly.

He also hated to take no for an answer and most of the time he didn't. He just found a way to go around people. There was nobody he wouldn't play my songs for, from the heads of major companies to the guy walking in off the street. He made me believe my career and my songs were the most important things in the world to him.

Throughout most of my career after college, I had wanted to be an artist / singer as well as a songwriter. However, Larry didn't want me to tour. I think he wanted all of my energy to go into songwriting, and I'm glad he guided me that way. He told me, "Just go write songs and play football."

Larry explained his reasoning.

"Jimmy was a good enough singer to express on tape what those songs represented," he said. "But his forte' was not on stage. His forte' was creating great songs. We probably could have developed the artist thing, but I just didn't think that would take him where he needed to go."

At the time, Larry said, "I kind of wanted to make him a mystique ... I felt that would help with his longevity and make him more in demand as a writer."

Larry was already a successful businessman when I came along. But he was determined to have even greater success.

"I gave up Harry Nilsson and Paul Williams to do this," Larry said. "We were right in the middle of success with them. With Nilsson, I was his partner on a movie made for TV ("Me and My Arrow"). Before signing Nilsson and Paul, I had a very successful business. I'd had my share of success but not my share of copyright success. And that's what I wanted. I feel even today Jimmy is one of the better songwriters that ever lived outside of the great old songwriters, the Gershwins and those kind of guys. I still haven't heard a contemporary songwriter that's really as good as Jimmy, especially with lyrics."

Less than a year before, I was depressed and feeling weary and seriously considering going back to Mississippi to coach football for a living. And just forget about music.

Larry Gordon and me

30 ——⚬

"Weatherly" The Album

It wasn't too long afterward that Larry got me a recording contract with RCA Records. My spirits were rising and my anxieties and insecurities were dwindling. I couldn't believe the way he was making things happen so quickly. Here was a guy who was taking the bull by the horns and was committed to the longevity of my songwriting career, which was exactly what I'd been looking for and thought I probably would never find.

I began to relax a little more day by day knowing I was in good hands. I felt secure enough to move out of my little apartment on Sycamore Avenue in Hollywood and relocate to an upgraded, one-bedroom apartment on Laurelwood Avenue in Studio City in the San Fernando Valley. It was situated in the middle of some tall pine trees and reminded me a lot of Mississippi.

Larry started setting up meetings with record producers who might work with me on my first album. He thought Jimmy Bowen would be a good fit. Jimmy had produced Frank Sinatra's "That's

Life" and Dean Martin's "Everybody Loves Somebody Sometime."

He was known for reviving Sinatra's and Martin's recording careers. Bowen had a great sense of humor and was very creative. He had also produced records for Kenny Rogers and the First Edition. I liked Jimmy at our first meeting. He was down to earth, one of the funniest people I had ever met and amazingly talented. And he agreed to produce my first album.

When the time finally came to go into the studio to record, to say I was excited would be an understatement. The session was at RCA Studios on Sunset Boulevard. Bowen hired some of the greatest musicians in the business. They included the great drummer John Guerin, world-renowned guitarists Al Casey, Larry Carlton, and Mike Deasey, with Ray Pohlman on bass, all of whom had played on many hit records. Larry Muhobarac was on keyboards and arranged the songs for the album. It was an unbelievable experience to hear my songs come alive, played by musicians who had been heard on hundreds of hit records.

Bowen worked really well with me, to do things the way I felt most comfortable. He gave me room to make suggestions about how I wanted to record my songs. Suddenly, I was doing what I had always wanted. If I was going to be a recording artist, I wanted to record my own songs. That was what was important to me – the songs.

We recorded four songs at that first session and four more at a session that night. Who knew then some of the songs on that album would become some of the most recognizable of the 1970s and beyond?

They included "Neither One of Us," "Midnight Plane to Houston," "The Finer Things in Life," "Between His Goodbye and My Hello," "Mississippi Song," "Loving You Is Just an Old Habit," and "The Prince, the Cowboy, and Me." We cut four more songs at a later session.

The musicians' reactions to my songs were incredibly positive. They really seemed to enjoy playing them. After we got all the tracks done, over the next two or three weeks Bowen sweetened the record with strings and other instruments, as well as background voices. Then it was time to mix all the tracks.

Once the tracks were mixed, RCA set a release date, which was a few weeks away. The album was called *Weatherly*. It was released in 1972. My first solo album as an artist and I had written all the songs on it. I had accomplished one of my lifelong goals.

Bob Talbert gave it a glowing review in the Detroit *Free Press*:

"This is the best debut album I have ever heard. Jim Weatherly is the most talented new songwriting talent since the likes of Neil Diamond and Jim Webb. It's honest music about the things we all share. Pride in something tarnished. Love over or love started too soon. Hopes and fears that tomorrow will only be like so many more todays. Things that kiss and kick the psyche. Little stories, big thoughts. I listen to literally hundreds of 'new' talents every year. None has ever hit me with the impact of Jim Weatherly."

I recorded my songs the way I heard them in my head. I never tried to record them to be hit records, be it pop or country. I hoped they would be hits, but on my own terms. I don't think the record companies appreciated that.

Being a successful recording artist was something I had wanted very badly at one time. But my songwriting career was becoming more and more important, and that's where I put my energy and focus. I was thrilled when I heard other artists sing my songs. Almost every song on that first album has been covered by other artists.

My friend Marty Gamblin picked up on my shift in focus.

"Jimmy was a little ahead of the curve as far as country went, because he wasn't a basic country guy. I don't think they knew how to define him as a recording artist. Had he wanted to be a pop or country artist, and that's all he wanted to be, he would have been successful at it just like he is successful as a songwriter," Marty said. "But he liked to take an idea and sit at the piano all day and night and work until he had the song he wanted. That's who he was and who he is.

"Jimmy loved watching performers like Elvis. And Jimmy was good too. Everybody who ever went to see him was entertained. But I just don't think that was something he could see himself doing for the rest of his life without making certain sacrifices that he didn't want to make."

Charlie Monk, my longtime friend and self-appointed Mayor of Music Row in Nashville, tells a funny story that also says a lot about the music business.

"I worked for ASCAP, the American Society of Composers, Authors, and Publishers, in Nashville. Jim's always said that the songs he writes are basically country songs that happened to be recorded in another genre. So this guy sent me a tape of Jim Weatherly, and I listened to it. I didn't hear anything that impressed me. On that tape was 'Midnight Train to Georgia' (still 'Midnight Plane to Houston' at the time), 'Neither One of Us,' all the songs that became his hits. He always kind of jabs me with that."

At the time, a lot of the Nashville music community still saw me as a football player. It hadn't been all that long since I'd played football in the SEC, including Nashville where we played Vanderbilt. Back in those days some people thought football players couldn't walk and chew gum at the same time, so some of them kind of dismissed me because of it. When my band and I had recorded in Nashville back in '64 when we were in college, we couldn't get anyone there to pay attention to the group or my songs. They could be hard on new guys. They could make you feel really insecure. Not a lot of encouragement.

Even with all that was going on for me in California, I missed my family and the Southern way of life. I would fly back as often as I could, which actually wasn't very often at all. But I knew I had to get back for one visit in particular in the fall of 1973. It was my brother Shan's last year of high school football. I really wanted to be there for him and watch him play. I had missed out on a lot of his growing up since I'd been in California.

A close cousin, Terry Wood, one of Aunt Jean's sons, also played on that team. Another one of her sons, Tommy Wood, was one of the coaches. So I was really looking forward to getting back and also catching a few Ole Miss games.

Shan remembers that visit. It was special for both of us.

"I remember the times Jimmy would get to come home, especially when he was trying to make it out in L. A. That was maybe once a year. It was always really exciting when he came home. It was neat to have him there for those games when I was a senior in high school. It was the first time he'd ever seen me play high school football."

I was home for more than a month for the first time in years and got to see Shan play six games. Pontotoc had a really good team and lost only one game that season. At the end of the year, Shan, who kept up the family tradition by playing quarterback, was voted Little Ten Conference Player of the Year. I was really proud of him.

I also got to see him play in the Mississippi High School All-Star Game in Jackson. Shan was a little smaller than some of the players they were recruiting in Division I college football. I'm convinced his size was all that stood between him and a major college career. He was certainly good enough to play.

31 —⚭

Hits, Hits, and More Hits

Among the producers and artists Larry pitched my songs to, was a man named Joe Porter, who was preparing to produce an album on Gladys Knight and the Pips for Motown.

"As I was promoting Jim and taking the songs around," Larry remembers, "'Neither One of Us' was on that first tape. I played it for Joe Porter at his house. I knew he was producing Gladys at the time. I felt like it would undoubtedly be a No. 1 record for her, and Joe felt the same thing. He fell in love with it. He said he was going to play it for Gladys, and he did. 'Neither One of Us' was the first song of Jim's that she heard and she loved it."

Gladys loved the sad song I thought nobody would ever want to hear. What amazes me is how they all heard that it could be an R&B/Pop record from the little Country version that was on my album. I never expected that.

Another miracle.

In the book *Motown – The Golden Years*, Bubba Knight, Gladys' brother and a member of the Pips, remembers recording the song:

"Our new producer, Joe Porter, was raving about this new writer that he had run across. His name was Jim Weatherly. The night we recorded 'Neither One of Us' we were supposed to fly back to Detroit. The group was recording the song at a studio in Los Angeles. We had gotten the lead vocal down and we had done a part of the background. We were singing the song on the way to the airport in the car. That song sure is sticking with us a lot.

"We got to the airport and were getting ready to get on the plane. And it just struck us: 'Go back to the studio. We've got a vibe, man, the spirit moved on us!' We got back in the car, called the studio and told 'em we were coming back. And they held the studio open 'til we got back, man. We went back there and laid down the background to 'Neither One of Us,' and man, when we played that thing back, we knew we had something great."

Larry Gordon was in the studio in L.A. when Joe recorded the track, so he heard the rough cut of it. As he put it, "I was 100 percent sure that, No. 1, it would be the single, and No. 2, it was going to be a monster success."

An A&R person from Motown called Larry and said they wanted to release "Neither One of Us" as a single. The only problem was they wanted part of the publishing. Larry was adamant about not giving away any portion of the publishing rights on any of my songs to anyone so he told them, "No publishing." Motown responded by saying if that was the case, then they wouldn't release the record. Larry said, "OK."

I waited. And waited. And held my breath. So did Larry.

Obviously the song was important to Motown, but how important was the question.

After some time had gone by, Motown called Larry again, asking for a portion of the publishing. Larry's answer again was, "No." Motown reiterated if that were the case, they would not release the song.

Then Larry said, "If you have a better song, put it out." Talk about nerve.

Finally Larry got a call from Motown's president, Berry Gordy, Jr. He told Larry they had to have a piece of the publishing. "So I just bullshitted him and told him that Warner Brothers was already putting it out. And I told him I didn't care if Gladys put it out or not," Larry said.

Motown caved.

They finally agreed to release "Neither One of Us" as a single without getting any portion of the publishing. Such are the wars of the music business.

Larry and I were beyond thrilled. They were now putting the record out, and I hadn't been at all sure they would. It was pretty nerve-racking.

"Neither One of Us" became the title of the album, and my first No. 1 record as well as Gladys' first. It had been a long, long, long time coming for both of us.

It's amazing how things work sometimes. Motown could have said they weren't going to put it out, put it on a shelf, and the song might never have been heard. And who knows? Gladys and the Pips might not have cut any of my other songs. Who knows if I would have ever had a hit? Again, everything fell into place and worked in my favor.

Another miracle.

I was sitting in Larry's office when he played the record for me.

At first, I was kind of taken aback because it was so different from the way I had written it. I wrote it as more of a country song with a different kind of groove. Larry played it a second time and I was more focused. I thought, "What a great record!"

Gladys sang the song in a way I never dreamed I would hear. She had made it her own, completely believable and with a deep, heartfelt emotion. They had slowed it down some and the track had a beautiful soaring string arrangement written by Artie Butler, with ethereal melodic keyboards by Michael Omartian.

The Pips' background vocals were shimmering magic. What they had given it was... Classic SOUL.

They had turned it into an international universal Pop and R&B classic. Something I had never dreamed of.

Another miracle.

Gladys had the perfect voice for the song. I couldn't believe how lucky I was to have a record like that with a voice like hers. And I can't say enough about the Pips' background vocals. They made the record something more than special.

It was released in January of 1973 and eventually rose to No. 1, not only on the *Cashbox* and *Record World* magazine Hot 100 pop charts, but also on the *Billboard* Best Selling Soul Singles Chart where it stayed No. 1 for four weeks. The song would become one of the most played on radio that year, according to *Billboard* magazine.

Years later, after it had become a hit by Gladys Knight and the Pips, Daryl Hall of Hall and Oates recorded the song on their "Our Kind of Soul" album. He said it was the saddest song he'd ever heard.

He also expressed other thoughts about the song.

"That's an amazing song that I always thought I could sing and bring a different sort of poignancy to it. Gladys Knight had done a fantastic job on that song. I wanted to break 'Neither One of Us' down to its raw emotion. And this was already one hell of a song written by Jim Weatherly, who was responsible for a number of (Gladys') biggest hits. We listened to that track after we cut it, and frankly, we started crying. It's a very powerful, soulful song."

I was 30 years old and this was my first real taste of success. I remember staring at the gold record of "Neither One of Us" hanging on my wall and thinking, 'Well, that's something no one can ever take away from me. It will be written in pop music history forever. Now you can really call yourself a songwriter."

Larry had been right about "Neither One of Us." Millions would hear it and love it and buy it. They continue to hear it today. It's still being played on traditional radio, satellite radio, and recorded by new artists.

I was so glad I'd been wrong about the sad song no one would want to hear. Now people were asking me to write more songs just like that.

At the same time Larry pitched Gladys and the Pips "Neither One of Us" and "Between Her Goodbye and My Hello," he also pitched them "Midnight Plane to Houston."

But there was something that didn't feel exactly right to them, so they passed on it.

Soon Larry got a call from Sonny Limbo, a record producer in Atlanta. Sonny was producing an album on Cissy Houston, who became a member of the Sweet Inspirations that backed up Elvis in his Las Vegas shows. She was also Whitney's mother. They wanted to cut "Midnight Plane to Houston." The kicker was that

Sonny asked if they could change the title. He and Cissy felt that "Midnight Train to Georgia" sounded more like an R&B title. And with Cissy's last name being Houston, they felt that might cause some confusion.

Cissy said that she loved the song the minute she first heard it but felt it needed the title change to make it real for her. She said her family is from Georgia and they didn't take planes anywhere. They took trains. It was a country song but she wanted to add some kind of a gospel feel to it. Cissy also mentioned that she personally arranged the background vocals.

Larry's immediate response was, "No! Don't touch that song. Absolutely not. It stays 'Midnight Plane to Houston.'"

Larry said he and Sonny went back and forth on the phone for two hours, and Sonny finally convinced him to change the title.

"I finally just said, 'OK. Go ahead and do it and record it.' I loved the song and I knew it would be a hit," Larry said. "But it didn't have the same impact to me as 'Neither One of Us' and 'You're the Best Thing That Ever Happened to Me.' So to me it was my third favorite of Jimmy's songs. All three of those songs became mega-hits."

Larry agreed to let them change the title as long as they understood that was all they changed and made sure they understood they would get no songwriting credit, no writer's royalties, and none of the publishing. And that was fine with me.

Cissy Houston recorded the song in Memphis with the new title of "Midnight Train to Georgia." It was released as a single in 1972 and peaked at No. 45 on the *Billboard* R&B charts.

MIDNIGHT TRAIN TO GEORGIA
(MIDNIGHT PLANE TO HOUSTON)

L.A. proved too much for the girl
So she's leaving the life she's come to know
She's going back to find what's left of her world
The world she left behind not so long ago

She's leaving on the midnight train to Georgia
Going back to a simpler place and time
I'll be with her on that midnight train to Georgia
I'd rather live in her world than live without her in mine

She kept dreaming someday she'd be a star
But she found out the hard way dreams don't always come true
So she's pawned all her hopes and sold her car
And bought a one-way ticket back to the life she once knew

She's leaving on the midnight train to Georgia
Going back to simpler place and time
I'll be with her on that midnight train to Georgia
I'd rather live in her world than live without her in mine

Gladys Knight and the Pips' contract with Motown was about to expire after "Neither One of Us" was released.

The people at Motown knew in order to re-sign her they had to get her a No. 1 record. I believe Gladys was not real happy at Motown and wanted to move to another label.

In a 2014 interview, Gladys said, "There was a stigma at Motown that if you ever left there you wouldn't make it. Nobody leaves. They were that cocky. Can you believe it? Nobody leaves Motown and makes good." According to Gladys, she and the Pips and the Isley Brothers were the first two groups to prove them wrong.

In 1972, after leaving Motown, Gladys and the Pips were approached by Neil Bogart, who wanted to sign them to Buddah Records. As they were getting ready to record their first album on Buddah, Larry kept sending Gladys my songs since he had already established a relationship with her. That made it easier to get songs directly to her.

Larry also sat down with Art Kass, Bogart's partner at Buddah, and pitched songs to him for Gladys. He pitched "Where Peaceful Waters Flow," which became their first single on their new label in early 1973. It went to No. 23 on the Pop charts, No.18 on the A/C (Adult Contemporary) charts, and No. 5 on the R&B charts.

I've always thought "Peaceful Waters" was a really good record, and because it followed "Neither One of Us" it got a lot of airplay. But it didn't sell as well because Motown released another one of my songs, "Between Her Goodbye and My Hello," by Gladys at the same time.

So Gladys had two songs fighting each other for radio play and chart positions, both of them mine. Crazy as it sounds, that actually slowed things down a bit.

I think Gladys liked "Peaceful Waters" because of its spiritual quality. I wrote it as a secular song, but many gospel artists have recorded it as well. Also, because I was an emotional songwriter and not an intellectual songwriter, I aimed for the listener's heart, not the mind.

WHERE PEACEFUL WATERS FLOW

Come and walk with me
We can go where peaceful waters flow

If loneliness surrounds you
And rain clouds always hang around you
If wakin' up each day gets you down
If the life that you're leading
Seems hollow maybe what you're needing
Is someone to turn your world around?

Come take my hand
And walk with me awhile
Let me teach you how to smile
I'll show you skies where gentle breezes blow
And I'll take you where peaceful waters flow

If the sunshine hurts your eyes, boy
It's time for you to realize, boy
Beyond this moment lies a better day
And if you let me I will guide you,
I'll always be there right beside you
Through each and every step of the way

Larry knew that Gladys and The Pips had already heard "Midnight Plane to Houston," so he sent them Cissy Houston's version of "Midnight Train to Georgia," which Gladys thought was a demo. It got rid of the uncertainty the group felt when they first heard the song under its old title. According to Gladys, they had already discussed changing the title to "Midnight Train to Georgia" before they heard Cissy's version.

"It was one of those songs that got four stars – we called them stars," Gladys said. "We all felt the same way about the song, so we knew there was something special about it. We're from Georgia, so I said it would make a little more sense to me if I sing it that way. Even though I would have taken the song either way, because it was constructed in a real wonderful way. We were just trying to personalize it, and Jim allowed us to do that."

"I think it just became a monster hit because of his lyrics, which is the way it is with all of Jim's songs," Larry said. "When they finally get heard and you listen to the words, it has a way of being infectious."

Tony Camillo, who had worked on many of the pop, soul, and disco records of the 1960s and '70s, was hired to produce Gladys' record of "Midnight Train."

Years later, *Goldmine* magazine celebrated the 40th anniversary of "Midnight Train to Georgia" by telling the whole story of the recording of the song. Some excerpts:

"The session where 'Midnight Train to Georgia' was recorded was at Tony Camillo's Venture Sound recording studio at his home in Hillsborough, N.J. All of the instrumental tracks for Midnight Train were done there in 1973.

"They recorded two different instrumental tracks with a big rhythm section, but Gladys didn't like either version. Camillo said

those tracks didn't have the magic. Gladys wanted the track to be more down-home with a more southern vibe, like an Al Green song or in the style of the Muscle Shoals sound. So Camillo hired just three musicians to cut the new basic track – Guitarist Jeff Mironov, bassist Bob Babbitt, and drummer Andrew Smith. Camillo later played keyboards.

"Before they started recording they all went into a back room to listen to some songs by Al Green to help them get the feeling Gladys wanted. When they cut the track, it was simpler and had a great down-home feel to it. Then they sweetened it with strings, horns, and acoustic piano, and Camillo playing the Hammond organ. Gladys recorded her vocals in Detroit. She recorded the song in one take and later she did punch in one line at a studio in New York."

The memorable background parts the Pips sang weren't written in. That was entirely their creative work. They came up with the "woo woo" that helped make the song a timeless classic that's lasted for decades. When Gladys was singing the fade she was ad-libbing, and her brother, Bubba, was in the control booth feeding her some of the ad-libs through her headset.

Gladys seemed to be sold on my songs from the start, and I've always been grateful for that. She gave an unknown songwriter the chance of a lifetime.

"I just love the way Jim writes," she explained. "It's simplistic. He writes about slices of life, real life. The way he writes, everybody can understand it. It's basic. It's not all out there. The melodies are wonderful. He gives me a chance to step out a little bit and add to whatever the melodies are. I love that about it, too. He leaves room for me to do it musically as I feel it."

The first album Gladys and the Pips recorded for Buddah after leaving Motown was titled *Imagination*. It peaked at No. 9 on the *Billboard* album Pop charts and No. 1 on the *Billboard* R&B album charts. It also went platinum, which means it sold more than a million copies. I wrote five songs on that album – "Storms of Troubled Times," "Once in a Lifetime Thing," "Where Peaceful Waters Flow," "Best Thing That Ever Happened to Me," and "Midnight Train to Georgia."

When the album was first released in October, 1973, it was reviewed by acclaimed music critic Robert Hilburn in the *Los Angeles Times*. Basically, he wrote there wasn't a good song on the album. Everybody has different tastes.

When Gladys and the Pips left Motown Records they showed a classic example of their good old-fashioned integrity.

"We didn't have to give Motown 'Neither One of Us' because our contract was up. But we decided that there were some things we got that were good." Gladys said. "You know nothing is all bad

Me, Gladys Knight, and the Pips – William Guest, Edward Patton, and Bubba Knight

and nothing is all good. We had some good things happen over there simply because they were Motown. They opened some doors for us. So we said, "OK. The fair thing to do is we'll leave one of these songs with Motown, and we'll take the other song to the new company that we're going to. So we left 'Neither One of Us' with Motown, and we took 'Midnight Train to Georgia' to Buddah."

"Midnight Train to Georgia" hit No. 1 on the Billboard Hot 100 Pop Charts on October 27, 1973. It stayed there for two weeks at a time when most songs only spent one week at No. 1. It spent four weeks at No. 1 on the R&B charts. It was No. 19 on the A/C and No. 10 in the UK.

After all these years, Gladys Knight and the Pips' recording of "Midnight Train to Georgia" retains its magnetism. On the Internet it's one of the most discussed and reviewed songs of modern times.

In January, 2018, this glowing review by Joel Freimark – which provides detailed histories of great songs and albums – declared it one of the best songs ever written.

Some excerpts:

> There are countless numbers of songs that tell tales of people aspiring for greatness, but ultimately falling short. While this theme has been famously explored by everyone from Tom Petty to Metallica there has perhaps never been a finer and more beautiful example of this theme than the 1973 hit from Gladys Knight and the Pips, the unrivaled, "Midnight Train to Georgia."

> Bringing together absolutely phenomenal orchestration, brilliant vocals and one of the finest lyrics in history, "Midnight Train to Georgia" would rise all the way to the top spot on the charts, as well as win a Grammy Award and become one of the most cherished songs in the history of music. The song remains the ultimate song for those who have traveled far in hopes of achieving fame in music or movies, and it also stands as one of the most

beautiful love songs in history. Having been featured in countless films, most notably in a rather iconic scene in "The Deer Hunter," "Midnight Train To Georgia" is without question one of the most perfect and iconic songs ever recorded.

Though it was actually originally recorded and released a year earlier by Cissy Houston, it is the Gladys Knight version that remains not only the definitive version, but one of the greatest songs in music history.

The soul of the music on "Midnight Train to Georgia" unquestionably comes from the rhythm section, and the bassline is one of the finest that was NOT written and performed by The Funk Brothers. It is within the rhythm to the song that sounds of Motown and funk shine through, and this is of very little surprise as the bass player was, in fact, former Funk Brothers player, Bob Babbitt.

The musicians found on "Midnight Train to Georgia" are without question some of the finest, and it is the combination of their performance with the magnificent vocals that makes the song such a timeless classic.

Without question, "Midnight Train to Georgia" is not only Gladys Knight's finest vocal moment but easily one of the most stunning vocals in all of music history. From the deep, soulful verses to the crying, heart-wrenching choruses, Knight excels across the music scales, and there are very few vocal performances that even come close to the power and emotion.

Perfectly capturing the feeling of the lover telling the cautionary tale of her boyfriend's quest for fame and fortune, Knight brings the story to life in vivid fashion. The basis for the song can be summed up in the iconic line "superstar, but he didn't get far," as the narrator chooses to stand with her love, though he initially left her behind. These subtle lyrical interjections from The Pips remain equally as iconic as the lead vocals, and the interplay between Knight and The Pips exemplifies the ideal way in which such a setup should function.

Truth be told, the 'woo woos' from The Pips are perhaps as memorable as the lead vocal, and they were highlighted in one of the most amusing parodies, when in 1976, The Pips performed the backing vocals sans Knight on 'The Richard Pryor Show.' Truly one of the most stunning vocal performances in history, few songs even come close to the perfection found on "Midnight Train to Georgia."

Standing today as one of the most iconic songs in music history, "Midnight Train to Georgia" is perhaps the essential song about the failed quest for fame and fortune. Strangely enough, the song was inspired by a conversation concerning a pre-"Charlie's Angels" Farrah Fawcett, though it is in no way a tale of her life. The song's writer, Jim Weatherly, was said to have had a conversation with Fawcett and she said that she was 'taking a midnight plane to Houston to see her family,' and this served as the beginning of the song's formation. Though the finished product in no way references the original inspiration for the song, "Midnight Train to Georgia" can be applied to countless situations, and the phrase itself has become a part of the vernacular of society. This crossover into so many different aspects of music and society as a whole serves as a testament to the overall impact of the song, and that is much the reason that it stands today as one of the most important songs ever written.

"Midnight Train to Georgia" is one of the most magnificent and truly unparalleled recordings in music history.

Gladys Knight and the Pips recorded 13 of my songs during their remarkable career. It was an amazing run and we moved the world of music.

I felt a sense of sadness after their final tour in the late 1980s when they finally disbanded. Gladys and her brother Bubba continued to tour, and Gladys still tours. She performed several concerts in my native Mississippi in 2017 and 2018.

I have gone to several of her concerts in Nashville. I always leave with a sense of contentment and amazement that she seems to still love to sing my songs, and of course I love to hear her sing them.

I was finally making enough money to buy my first house. It was located in Sherman Oaks on Valley Vista Boulevard. I furnished it with turn-of-the-century American antiques, including cigar store Indians, which kind of became my hobby. I was finally living my own "American dream."

Back home, my brother Shan was in high school when my music with Gladys began to climb the charts. He had an old radio/cassette tape player and he would lie in bed at night and tune it from station to station to station, hunting for those songs.

"I was amazed that Jimmy's music was suddenly everywhere. Most of his songs I like the most were not the hits," Shan said. "I always loved the earlier songs, the ones he wrote by himself. He's got some really good songs with co-writers. But the ones he wrote by himself tended to come from the heart and from his past growing up. There were songs about Mississippi and about growing up in Mississippi.

"Jimmy talks about how his songs are sad. A lot of them are. But there are some really, really great songs that I don't know if anybody will ever hear or ever record. Someday maybe they will and music will change to the point that they mean something again."

On the Mississippi Gulf Coast in 2013, not far from the spot where Jim Weatherly and the Vegas spent a summer playing at the Fiesta Club almost 50 years earlier, Gladys Knight's tour bus stopped for a concert at the Beau Rivage in Biloxi. That night, among the many stories she told between songs, she recalled "Neither One of Us."

"My mother always taught us not to ask for anything we really didn't need. But we had been performing a long time by then. I said, 'Lord, we do need a Grammy.' We even prayed about it," Gladys told her audience.

On March 2, 1974, at the Hollywood Palladium, with Frank Sinatra and Tony Bennett as hosts and millions watching on CBS, Gladys Knight and the Pips won their first Grammy.

Best Pop Vocal Performance by a Duo, Group or Chorus for "Neither One of Us."

The fun was just starting. After years of working and waiting and praying for one Grammy, they suddenly had two.

Best Rhythm and Blues Vocal Performance by a Duo, Group or Chorus for "Midnight Train to Georgia."

I was there that night. I had been nominated in the R&B songwriter category for "Midnight Train." But I lost to Stevie Wonder, who won the Grammy for "Superstition."

It was still a very proud moment for a kid from Mississippi, a guy whose world had been turned upside down in such a short period of time. I still felt a little bit like a fish out of water. But I was a happy fish.

It didn't end there. It wasn't long before "Best Thing That Ever Happened to Me" became another huge hit for them.

"'Best Thing That Ever Happened to Me' wasn't in the package that Larry first sent us." Gladys said. "We went to the Sands Hotel one night. Danny Thomas was a friend of ours and he was on stage doing his show. He sees us in the audience. He says, 'Hey Gladys, when the show is over meet me backstage. I've got a song for you.' He was on stage when he said that. So we met him backstage and he was telling us about his connection to Larry's publishing company that had this song. It was one of his wife's favorite songs. So he gave us this song, and we loved it. We eventually got around to getting it all together with Jim and everybody and doing it. And it became one of our signature pieces of music."

When Gladys published her autobiography, the title of the book was a line from that song – *"Between Each Line of Pain and Glory."*

"Best Thing" was a really simple song. The line that still sticks out in my mind is at the top of the chorus: *"If anyone should ever write my life story, for whatever reason there might be."* I don't know where that line came from. It just came from out of the blue. It just felt right.

At the time I didn't know there was such a thing as crafting a song. Had I known, I might have written "Best Thing" differently. I might have tried to control it more intellectually rather than letting my emotions flow. But since that was the way I wrote all my songs then, through a stream of consciousness and emotion, I didn't think of that song as overly special when put up beside all the other songs I'd written.

But the public often knows better than the writer what a hit song is. The people who listen to songs and buy records will let you know.

"Best Thing That Ever Happened to Me" reached No.1 on the R&B charts, No. 2 on the Pop charts, No.10 on A/C, and No. 7 in the UK. Another song of mine Gladys and the Pips released on Buddah was "Love Finds Its Own Way." It went to No. 33 Pop, No. 3 R&B, and No. 40 A/C.

I felt like I was in a dream.

Not long after "Best Thing" became a hit, a beer company wanted to use it in a commercial. Larry said they would pay $10,000 plus royalties each time the commercial was played. He asked my opinion. I told him I didn't want the song associated with any alcohol product. I had written it as a romantic love song, and I didn't want to romanticize beer. Larry agreed and we passed. My songs had meaning to me. I wanted to make a good living, but it wasn't always about the money.

Later when the song became a gospel classic by Reverend James Cleveland, I wondered if that would have happened had we gone for the beer bucks. God does work in mysterious ways.

Larry Gordon, me, and Glenn Sutton

32 ——⚜

Nashville Connection

By the 1970s Ray Price, one of country music's most recognizable and legendary stars, had been performing on the Grand Ole Opry for two decades. Ray was one of my favorite singers, and Larry started sending my songs to him.

Larry sent "Neither One of Us" to CBS in Nashville to producer Ron Bledsoe, who was looking for songs for Ray. Before Ray had a chance to hear it, another CBS producer, Glenn Sutton, saw the tape on Ron's desk and grabbed it. He listened to it and decided to produce it himself on a great country singer he was recording named Bob Luman. The song was released on Epic Records and peaked at No. 5 on the Billboard country charts.

Later on, Glenn Sutton became a great friend of mine. Like Jimmy Bowen, he was one of the funniest people I'd ever met, if not the funniest. Stealing a tape off another producer's desk and recording it on one of his artists sounded exactly like something Glenn would do.

At the opening of a new swimming pool on Music Row next to ASCAP in the '70s, a black limo pulled up on Seventeenth Avenue and Glenn jumped out. He was dressed in an Esther Williams swimsuit, a "Creature from the Black Lagoon" mask, and flippers. He ran and jumped in the pool and swam to the other end. When he climbed out he turned and faced the crowd of people standing around and like a ringmaster at a circus he waved his arms and said, "Thank you!" Then he ran and jumped in the waiting limo. That was just who Glenn was.

Glenn was married to Lynn Anderson at the time and he produced her hit record "I Never Promised You a Rose Garden" written by Joe South. Later on, Lynn would record a great version of "Midnight Train to Georgia." Glenn would do anything in the world for a laugh. But he was an amazingly talented songwriter and producer. And he was my friend.

Larry Gordon, never one to give up, sent another song to Nashville for Ray Price, and this one did get to him. It was "You're The Best Thing That Ever Happened to Me." Ray loved it and wanted to record it.

Even though I had written the song at Danny Thomas' request, I had actually written "Best Thing" with Ray Price in mind. I just thought that might be something he would say in a song. He had an understated way of saying simple things that touched the hearts of his fans. And he liked mature lyrics. I was in the studio at CBS in Nashville when Ray recorded it. That was a once-in-a-lifetime experience for me, a young songwriter, getting to watch a legend like Ray in the studio.

A good interpreter of a lyric can make simplicity so poignant if the lines are there. It's just like an actor. An actor can only be good if the script is good. Same thing with writing a song and an artist singing it.

I was actually surprised when Ray cut "Best Thing," although I felt it was perfect for him. Rarely does an artist you have in mind to sing a song actually record it. At least that's been my experience.

Ray's record of "You're the Best Thing" climbed all the way to No. 1 on the *Billboard* Country charts as well as *Cashbox* and *Record World.*

He wound up recording an entire album of my songs titled, "You're The Best Thing That Ever Happened to Me." For a legend like Ray Price, a member of the Grand Ole Opry and later the Country Music Hall of Fame, to record a whole album of my songs was way beyond anything I'd ever imagined.

To Charlie Monk, it was beyond anything Nashville had ever imagined.

"To have Ray Price do a whole album of Jim Weatherly songs, that was unheard of," Charlie said. "Somebody might have done a Hank Williams tribute album, who had been dead for 20 years. But Jim was at the height of his career. I was stunned. I must admit the songs were there, but Larry Gordon did that with his salesmanship. He just went in and said this is what you ought to do and everyone agreed. It was a compliment to Jim and to Larry to pull that together, but ultimately Ray Price had to make that decision. Anyone would have been tickled to have one song on a Ray Price album. Jim will tell you he would have been tickled to have gotten one song on a Ray Price album at that time. But he got them all."

Gladys Knight – to me the greatest female singer in the world – took "Best Thing" in a whole different direction. She has so much power and emotion in her voice. It had more drive than Ray's more understated intimate tone. Gladys sang it with more fire. Ray's record was slower and more romantic. Both cuts were incredible, each in a different way. And I was certainly proud that two music superstars had chosen to record it.

Larry had become good friends with Ray. And Ray liked what Larry was doing with my career.

"Ray asked me to manage him. I didn't want to be a manager anymore but I was close to him and we had a great relationship," Larry said.

"He wanted me to produce him. And we were having a lot of trouble back in Nashville, because it was right after Keca Music won the Nashville ASCAP awards in 1974 and Jim was ASCAP's Country Songwriter of the Year. Being from L.A., Nashville didn't exactly love that. It's like they wanted Nashville people to win those country awards. We had, I think, nine hits in Nashville that year. So after he left CBS Records, Ray asked me to represent him with Word Music and represent him on ABC Records. All the cuts came really from the relationship we developed. When Ray found out that I won the ASCAP awards, then the following year we were almost ignored in Nashville because they didn't like the idea of an L.A. publisher and a writer living in Los Angeles, which Jimmy was at the time, winning their awards – he decided to do another album of Jim's songs."

Larry had previously been to Ray's house in Dallas and played a lot of my songs for him and his wife and he was picking out Weatherly songs he was going to sing.

"That's how the album came about," Larry recalled.

Later, when Ray was in L.A., he and Larry had a slight disagreement as to how they would get to Nashville.

"Ray had his own plane at the time. He had already committed to doing the album. I told him I would meet him in Nashville and we would do the album there," Larry said. "I told him I was going to drive to Nashville. He didn't like that. He wanted me to fly back with him on his plane. But I really had an aversion to flying. So he said, 'I'll tell you what, I'll give you a choice. If you fly with me, we'll go ahead and we'll do the Weatherly album. If you don't fly with me, I'm not going to do the songs.' Ray wasn't a bullshitting guy. He meant it. I believed him. Obviously I flew.

"Ray said he would only record songs that he felt had a chance to be special," Larry continued. "I think the connection was simply great songs. Period. Jimmy's songs have a way, at least for me and somebody like Ray, you listen to the music and listen to the lyrics, they're just infectious. They talk about real life. And they did the same thing for him that they did for me. I used to sit around with Ray and his wife all the time and talk about what a great, great songwriter the guy is."

Many of the Nashville music people thought Ray was out of his mind to move away from his hard country, honky-tonk image, which had been so successful, to what they called Cosmopolitan Country or Countrypoliton. It was a little slicker sound and he would sometimes use strings and horns. Ray's record of Kris Kristofferson's "For the Good Times" was the first step in that direction. It was a huge hit.

I think the change in style extended Ray's recording career by several years. A lot of people liked his new style and thought he was country's answer to Frank Sinatra. As it turned out, Ray went on to record three more full albums of my songs – 38 songs in all. I was amazed.

Underneath the good news of Ray recording so many of my

songs, I sensed trouble. I was afraid it would cause a backlash from the Nashville music community. To some extent, that's exactly what happened. I was living in L.A., which made me an outsider in Nashville. It got back to me that some people involved with Country music, especially at Columbia Records, didn't like the fact that Ray was cutting so many of my songs. They wondered why Ray would even do one album, much less four. Some people asked me about it. I could only say that I guess it was because he liked the songs.

I do know this. Ray Price would not do anything Ray Price didn't want to do. And no one could talk him out of doing what he wanted to do or into what he didn't want to do. He was his own man. And he did things his way. Period!

Ray had several hits with my songs, starting with "You're The Best Thing That Ever Happened to Me." He followed that up with "Roses and Love Songs," which went to No. 3, "Like Old Times Again" got to No. 4, "If You Ever Change Your Mind," No. 31, "Farthest Thing From My Mind," No. 17, "Like a First Time Thing," No.15, and "Storms of Troubled Times," No. 23 – all on the country charts.

Ray Price was a legend. I was certainly honored, although flabbergasted may be a better way to put it. And grateful.

When Kris Kristofferson inducted Ray into the Country Music Hall of Fame in 1996, in classic Ray Price fashion his first words to the audience after "Thank you" were, "It's about time."

And he was right.

The one thing I didn't like to do was pitch my own songs. I just didn't feel like I was good at it. Charlie Monk knew that, so every now and then he'd call and say, "Get up off the couch and go pitch a song to somebody." I hated rejection. I'd had enough of it, but

My good friend Charlie Monk and me

Charlie kept trying to motivate me.

"As I got to know Jim, he was a very convicted man about what he believed in," Charlie said. "Going back to Pontotoc (for Jim Weatherly Day in 2010) and having heard how he grew up, being the man of the house at such a young age, pretty much helping his mother raise the other children, he had to be a role model for them. That was tough. You had to be a tough man to do that. His mother was obviously a tough woman, because the other kids are fine, fine people. Having filled that fatherly role just really impressed me."

Charlie is one of my closest friends and I trust him.

"Over the years Jim and I have done a lot of business and never had a contract," Charlie said. "It's always been a handshake. I never once worried about that. It never crossed my mind that he might not live up to what he said he was going to do. And that's really very strange in today's business environment. He's taught me, 'Don't ask me my opinion about something unless you want it. I'm going to tell you the truth, because I don't want to have to worry about what I told you today tomorrow.' I think his songs are kind of that way, too.

"It's a story. It's a truth-telling process. I know him so well it's hard for me to say he's a genius. But when you look at his lyrics and his story-telling ability and the musicality of it, he's enormously blessed in so many areas. I think he felt like he had to do better than most. God gives you the talent and you enhance it by working at your craft. I think he's done all of that because he wanted to be the best at it," Charlie continued.

"Again, the dichotomy of having success both in the sports world and in music. Although he didn't play professional sports, I do think he could have played professional football. He wanted to be good at sports, and he was."

Sherrie, me, Elise, and Shan on Jim Weatherly Day in Pontotoc, 2010

33 ——⚜

The Artist Thing

While Gladys Knight and Ray Price, as well as others, were having success with my songs, I was having some success of my own singing them. I enjoyed making records and hearing my songs played by great musicians, but my true love was songwriting. I just enjoyed the creative writing process, to start with nothing and end up with a song. What a powerful feeling.

I do remember another powerful feeling. So powerful, in fact, that it almost put me in a trance. Shortly after my first album was released in 1972, I was driving west on the Ventura freeway in the San Fernando Valley. I had to turn south on the 405 freeway headed for Brentwood to get to my destination. I was listening to KISS AM out of L.A. I was cruising along, not paying much attention to anything, when I heard a song that sounded familiar. Then I realized, "Hey, that's me." I was singing, "Loving You is Just an Old Habit," a song from my first album. That was the first time I had heard myself on Los Angeles radio. I started listening intently, lost in the music and the moment.

When the song was over and I came back to reality, I didn't know where I was. I had driven right by my exit and was past Encino still headed west. It dawned on me I'd missed my turn. It was a surreal moment, realizing there were people all over Los Angeles and southern California hearing me sing on the radio while I was going about my day as usual.

I recorded three albums for RCA – "Weatherly" in 1972, "To a Gentler Time" and "Jim Weatherly" in 1973, but only had a minor hit with a song called "High on Love," which peaked at No. 40 on the A/C charts. "Loving You Is Just an Old Habit," the song I heard on radio that day, got on the Pop charts but never rose above the high 90s. So without any real record sales to speak of, RCA dropped me.

Since Gladys Knight and The Pips had signed with Buddah Records, Neil Bogart thought it could be a good promotional situation to have all of us on the same label. So Larry worked out a deal and I signed with Buddah. I did two albums for their label – "The Songs of Jim Weatherly" and "Magnolias and Misfits."

That's where I had my most success as an artist. "The Need to Be" rose to No.11 on the Pop charts and No. 6, A/C and "I'll Still Love You" got to No. 9 Country. I also had another Country chart song with "It Must Have Been the Rain," which peaked at No. 58 in 1974.

One day Larry told me that Marlo Thomas, Danny Thomas' daughter who is a spokesperson for St. Jude Children's Research Hospital, was going to do a TV special called *Free to Be You and Me*. Marlo gained TV fame as the star of *That Girl* from the late 1960s.

Larry said they needed an 11 o'clock song, which was a big song to close the show. Based on the title of the special, I wrote a song called "The Need to Be." I wrote it for a female to sing – There's the need to be something more than just a reflection of a man – was a line from the song. They didn't end up using it, which is how it turns out sometimes. So Larry had me record it on my first Buddah album, even though I'd written it for a woman's voice.

There were some intense negotiations as to what would be the first single. Larry wanted "The Need to Be" and Art Kass didn't. He said his promotion team didn't like the record. They weren't satisfied with the vocal performance. To be honest, I didn't much care for my vocal performance either. Art and Larry went back and forth for a while and finally Larry said, "Art, if you want this relationship to work, you'd better release 'The Need to Be.' It's a No. 1 record."

Eventually Art relented and released the song as the single. It became the biggest hit I ever had as an artist.

The Need to Be

To fulfill the need to be
Who I am in this world is all I ask
I can't pretend to be something that I'm not
And I won't wear a mask
You've touched my face with love in your eyes
But will you touch my heart
With the understanding that it takes
To realize I just can't play a part

There's the need to be true to myself
And make my own mistakes
And not to lean too hard on someone else
No matter what it takes
So if you're sure it's love just be sure it's love
For this thing called me
'Cause I am what I am
And I have the need to be

I'm not fool enough to think
That I could be the master of my fate
But it's up to me to choose my roads in life
Rocky may well be the ones I take

There's the need to be something more
Than just a reflection of a man
I can't survive in someone's shadow
I need my own spot to stand
So if you're sure it's love just be sure it's love
For this thing called me
'Cause I am what I am
And I have the need to be

I re-recorded the song in 2001 on my own Brizac label, and it's a much better recording than the original.

Sandra Feva recorded and released the song as a single. It peaked at No. 45 on the *Billboard* R&B charts. Gladys Knight and the Pips also recorded "The Need to Be." It was released on their million-selling "Imagination" album but never released as a single.

I believe it would have been a No.1 record for them. However, Gladys did sing it in the Tyler Perry movie *I Can Do Bad All by Myself.* She gave a tremendous performance. Ray Price also recorded it.

In an interview with Kam Williams posted on aalbc.com, the No. 1 site for African American Literature, Gladys revealed a special fondness for "The Need to Be."

"Most people who ask me what's my favorite song expect that it's 'Midnight Train' or 'Neither One of Us.' But actually it's always kinda been 'The Need to Be,' because of what it says. I love the way that song was written. I love the melody. I love everything about it," she said.

Not long after "The Need to Be" became a hit, I received a letter from a lady telling me how special that song was to her. She told me that after years of trying, it gave her the courage to finally leave an abusive marriage that was destroying her life. That made me stop and think about how powerful songs can be. They touch people in ways that can cause them to be happy, sad, emotional. That song gave a woman the inspiration to move forward with her life. That made me realize that somewhere out there in radio land, real people were making critical decisions based on my songs. What a gift to a songwriter and to the people who are moved by their songs. But what a responsibility.

I didn't sell too many albums on Buddah so they dropped me. After that I recorded three albums for ABC Records – "Pictures and Rhymes" in 1976, "The People Some People Choose to Love" in 1976 and "Dancing Moon," which was not released at that time. I had a single for them called "All That Keeps Me Going." It peaked at No. 27 in *Billboard*.

It was becoming more and more clear to me that I was more of a songwriter than a recording artist. I tended to record my songs the way I heard them in my head, and sometimes that wasn't what the record company wanted. I didn't always like to make records just for radio. That was very limiting. I hoped that radio would accept what I did and sometimes that happened, but most times it didn't. Larry still didn't want me to tour to help promote my records because he felt that my strong suit was writing songs. And thank goodness other artists were recording them.

Performing with Dorothy Moore at a North Mississippi Medical Center benefit in Tupelo

34 —

A Song About Home

Around 1971 I wrote a song about my home state. "Mississippi Song" is about her beauty, her struggles, and my feelings about her. My years at Ole Miss contributed to some of my thoughts in the lyrics of that song as well. Some people have tried for years to make it the state song, but for political reasons it has always been blocked. Dorothy Moore, who had her own huge hit with "Misty Blue," was one of the artists who recorded it.

"When I first heard 'Mississippi Song,'" Dorothy said, "I felt from the very beginning that song was for me. There is just something about that song and what it says. It's self-explanatory. 'She was once a great lady standing tall with her head held high.' Such a great song. I wanted that song to be the state song. I sang it for the entire Mississippi legislature in the late '70s. I sang it acapella.

"That would be my biggest dream if that could happen. It says such great things. The lyrics are really wonderful. I don't know any other way to say it, but it is from his heart. The songs Jim has written are from his heart with feeling. It's the same thing with me. I was singing before an audience in the church choir when I was five years old. Maybe we've got a deeper story in Mississippi."

The Lyceum at Ole Miss

MISSISSIPPI SONG

She was once a great lady standing tall
With her head held high
Then a war came along, broke her heart
And left her there to die
With her gown in tattered shreds she raised her weary head
And vowed she'd rise again
Looking back to yesterday
She's come a long, long way since then

Mississippi this is your song
Sung for all the righteous people
Who won't let you forget when you were wrong
In the past they've written songs
For everything that's red, white and blue
It's been a long time coming
So Mississippi this one's for you

I was born into her family
And raised on the labors of her fields
Beneath the summer suns warm haze
She let me run across her meadows and her hills
But she's still the last in line when they pass out poems and rhymes
About the land of the free
Lord, she's still misunderstood
But she's been mighty good to me

My friend Marty Gamblin thought Dorothy Moore was the perfect choice to sing "Mississippi Song."

"She sang the fire out of it," Marty explained. "It has also become the signature song for Guy Hovis of the Lawrence Welk Show, a Tupelo native.

"I think the songs Jim writes require a person that really sings with emotion," Marty said. "He didn't often write ditties. It wasn't the kind of stuff that people just got out there and did. It was those great interpretive singers, some of them great country artists who sang from the heart, and a lot of the R&B artists as well, singing that real soulful music that would strike that emotional chord. Those are the people that reached out to sing Jim's songs. And back in those days people really looked for great songs, country artists and soul artists. It wasn't unusual to see a great song covered by both. There was a message and substance in the lyrics. It wasn't just about a groove for the most part."

In 1979 legendary Mississippian, country singer Charley Pride, had a big hit with a song I wrote called "Where Do I Put Her Memory." It went to No. 1 on the *Billboard* Country charts.

Rolling Stone magazine has it listed as one of their top 40 saddest country songs of all time. The magazine had this to say about it:

"This Jim Weatherly-penned Charley Pride track never specifically says what happened to the woman whose memory can't be put away, but the way Pride sings it, it's safe to assume she's probably dead. The song, which became his 21st No. 1 on the Country chart when it came out in 1979, walks through all the things the narrator hid of his lost love. Gifts she gave him, the pillow she slept on and her drawers of clothes are all par for the course, but the lyrics get particularly sob-worthy with the devastatingly realistic mention of picking up "her hairpins and curlers/ That she dropped on her side of the bed."

WHERE DO I PUT HER MEMORY

I've taken down all of her pictures
I've cleaned out all of the drawers
I've painted over the scratches
From all of our little wars
I've put away every gift that she ever gave to me
Now everything is in its place except for her memory

Where do I put her memory, it's always in my mind
I can't hide it in the closet
And Lord I can't throw it away
Where do I put her memory, it's always in my mind
I can't chase it, erase it, I just have to face it
It's gonna be there a long, long time

I got rid of the pillow
Where she used to lay her head
I've picked up the hairpins and curlers
That she'd dropped on her side of the bed
I've locked away each souvenir and thrown away the key
Now everything is in its place except for her memory

Where do I put her memory, it's always in my mind
I can't chase it, erase it, I just have to face it
It's gonna be there a long, long time

I've known Charley Pride for years and we have some things in common. We are both north Mississippi natives, although on different sides of the state. I'm from Pontotoc in the northeast hills and he's from Sledge in the Delta. Charley's birthday is March 18, one day after mine. Every time I run into him, he reminds me of that. I've always been proud that he recorded "Memory" and had a No. 1 hit with one of my songs.

Later on, Charley recorded another one of my songs that I wrote with Bob McDill called "Soft to Touch, but Hard to Hold." It's on his album, "I'm Gonna Love Her On the Radio."

Charley Pride, me, and former Mississippi Governor Cliff Finch

As the 1970s drew to a close, I was still writing songs and artists were still recording them. And Larry Gordon was still working to get even more people to notice my work. I asked Larry once why he didn't sign a couple of more writers to his publishing company. He said, "I can't tell people I've got the greatest songwriters in the world, but I can tell them I've got the greatest songwriter in the world."

He got me a new record deal on Electra Records with Jim Ed Norman producing. I never did an album for them, but I had some chart singles. "Smooth Sailin" peaked at No. 32 in 1979, "Gift from Missouri" made it to No. 34 in 1979, and "Safe in the Arms of Your Love" topped at No. 82 in 1980, all on the *Billboard* Country charts. With not much in the way of record sales, Electra let me go.

"Jimmy and I were really pretty much inseparable," Larry said. "I never desired to take on another writer. And after the success, I had plenty of opportunities. But I never thought anybody would be as good as Jimmy...I was just really into Jimmy. My philosophy was he was the best writer on the planet, so I was just willing to put whatever credibility I had on that fact and to sell him as a songwriter. We kind of toyed with the entertainment end and the stage end. His real love and passion was writing songs. And that showed."

Through it all, Larry never stopped believing in me. And I never stopped believing in him.

"I think there was a sense of loyalty," Larry explained. "I never expected in the music business for Jimmy to leave me. And I think he was very, very honest in his way of doing business. He is a very great and decent guy. I love being around him. I liked hanging out with him, and I felt comfortable that for all the business that we did, he just liked what I did and I liked what he did. I wasn't interested in anything other than his wellbeing and protecting him both as a human being and as a songwriter. And I think that he respected me enough at the time to be the other end of that. So whether we had a contract or not, I don't think he was going to leave me and I wasn't going to leave him. I was never really worried about the normal Hollywood story where you leave your agent, you leave your publisher, you leave somebody.

"It's never smooth sailing, because cuts don't come that often at the time that we were building. It's hard to get anybody to record your songs, and then they want the publishing, and they want this or they want that. So there are always hard times. But to me it was smooth sailing, because I had a good time every day I represented him. I just believed in his songs and was able to sell them. That's really basically what it takes. I don't care how good the song is, you've got to sell it to somebody," he said.

I expected to work with Larry for as long as my career lasted. But in the early '80s he got chronically sick and decided to sell his publishing company. That was a sad time, but I understood. That was the only reason we ended our business association.

Larry thought I was upset.

"When I sold the company I'm sure Jimmy was pissed off, and we didn't talk for a long time, even though there were always very, very good feelings. We didn't talk for several years. This was around 1981," Larry recalled.

In truth, I was afraid that if I remained close to Larry I would constantly call him and ask him for advice and what direction I should take next, like he was still my manager. I had become really dependent on him. He was the one person I leaned on most and I trusted him completely. When he got sick he just didn't feel like he had the energy to keep up the pace he was used to. I think that frustrated him. He didn't think he was capable of doing the job anymore. That was the only reason he sold his publishing catalog and we split up.

I didn't want to put any extra strain on him, so I felt the only fair thing to do was to move away from Larry on a personal basis while we were ending our business relationship. I hated losing him. I knew I'd never find another publisher who believed in me and my songs the way Larry did. He was the perfect publisher for me. And he was a great friend. He was like family to me.

I left Larry's company, Keca Music, feeling truly grateful for all Larry had done for me. I wasn't particularly angry, but one thing did bug me some, and that was the fact that he sold my songs to K-Tel Records and my contract along with it.

K-Tel was a record company that specialized in putting out "oldies but goodies." They would have some of the original artists go in and re-record their hit songs so they would then own the new master recordings. They could release them on their own label and not have to pay another record company or any publishing royalties. I think I had about a year left on my contract, and as soon as it was up I would be free to move on.

I started to get that old sick feeling again. I began to think, "What happens now?" Larry and I had worked together for about 10 years, and my career was far better than I could have imagined. Now I was back at square one. I was lost again. I really didn't know what to do next, but I couldn't call Larry and ask him.

K-Tel couldn't get my songs cut because they didn't have Larry's all-consuming belief in me or his kind of commitment. They didn't have his drive, salesmanship or conviction. There was a guy who worked there named Bill Issacs. We became friends. Bill tried his best to get me cuts, but he just wasn't Larry. The momentum that I had enjoyed tapered off. A year passed and when my contract with K-Tel was up, I started publishing my own songs.

Eventually K-Tel sold my catalog to Welk Music, Lawrence Welk's company. They had a hot streak going, especially in Nashville. At least I had a better chance of continued success there. Later Welk was bought by Polygram Music and sometime after that Polygram merged with Universal Music. That's where my older songs remain to this day. Universal Music Publishing is a worldwide organization. They collect royalties from every country in the world and make sure I receive the money from record sales that my songs have earned.

Cynthia and me at the Birmingham premier of "The Bear" in 1984. Cynthia played the role of Mary Harmon Bryant, the wife of Coach Bear Bryant.

35 —❧

Acting Class Miracle

Meanwhile, I had decided to take some acting classes at Vince Chase's workshop on Hollywood Boulevard, a well-established, highly-reputable place for actors to advance their craft. I wasn't sure I wanted to be an actor, but I did want to learn what acting was all about. I thought it could only help me in my songwriting.

While taking the classes, I met a beautiful girl from Oak Ridge, Tennessee, named Cynthia Leake. We discovered we had a mutual friend in Charlie Monk. Cynthia had worked on a TV show in Nashville called "Hee Haw Honeys." That's where she met Charlie, who was always involved in some way in the music and entertainment industry. She was dating someone else at the time and so was I. After some time passed and we were both free, we started dating and gradually became close.

One day Cynthia and I were having lunch at a small outside café in Burbank. I noticed Jonathan Winters, the off-the-wall comedian with a quirky comedy style so popular on TV and movies in those days, sitting alone two tables down. In a few minutes he got up and walked over to our table and sat down. Without saying hello he immediately started cracking one joke after another. Cynthia and I were in stitches with laughter. This went on for about twenty minutes or so, and then he just abruptly stopped. He told us he was working on a new comedy routine, and he wanted to try it out on people he didn't know. He thanked us for letting him sit with us and for being such a great audience. Then he got up and was on his way. Cynthia and I looked at each other like "What just happened?" Only in Hollywood.

I floundered for a while before making the decision that I would start going to Nashville to co-write. Larry had never wanted me to co-write because he thought it would get in the way of how I wrote by myself. That's probably true, but I needed a fresh start, and co-writing seemed like a good way to do it.

I began commuting to Nashville, and one morning in 1983 I had a writing appointment booked with a singer/songwriter/producer named Keith Stegall. I was staying with my close friends Marty and Cherie Gamblin in Franklin, just south of Nashville. Cynthia was with me.

As Cynthia drove me to Music Row for the appointment, she started talking about her grandparents and I found myself staring at her. They seemed to be very special to her. I was thinking just how lucky I was to have her in my life. The words "A Lady like You" popped into my mind. I thought it would be a great song title.

When I got together with Keith we began to write a song with that title. He understood where I was coming from. I wanted it to be a loving tribute to Cynthia.

A few days later Keith demoed it with some outstanding Nashville musicians, and I played it for Marty who was now running Glen Campbell's publishing company in Nashville. He loved it and thought it would be a great song for Glen. So he sent the song to Glen, who was living in Phoenix. We never heard anything back, so we didn't really know if he'd even listened to it. Marty sent him another copy. No response. We still felt like maybe he hadn't listened to it yet.

When Glen came to Nashville to record a new album at Harold Shedd's Music Mill Recording Studios, with Harold producing, Marty had another plan. Glen's publishing company office just happened to be in the Music Mill as well. Glen's wife, Kim, had come with him to the recording session and Marty got her to come to his office. He played the song for her.

Kim said, "Has Glen heard this?" Marty said he had sent the song to Glen a couple of times and never heard anything back.

"Give me a cassette of the song," Kim said.

She took the tape upstairs to the studio where Glen was recording. When he had a break, Kim walked in, laid the cassette on the recording console and said, "Glen, you need to hear this." Then she turned and walked out. Glen asked Harold to play the tape for him. His reaction: "Yeah, this really is a good song. Let's cut it."

So with Kim, Marty, and me standing there, the musicians rehearsed the song with Glen and got the track they wanted in one take. Glen sang it great and never punched in one line. So his vocal was in one take as well.

Glen had a mint in his mouth to keep from getting "cottonmouth" as he sang. There's a line in the song that says, "It's a mystery how someone like me was chosen to be blessed with a lady like you." Evidently the mint was in the wrong place in his mouth, because when he got to that line he sang "It's a 'ristery' how someone like me..." Glen was leaving Nashville on a European tour and he never replaced the line. It came out on the record that way. If you listen closely you can hear it.

Marty and I were elated. If it hadn't been for Marty's persistence and Kim's assistance, I don't think Glen would've ever cut the song.

When the album came out, it was a beautiful recording and I was really proud to have it. Glen had sung it beautifully. The record company put out another song as the first single. It was a great song called "Faithless Love" written by J.D. Souther.

Several weeks later when Glen came back into town to tape "Nashville Now," Ralph Emery's popular television show, I ran into him and he said, "You've got the next single." I was totally surprised. Singles are important because that's the song they promote to radio stations and hope it will become a hit. After all it had taken to get Glen to record it, "A Lady like You" was now a single.

It turned out to be the last No. 1 record of Glen Campbell's remarkable career. It peaked at No. 1 on the Radio and Records Charts and at No. 4 on Billboard's Country charts in 1984.

Cynthia and I continued to grow closer, and we talked about getting married. But I didn't want to get married in Los Angeles and try to raise kids there. Not that there's anything wrong with raising kids in L.A., but I was from the South and that's where we both had family. Neither of us had family in L.A., and I've always believed that kids need family.

I decided to move back to the South. Nashville was the obvious choice. There, I could continue to write songs and get them published and recorded. Cynthia was a working actress and wanted to stay in L.A. to pursue her own career.

So we parted ways, and I bought a house on Farrar Avenue in the Green Hills area of Nashville, where my career was already taking a turn for the better.

A Lady Like You

Here I am just an ordinary man, my virtues are few
And I'm amazed every morning when I wake
With a lady like you
You're all the good things God put on this earth
And you're so much more than I deserve
What did I ever do to win a lady like you.

Look at me, I'm as common as can be
But you make me shine
Look at you, you're a lady through and through
So gracious and kind
And when you're sleeping softly by my side
Oh I look at you and I'm mystified
What did I ever do to win a lady like you

Heaven knows I'm less than perfect
And I've found the very best
But it's a mystery how someone like me
Was chosen to be blessed with a lady like you

You're all the good things God put on this earth
And you're so much more than I deserve
What did I ever do to win a lady like you
A lady like you

36 ——⁂

Co-Writing

I made some good friends in Nashville while co-writing. It helped my social life and got me out of the house more often. My friend, Charlie Monk, was a big help in introducing me to Nashville songwriters. It was like he knew everybody in town.

One of my favorite co-writers was a great songwriter named Bob McDill, who became a good friend. He had written many country classics like the brilliant "Good Ole Boys Like Me."

Bob wrote for Welk Music and was a master at crafting a song. I had always written stream of consciousness but while working with him, I learned how to "craft" a song. It was an intellectual thing instead of an emotional thing. I learned quite a bit while working with him. I remember when I would contribute a line and Bob would say, "That's not very interesting."

We had two Top Ten hits on the *Billboard* Country charts together in 1985 – "You Turn Me On Like a Radio" by Ed Bruce which peaked at No. 3, and "All Tangled up in Love" by Gus

Hardin and Earl Thomas Conley which peaked at No. 6. We also had some album cuts together.

I had a lot of other cuts during that period, but most were old hits from my catalog. One that stands out was a cut by Julie Andrews. That's right. THE Julie Andrews of stage and film, best known for her iconic roles in "Mary Poppins" and "The Sound of Music."

Larry Butler, who produced many hits for Kenny Rogers, was going to record a country album on Julie. One of the songs they picked was "The Closest Thing to Love" which I had written in the early 1970s. The album never came out or maybe it was never completed. But Larry Butler gave me a copy of the cut. It's a beautiful recording and I treasure it. Mac Davis, another fine songwriter who I admire, also cut that song on one of his albums. I took that as a great compliment.

A short while later I sold my house in California and became a permanent Nashville resident. It was good to be living in the South again. I could watch more SEC football.

Around 1989, I signed a songwriter contract with Opryland Music Group, mainly because Charlie Monk had gone to work there. Jerry Bradley, who was head of the company, had been a friend for years. It was the first publisher I had signed with since Larry Gordon.

I felt like at this point in my career I needed a big company's power behind me. The only drawback was that I was now one of a stable of writers, which meant my songs wouldn't get the concentrated individual attention that I got from Larry.

Most of Opryland's (now Sony Music) success was with Country music artists, and I'd had a lot of success in R&B and Pop. We got some good album cuts in Europe. One was a beautiful song called "If I Love You" by Elaine Page that I wrote with Toni Clay.

I also wrote a song during this time with Skip Ewing called "Someone Else's Star." It would become a No. 1 Country song for a talented young artist named Bryan White.

Bryan was generating excitement as an up-and-coming singer, and Marty Gamblin managed him.

"Someone Else's Star" was the only song Skip and I wrote together. A friend of mine got that cut. Derek George who was a member of the band, Pearl River, pitched that song to Bryan. Marty had given the song to Pearl River to record but their producer Jimmy Bowen – the same Jimmy Bowen who produced my first three albums years earlier – turned it down. Derek thought it would be a great song for Bryan, who was looking for a hit.

Bryan went into the studio with Billy Joe Walker, a first-class guitarist and an A-list player, to do a simple demo. They did a killer guitar-vocal. Everyone thought it could be a hit record so Kyle Lenning, Bryan's producer, booked studio time with a full band to re-record the song. They tried and tried but they couldn't recapture the magic that Bryan and Billy Joe created on their simple demo.

So Kyle took their original guitar-vocal demo and built the entire track around it. It turned out to be a wonderful record. It went to No. 1 on the *Billboard* Country charts and was Bryan's first No. 1 record.

SOMEONE ELSE'S STAR

Alone again tonight without someone to love
The stars are shining bright
So one more wish goes up
Oh, I wish I may and I wish with all my might
For the love I'm dreaming of and missing in my life

You'd think that I could find a true love of my own
It happens all the time to people that I know
Their wishes all come true so I've got to believe
There's still someone out there who
Is meant for only me

Guess I must be wishing on someone else's star
Seems like someone else keeps getting
What I'm wishing for
Why can't I be as lucky as those other people are
Guess I must be wishing on someone else's star

I sit here in the dark and stare up at the sky
And I can't give my heart one good reason why
Everywhere I look it's lovers that I see
Seems like everyone's in love with everyone but me

I had some of the lyrics for "Someone Else's Star" written down for a long time, and I had tried to write the song by myself. I just wasn't happy with the melodies I kept coming up with, but I knew it was a unique idea for a song.

So I filed the lyrics away until I had more inspiration. I had a writing session with Skip, a really talented and well-respected songwriter, and I decided to pitch the idea to him. He really liked it and said, "Why don't we take the chords to 'Twinkle, Twinkle Little Star' and try to write the melody around those chords?"

Skip began to play his guitar and sing a melody to some of my lyrics. Little by little it started to take shape. We edited some of my lyrics and rewrote some of them to fit the meter of Skip's melody. It wasn't long before we had what I thought was a really classy song, and it sounded like it could be a hit record.

Skip was just the right guy to add the touch it needed. I always thought it could have been a pop hit for one of the boy-band groups popular at the time, in the vein of "I Swear" written by Gary Baker and Frank Myers.

I was with Opryland Music for three years. After that I went back to publishing my own songs through my Bright Sky and Bright Leaf publishing companies.

In the June 11, 1989, edition of the Jackson *Clarion-Ledger*, 25 years after my last football season at Ole Miss, sportswriter Butch John wrote a story headlined "A Rebel Seeks Harmony." It hearkened back to the disappointing '64 season.

In the story Coach John Vaught spoke about that season:

"Weatherly had an 'outstanding' senior year, in spite of the fact that he had played the entire season with an injured toe on his right foot, known today as turf toe."

In the interview with Butch John, I unloaded some of my feelings of despair about the '64 season. It still nagged at me. Our final record, with so many close losses, just wasn't up to the standard set by Ole Miss teams of that era. I've carried that burden my entire life. After all, I was the quarterback.

We kept our bowl streak going, but we finished 5-5-1, and Ole Miss wasn't used to that.

At one of our football reunions, Bob Bailey, another Rebel quarterback on that team, came up to me, got in my face, and told me that season wasn't my fault. He said, "We all lost the games that we lost and we all won the games that we won. It was a team effort both ways."

I appreciated Bob saying that. I have to admit I probably needed to hear it.

In the early 1990s I was diagnosed as being clinically depressed. For a long time I hadn't quite felt like myself. I was doing and saying some things that were out of character for me and I knew it. I was wondering why.

It was something I had dealt with off and on for years. Now that I wasn't playing sports anymore, it had reared its ugly head again. I had some tests run and the doctor concluded that it was depression. He prescribed medication and eventually got it under control.

I was enjoying being back in the South again, closer to my family and friends. Life was getting better.

But I still missed Cynthia.

I never will forget the gut-wrenching pain I felt when I picked up the phone one day and heard my brother Shan say, "Jimmy. Mom died."

It was the morning of July 16, 1991. She was only 68. I thought she would go on forever.

Edith Roberson Weatherly had lived in Pontotoc all her life. She had practically been in the same neighborhood the entire time, and for all her adult life had lived in the same house on Warren Street that she and my dad built early in their marriage. That's where she died.

Ten years earlier she had been hospitalized with a clogged carotid artery that was about to cause a stroke. The doctors believe that during surgery she did have a stroke. For a few days we lived with the possibility she wouldn't pull through. But she was tough. She had always been a fighter, especially for her children and family, and she made it through to not only survive but to thrive.

She was able to continue to live alone those last 10 years and made a full recovery. My sister Sherrie and her husband Ronnie built a home right up the street from her and they kept an eye on her.

Mom seemed to enjoy life even more those last 10 years. The years of depression and anxiety attacks, like the ones she'd experienced on her way to watch me play football at Ole Miss, seemed to be slacking off. She visited me in Nashville a few times. She loved her time with family, especially her grandchildren.

I was devastated. I couldn't imagine life without her. Every now and then I would drive down to Pontotoc to see her. I'm so thankful we were in close touch for the last years of her life. I called her all the time. I still miss picking up the phone and hearing her voice. My mom was my rock. I loved her very much. Still do. She never remarried. Her devotion to her children always came first.

When someone you love dies suddenly, you look for answers. I needed reassurance. In my grief, the night after Mom's funeral, I turned to God and asked him to give me a sign that she was okay.

The next morning when I walked out the front door of Mom's house, in the middle of the sidewalk not eight feet away, was the most beautiful redbird looking straight at me.

I stopped and watched it. It remained there without moving for what felt like almost a full minute, looking straight at me. Then it flew away. I felt an overwhelming sense of calm. I felt my prayer had been answered. Silly? Not if you believe.

Now, every time I see a redbird, I think of my Mom. And I know she's at peace.

Me with my biggest fan, my rock, my mom

WHERE SHADOWS NEVER FALL

Once I stood alone in darkness in the valley of the shadows
In a world so cold and heartless filled with anger, greed and sorrow
I knew my life was in a stormy rage

Then I fell down on my knees and prayed
And I could feel his light surround me, and the darkness it was shattered
Then he wrapped his love around me and healed a heart, torn and tattered

He cast away the shadows of the night
And I was saved once and for all
Now I'm standing in his light where shadows never fall

The way is clear now and his truth shines bright
For I've been saved once and for all
Now I'm standing in his light where shadows never fall

My longtime great friend and the biggest Ole Miss fan I know, Carl Jackson, and I wrote a song together called "Where Shadows Never Fall." In 1992, we received a Dove award for "Southern Gospel Song of the Year" from the Gospel Music Association. It was recorded by Glen Campbell who sang it with grace and heart.

Glen recorded three of my songs in his long and storied career – "A Lady Like You," "On A Good Night," both co-written with Keith Stegall, and "Where Shadows Never Fall."

Carl, one of my favorite co-writers, and I have written several songs together over the years. I always enjoyed writing with him because he always had such great ideas both musically and lyrically. And he's one of the best musicians in Nashville, if not the best. He made a fantastic record of a song we wrote called "Dixie Train." It was a barnburner and peeked at No. 45 on the *Billboard* Country charts in 1985.

Ken Weeden, Jeff Roberson, me, Carl Jackson, and Uncle Billy Roberson back stage at the Ryman in Nashville

37 —⚮

Love and Marriage

After the final beak-up with my high school girlfriend when I was a junior in college, I found it hard to move on. On the outside I seemed like a normal college athlete. Inside I had a shy and painfully insecure nature. I found it extremely difficult to ask a girl out on a date. I had a crippling fear of being rejected. I would agonize, sometimes for weeks before I would get up the nerve to call someone and ask her out. Through playing music, it became somewhat easier because sometimes girls would come up and talk to me. If I felt accepted, I was more at ease. I finally grew out of some of the shyness, but that insecure nature still lives inside of me.

Through high school, college, and adulthood, I dated several nice ladies, but nothing ever led to serious talk of marriage. There was always something that didn't feel right. And it may have been me. I was scared to death of divorce. I had once heard, "A bachelor is someone who never made the same mistake once." That little joke was always in the back of my mind. I wanted to be married only once, to someone I loved and to someone who loved me, to someone who shared the same values. Divorce was a fast-growing epidemic in America and I had witnessed people going through it. It sure didn't look like a lot of fun.

For a long time I didn't know if I could even afford to be married. I had made some money but I wasn't sure how long the royalties would last. I felt marriage wouldn't allow me to pursue my career the way I wanted. I didn't want to have to choose one over the other. As I neared 50, I resigned myself to the fact that it might never happen.

In the early 1990s Cynthia was ready to come back to the South. She was familiar with Nashville because she had worked at Opryland theme park as a dancer before moving to L.A. I drove to L.A. to get her. We had a lot of time to talk about things on the way back, and we started dating again after three years apart. I was still in love with her. I think Cynthia was ready to have kids and I felt more secure financially, so I pushed my fears aside and we got married. It was the best decision I ever made.

On September 20, 1993, at age 50, I married someone who felt like home to me. Our daughter, Brighton, was born in June, 1995, and our son, Zack, was born in August, 1997.

There was a time when I'd resigned myself to the fact that I might never have children. But God had other plans. So I'm constantly thanking Him for not letting me miss out on this wonderful adventure. The children have been a blessing to both of us and because of them this has been the best part of my life

Another miracle.

Gordian Knot bass guitarist Leland Russell recognized what God had done.

"God's taken care of Jimmy Weatherly," he said. "Jimmy did what he was supposed to do and God blessed him with that family. That family is beautiful and amazing, and Cynthia is a miracle."

I kept right on writing songs. In the early 1990s after I had departed Opryland Music Group, I had the opportunity to write with a super talented guitar player and songwriter named Bob Welch. Bob had a huge hit record as an artist called "Sentimental Lady" in 1977. He had also been a member of the super-group Fleetwood Mac in the early '70s.

When we got together, I pitched him an idea I'd gotten from the 1989 movie *Miss Firecracker* starring Holly Hunter and written by Mississippian Beth Henley. Toward the end of the movie, Holly Hunter's character starts walking away from the man she had been seeing. When he asked where she was going, she stopped, turned and said, "to find some grace."

To me it was a sentimental moment in a sentimental comedic movie about people in the South. "To find some grace" touched me and I felt like it could be a song. Bob and I talked about it and decided to write it as an ode to old rock and rollers.

Bob came up with a great line in the bridge that summed up what the song was about.

"I've paid a high price for small change."

I thought it was the best line in the whole song. "Find a Little Grace" was recorded by Bruce Channel of "Hey Baby" fame and also by superstar legend Kenny Rogers.

Find A Little Grace

I've put too many miles on the soles of my shoes
Running from place to place
Now it's time to stop and put down some roots
And find a little grace

I've danced with the devil beneath a pale moon
Confronted him face to face
Now I'm gonna dance to a different tune
And find a little grace

I've been too long at a fool's game

And it's about taken its toll
I've paid a high price for small change
But it's not worth the price of my soul

I must admit, it's taken some time
To tame my restless ways
Now I'm gonna leave those struggles behind
And find a little grace

I'm gonna walk where the light always shines
And find a little grace

38 ——꒚

The Tennessee Plowboy

The kids were growing up and Cynthia and I were enjoying a new house we had built in Brentwood. It had a studio in it where I could work. We stayed there a few years and then built another house a little further south near Franklin where we live today. It's off the beaten path on ten acres of land where Brighton can work with her horses.

One day in 2005, Charlie Monk called and said, "Let's go have lunch with Eddy Arnold."

I had always been a huge fan of Eddy Arnold and had met him at a country music event a few years before. So I jumped at the chance.

We went to a small Thai restaurant in Brentwood near Eddy's office. Known as the Tennessee Plowboy, Eddy had grown up poor in Henderson, Tennessee, and had never forgotten his roots. He told me the best Christmas he ever had when he was growing up was when he got an apple. That tells you something about how poor he was.

He became a true music legend yet had no ego at all. He was the nicest guy in the world. Real class.

I was honored when he recorded two of my songs – "A Lady Like You," which had been a No. 1 hit for Glen Campbell, and "How's the Weather Back in Tennessee," which I had co-written with a talented L.A. writer, my friend John Durill.

After that first lunch, from time to time I would call Eddy up to ask if I could come by and play some songs for him. He was always looking for good songs. He was in his 80s then. We'd talk a bit as we played songs and I began to look forward to those visits. He was as genuine as they come and often had a funny story to tell.

Like this one:

"One day I was mowing my front yard on my riding lawn mower down close to the street where cars were passing by. A woman driving by in her car stopped, got out, and got my attention. I turned the mower off and asked 'What can I do for you?' She said, 'How much do you charge to mow yards?' Eddy, with his dry wit and Southern drawl, said he thought for a few seconds and finally said, 'Well … the lady who lives here lets me sleep with her.'"

He laughed when he told it and said the lady just got in her car and drove on off.

I went to lunch at Sylvan Park Restaurant in the Berry Hill section of Nashville one day, and Eddy was there with some friends. He motioned for me to come over. He said, "You got any songs for me? I'm doing a new album."

I said, "I'm sure I do. I'll call you and bring something over."

I took him a song that he loved – "If I Had Lived My life Without You." The first verse was written for Cynthia. The second verse was written for Cynthia, Brighton and Zack. Eddy recorded it on an album called "After All These Years." It was the last album the legendary singer and entertainer ever recorded.

IF I HAD LIVED MY LIFE WITHOUT YOU

Every now and then I think to myself
What if you had fallen in love with someone else
If I had never known the sweet taste of your kiss
Or held you in these arms of mine, I think what I'd have missed

If I had lived my life without you there would still be stars above
But they wouldn't shine as bright if I had never known your love
And I am sure I never would have loved the way I do
If I had lived my life without you

Everything you do, everything you are
Makes ordinary moments memories in my heart
Flowers in the spring, autumns golden leaves
Wouldn't be as beautiful if you weren't here with me

If I had lived my life without you there would still be stars above
But they wouldn't shine as bright if I had never known your love
And I am sure I never would have loved the way I do
If I had lived my life without you

Eddy Arnold died on May 8, 2008, at age 89. Billboard Magazine had him ranked as the No. 1 Country artist of all time.

In 2008 I got a call from a Canadian named Douglas Hutton, who was producing an album project in Nashville called "This is My America." He asked if I would write a song about Elvis. I had started one some years earlier but never finished it.

I dug out the old lyric and finished the song. It was called "Hot Night in Memphis" about Elvis Presley's first recording session at Sun Studios in 1954 with his sidemen, Scotty Moore on guitar and Bill Black on bass. Elvis played rhythm guitar. I played the song for Douglas and he loved it.

We recorded it with Billy Burnette singing and it's on the "This is My America" CD. Bekka Bramlett, the daughter of rock icons Delaney and Bonnie Bramlett, sang the harmonies.

HOT NIGHT IN MEMPHIS
(ELVIS AND THE BLUE MOON BOYS)

On a hot night in Memphis, July '54
A sleeping world could not have dreamed
What fate held in store
Down on Union Avenue things were about to change
The music that we listened to would never be the same
Three ole boys with two guitars and a thumping standup bass
Went in to make a record down at ole Sam Phillips' place
At Sun recording studio when they began to play
A haunting voice with strange echo
Was captured on the tape

They mixed a little country with a little blues and soul
Threw some southern gospel in and called it rock and roll
They played with so much passion it would give you chills
Elvis and the Blue Moon Boys
Scotty and Bill

Well 'That's all right now Mama' Elvis wailed as he cut loose
He sang with raw emotion and the innocence of youth
When the song was over no one could say a word
They knew they'd stumbled on a sound no one ever heard
Sam, he called ol' Dewey up down at HBQ
Dewey had a night time show called Red, Hot and Blue
Sam said I'm coming over with a song you gotta hear
But you better be prepared boy
'Cause you won't believe your ears

Ol' Dewey played the record it lit up the phones
So he played it once again and then he played it all night long
The kids were going crazy Elvis was in shock
Overnight he was a star and headed for the top

Well like the man once said boy the rest is history
That's how it started long ago way down in Tennessee
That driving rocking rhythm changed the world forevermore
On a hot night in Memphis, July '54

I wrote another song for the "This is My America" project with another great writer, my good friend Wood Newton. It's one I'm really proud of.

We came up with a beautiful patriotic song called "Wave On, Old Glory, Wave On." Country music star Billy Dean sang it and did an amazing job. It was recorded at Ocean Way Studios with the Nashville Symphony Orchestra and the Fisk University Jubilee Singers.

Michael Peterson also has a beautiful version of the song. Both can be found on YouTube. It's also available on iTunes and is being sung in churches all across the United States. The song hasn't found its way into America's consciousness yet, but I have hopes that someday it will.

WAVE ON, OLD GLORY, WAVE ON

It was Betsy Ross who made you Ole Captain Driver saved you
Some brave Marines raised you on an Iwo Jima hill
You've been ripped and torn in battle as guns and sabers rattle
But you survived to fly again and you always will

Wave on, Old Glory, Wave on
Keep us united, free and strong
In the face of all adversity, attacks upon our liberty
Remind us where our loyalty belongs
Wave on, Old Glory, Wave on

You rode with Teddy Roosevelt
You were at Pearl Harbor when bombs fell
You followed our troops into hell on the beach at Normandy
You came crashing down with the towers
One of our nation's darkest hours
But you rose from the smoke and ash for all the world to see

Wave on, Old Glory, Wave on
Keep us united, free and strong
In the face of all adversity attacks upon our liberty
Remind us where our loyalty belongs
Wave on, Old Glory, Wave on

All throughout the course of history
You've inspired our hopes and dreams of peace

39 ──❧

Entering The Digital World

Around 2000 I went to the Guitar Center in Nashville to buy a new piano keyboard. The guy that waited on me sat down to demonstrate and turned out to be an incredible keyboard player. I asked him if he did demos and he told me he did. His name is Jonathon Willis and he also happens to be a computer genius. He knew all about digital recordings and how to program them. I asked him if he would help me do an album of my songs on computer. Not only did we do the album together, he taught me how to program the instruments so I could record by myself. The album we did at his house was "Songs I've Written." I released it on my own label, Brizac Records, in 2003.

Jonathon set up a digital recording studio for me in my house, and I began to make my CDs there. I've recorded and released four CDs since learning about computer music. They are "Autumn's Light," "this & that," and "You Hold My World in Place" as well as a Christmas CD called "Christmas Like Christmas Used To Be."

Hopefully there'll be more to come. I really enjoy recording these CDs because it keeps my creative juices flowing and keeps me busy. I keep writing because I'm grateful that I've been blessed with the ability to do it.

One day, Jonathon asked me if I would listen to a melody he had written. He played me one of the most strikingly beautiful melodies I've ever heard. I asked him, "Are you sure you wrote that?" It had an otherworldly, timeless quality to it. It grabbed me by the heart and has held on since the first time I heard it.

He told me he had played it for other writers but no one had been able to come up with a lyric for it. I asked him if I could try. The next day I gave him a lyric called "My Heart Will Always Remember" that he thought fit perfectly. We recorded it with a great singer we were producing named Bryan Lane. It is on his album called "My Eternal Love." I also recorded the song on my new album called "Songwriter."

My Heart Will Always Remember

These are the days that my heart always will remember
Looking back at love it's you I'll see
I won't forget one glorious moment of the splendor
Part of you is now a part of me

Walking together hand in hand along life's roads
The joys and sorrows I will treasure as if they were gold
As long as there's a star that shines somewhere above me
My heart will always remember you

These are the days that my heart always will remember
Through the years they never will grow old
The bloom of May will light the warm fires of December
Mem'ries that my heart will always hold

I'll see the beauty in your eyes as clearly then
And know that we shared something that will never ever end
This love of mine will go on longer than forever
My heart will always remember you
My heart will always remember – you

In the springtime, you in the fall
There's not a season that I won't recall
Laughing in the snow as it covers fields in white
Memories so vivid as when colors catch the light

My heart will always remember – you
In the sunlight, you in the rain
Dancing on green grass to summer's refrain
Sheer exhilaration in the smile on your face
Passions exploding, your spirit ablaze

40 —⁂

Music Today

Stylistically, songs are more different today than they've ever been. The key word tossed around is "fresh." All the record companies want something "fresh." Today's songs seem to have been born out of a more hard-hitting reality. There doesn't seem to be as much romance.

Sometime around 2010, I went to an A&R person's office at a major record label down on Music Row. I played a song called "Turn Out the Stars (When You Leave)," It had been an Urban A/C hit for the R&B group The Manhattans peaking at No. 23 on the Radio and Records chart. It's another song I wrote with John Durill. The A&R person went crazy. "This is a great song! A really unbelievably great song! Wow!" The rant went on and on. And then he lowered his voice and added, "But we're not looking for great songs." I left scratching my head.

I've never followed trends in music, not even when I was having hits. I've always considered myself a love song writer or a romantic writer about relationships and emotions and the feelings they evoke. I write more in what is called the classic vein.

I came along when those songs were popular. It was during the singer-songwriter period in the '70s, and I feel grateful to have been a small part of it. Now and then I've ventured outside that box, but mostly I write love songs. Sadly, they don't seem to be in vogue in today's music world.

Attitudes toward relationships have changed, and that has changed our culture and our music. I still write the way I've always written – from the heart. It's far more satisfying.

A great quote by Jay-Z on the *Rolling Stone* magazine website expresses it even better:

> *"A great song doesn't attempt to be anything – it just is. When you hear a great song you can think of where you were when you first heard it, the sounds, the smells. It takes the emotions of a moment and holds it for years to come. It transcends time."*

I would rather have other artists record my songs, but since they are few and far between now, I record them myself in my home studio and put the CDs out on my own Brizac Records label, named for my two children, Brighton and Zack. My songs are on my website, jimweatherly.com, on Amazon and CD Baby and iTunes. Many are on YouTube. Some of the older ones can be found on eBay. I do this because I want them to be heard by as many people as possible. And besides, it's still fun for me.

41

Faith

I'm not a perfect person. Not by any stretch of the imagination. I've done things in my life I wish I hadn't done or at least had done differently. At the time I was having success with Larry, I was so caught up in the excitement that I was only somewhat aware of the role God was playing in my life, although I had called on Him for guidance and direction and forgiveness many, many times.

It wasn't until later in my life that I began to see the picture more clearly. As I write this book, I can see how the hand of God was always at work helping me find my path, even at those times when I doubted myself. I can see how God guided me when I felt lost and unsure of my footing. When I felt like a failure. He kept me sane when I thought my world was caving in. He kept leading me to places where I should be. He kept providing those miracles I've been talking about. He must have wanted me to be a songwriter because He led me to the one person who could make that happen.

I could have never written songs if it hadn't been His plan. I certainly could have never raised children without His help.

No matter what was happening on my journey, I always stayed close to God through prayer. I silently prayed before every football game I ever played. Not to win, but for safety and guidance. I've prayed before every game my son, Zack, has played and for the same reasons. I pray for my daughter, Brighton, that God will direct her paths and watch over her. And I pray for Cynthia. It makes me feel better knowing that God is in control.

I have always felt God's presence, even when I wasn't consciously aware of it. I know He gave me the talent that I have and He gave me the strength and courage to continue, even when I was close to giving up. He kept me out of harm's way. His love is amazing.

Brighton, Zack, and me

42 —⁊⁊

Honors

As the years have passed, my songs have received some significant recognition that I could never have dreamed of back in those youthful days in Pontotoc when I was trying to write cowboy songs or through the college years at Ole Miss and into the L.A. years with the band, or even after I began my solo career.

In 1999 "Midnight Train to Georgia" was inducted into the Grammy Hall of Fame.

On March 7, 2001, the National Endowment for the Arts and the Record Industry Association of America released the list of the 365 Songs of the Century chosen by voters across America. "Over the Rainbow" sung by Judy Garland and "White Christmas" sung by Bing Crosby were No. 1 and No. 2.

"Midnight Train to Georgia" by Gladys Knight and the Pips came in at No. 29, sandwiched between the Beatles' "I Want to Hold Your Hand" at No. 28 and "Imagine" by John Lennon at No. 30.

On April 7, 2011, *Rolling Stone* magazine announced its list of the "500 Greatest Songs of All Time."

"Midnight Train to Georgia" was No. 432.

Back in 2001 Gladys Knight and the Pips were inducted into the Vocal Group Hall of Fame. Prior to that, in 1996, they had been inducted into the Rock and Roll Hall of Fame.

The presenter for the latter induction was legendary singer Mariah Carey, who introduced them with these words:

"When I was a little girl and a budding insomniac, I used to sneak out of my room, steal a portable radio from the kitchen, hide under the covers and sing along with 'Midnight Train to Georgia,' 'Neither One of Us,' and 'The Best Thing That Ever Happened to Me.' The voice of Gladys Knight pulled me through a lot of lonely times, and I just wanted to thank her for that tonight. Unlike some who came after her, she's not about image or shock value. Gladys is a singer's singer. She's as real as it gets. All she has to do is stand there and sing, and she'll blow you away. She doesn't have to follow trends or set them. It's all about that voice, her incredible gift from God."

Hearing such effusive praise for someone singing songs I wrote had me shaking my head in wonder.

Some of my songs several decades old are still finding their way onto CDs, even today, by some of the world's greatest artists as well as unknown new artists.

In 2010 Neil Diamond recorded a beautiful ballad version of "Midnight Train to Georgia." It's one of my favorite versions. Neil did an awesome job, and I'm honored that such a legendary artist and songwriter chose to record one of my songs. Neil wrote me a personal note saying it was one of his favorite songs on the album.

In 2013 Garth Brooks recorded "Midnight Train to Georgia" on his "Blame it on My Roots" six CD set album.

In 2014 Aretha Franklin put "Midnight Train to Georgia" on her Diva Classics CD.

I went back to the Ole Miss campus in the fall of 2012 for a football game and to see my old teammates in the Grove again when the 1962 undefeated national championship football team held its 50th reunion. At long last we received national championship rings. It had been a long time coming.

Larry Johnson, a former teammate helping coordinate the event, asked if I would sing at the dinner. I told him I'd be honored.

Leland Russell remembers.

"I was talking to Jimmy, and it was a few days before this fiftieth anniversary reunion event for the 1962 team, and he was like, 'Leland, my teammates asked me to sing at the reunion dinner.' The way he said it to me on the phone, I just got the feeling it was really, really important to him."

I have to admit I was nervous about singing before my old teammates, even though they had asked me to do it often 50 years earlier. I just wasn't sure how I'd be received. But at least I felt like I had something to offer in some of the songs I'd written.

I sang "Midnight Train to Georgia," "Mississippi Song," and "Best Thing That Ever Happened to Me."

When I finished they gave me a standing ovation. It was one of the proudest moments of my life. They'll never know what that meant to me.

Along the way there have been other moments I cherish but never expected.

In 1979 I was named to the Mississippi Song Festival Hall of Fame in Jackson.

In 2006 I was honored with induction into the Nashville Songwriters Hall of Fame and also that year I was inducted into the Mississippi Musicians Hall of Fame. In 2011 I was honored by my alma mater, the University of Mississippi, with induction into the Ole Miss Alumni Hall Of Fame.

In 2013 I was honored to be at the Library of Congress in Washington, D.C., as a part of ASCAP's annual event "We Write the Songs." I performed with other songwriters of note, including Mary Chapin Carpenter, Alan Bergman, Paul Williams, Roger Cook, Roger Greenaway, Elvin Bishop, and more before an audience of members of Congress and their spouses. I sang "Neither One of Us" and "Midnight Train to Georgia." My hometown friend, U.S. Senator Roger Wicker, introduced me.

In 2014, I accepted the Governor's Award for Achievement in Music in a ceremony in Jackson. I told my fellow Mississippians what Mississippi and its people mean to me.

"I lived in California for 25 years and I've lived in Tennessee longer than that. But I've never considered myself anything other than a Mississippian."

Being inducted into the Ole Miss Alumni Hall of Fame in 2011

Our children are young adults now trying to find their way in a much different and more chaotic and divided world than I knew growing up. I cherish the years that Cynthia and I spent raising them. My prayer is for life to be as good to them as it has been to me. I want them to feel as safe as I did growing up in the little town of Pontotoc. I think back to those Sunday afternoons when I was a little boy at my grandmother's house and recall how easy going and calm life was. I remember fun and laughter and how at peace I felt. Everybody got along. It was the most content I've ever been. It was a much gentler time. I wrote a song with that title around 1972 while I was living in Califorrnia.

Cynthia, the kids, and me with the Sugar Bowl trophy

To a Gentler Time

Go stand before some mirror
And ask yourself just who are you
And just where you are going
And what you're gonna do
If you dwell there too long
Maybe that's a sign
That you just like me belong to a gentler time

If protesting is not your way
But still you feel concerned
If you wish you could take
The best of everything you've learned
And share it with the world
In peaceful frame of mind
Maybe you just like me belong to a gentler time

When there was less to give
People seemed to give much more
They were too concerned with how to live
To be concerned with what they were living for

If you stand before that mirror
And right before your eyes
If You don't find the answers
To your whos and wheres and whys
If you can't see the reason
And if you can't hear the rhyme
Maybe you just like me belong to a gentler time

43 —

New York 2014

In early 2014, I got a phone call that I never expected. I was being notified that I was to be inducted into the Songwriters Hall of Fame in New York City in June. It's such a prestigious group of songwriters. I was completely overwhelmed. I always felt it was far beyond my reach.

In my mind Jimmy Webb, Paul Simon, Willie Nelson, Paul Williams, Cole Porter, Irving Berlin, Stephen Foster, and so many, many others who were already enshrined among the – at the time – less than 400 members of the Songwriters Hall of Fame are all legends. I just didn't see myself in that category. I almost suffered a panic attack. My mind couldn't handle such a prestigious honor. I was deeply moved and really stressed out at the same time. The football player and the songwriter were colliding.

This was a worldwide hall of fame for people who have achieved legendary status for their works in music, and now I was being similarly recognized by a group of my peers.

I remembered all too well the many rejections and years of struggles when I thought maybe I should coach football for a living. And now to end up among legendary songwriters like Hank Williams and George Gershwin was just about too much for me to comprehend. I had gone to the Grammys when I was nominated for "Midnight Train" and to the American Music Awards when Gladys was nominated for the same song, but I never felt like I was in the same league with the artists and songwriters that had influenced me all of my career. And now they were all sitting around me.

I felt like they all knew something that I didn't.

On June 12, 2014, I was inducted into the Songwriters Hall of Fame at the Marriott Marquis Times Square in New York City. The 2014 class also included legendary songwriters and performers Donovan, Graham Gouldman, Mark James, and Ray Davies.

Marty Gamblin, me, and Jeff Roberson in New York's Central Park during the 2014 Songwriters Hall of Fame weekend

Sharing a laugh with Mississippi country music legend Marty Stuart in Central Park, 2014

Ole Miss Chancellor Dan Jones and his wife, Lydia, were there, along with other university officials and student leaders, as well as several members of my family and friends from Tennessee, Mississippi, and Los Angeles.

My brother Shan remembers that trip.

"Going to New York to see Jimmy inducted into the Songwriters Hall of Fame is probably the highlight of it all. That's the pinnacle for a songwriter, and when you look at the list of people who are in there, people like Francis Scott Key, Irving Berlin, Bob Dylan, Paul McCartney, John Lennon, it's quite a list of accomplished songwriters. And my brother is on that list now. I have to say that's pretty overwhelming.

"When we got to New York, the first place we all went as a family was to a restaurant across the street from our hotel," Shan said. "We ordered and the next thing we know, 'Midnight Train to Georgia' is being piped in throughout the place. That song is everywhere you go, and that's pretty wild."

Among those who performed that night were Chubby Checker, Jon Bon Jovi, Martina McBride, Rosanne Cash, Chita Rivera, as well as a host of new performers just beginning to make their mark in the world of music.

Gladys Knight was unable to attend due to a conflict in scheduling so Candice Glover, who burst onto the scene by winning Season 12 of TV's "American Idol" in 2013, filled in and performed "Midnight Train to Georgia" superbly. Then the South Carolina native introduced me as the newest member of the Songwriters Hall of Fame.

Following a few remarks, I sang "Neither One of Us" and received a standing ovation from an audience filled with songwriters whose songs had inspired me all my life. Then I returned to sit with my family near the stage. I was so overwhelmed I couldn't quite gather my senses. Moments like that are rare and life changing, and I tried to soak it all in.

The man I'd met years earlier in California on the night that changed my life, the man who inspired me to try to write great songs, Jimmy Webb, was chairman of the Songwriters Hall of Fame. He was the master of ceremonies that night.

How fitting is that? One of the people who influenced me the most directed the evening. Not everybody gets to see their dreams come true.

44 ——🎝

A Return To The Past

On an overcast afternoon in January 2015, I drove up to a converted metal building at the corner of Westwood and Inverness in the Berry Hill section of Nashville. As I got out, a brisk winter wind raked across my face. Another couple of months would pass before spring would arrive in Music City.

Inside, people scurried about, preparing for the following night's inaugural production of a musical venture called Skyville. Viewers around the world could click on SkyvilleLive.com, and watch a world-class concert featuring some of the best entertainers in the business.

Martina McBride, a four-time country music vocalist of the year, was one of the headliners. So was Estelle, a young British rhythm and blues artist, and my old friend, Gladys Knight, known to her legions of fans as the Empress of Soul.

I walked into the dimly lit studio and was greeted by Wally Wilson, the producer of Skyville. We'd known each other for years and had written songs together. From the back of the room I could see Gladys, Martina, and Estelle on stage and I made my way toward them. That's when the music stopped.

Although we'd stayed in touch, it had been several years since Gladys and I had seen each other.

"Hi Jim," she said as I sat down near the stage.

"Hey Gladys," I responded, as we both smiled.

To a casual observer, it was a meaningless conversation. Not to me. And not to Gladys. We had history.

By 2015 Gladys and I had been involved in music for more than half a century. For most of that time I was writing songs, while Gladys performed all over the world. We had seen major changes in the music industry, marveled at rapid developments in technology, and witnessed social change sweep the South where we'd grown up.

Cynthia, Gladys, and me

Brighton, Gladys, and Zack

On stage, Gladys ran through "You're the Best Thing That Ever Happened To Me" with the band. Gladys' soulful voice was as beautiful and robust as ever, and her onstage presence just as commanding.

After the rehearsal Gladys and I spent time reminiscing. Our paths would not have been nearly the same without each other, and these moments mean something, however infrequent they are.

"I still get chills when I hear you sing my songs," I said to Gladys. "To me, you always sing them like it's the first time."

"You know I still love your songs, and they always move my spirit," she said.

The following night, SkyvilleLive.com debuted. The small studio was packed with fans and music executives. I sat near the stage, set up like a nightclub with tables and chairs throughout, lights dimmed, creating an intimate, interactive feel between the performers and the audience. Gladys introduced me and graciously told the worldwide audience that my songs had made much of this night possible.

After the show my wife Cynthia, daughter Brighton, son Zack and I made our way backstage.

"Is that my girl?" Gladys asked, smiling at Brighton as she walked into the room.

"This is the one," I said. "She's all grown up."

Years earlier I had written a Christmas song called "Happy Birthday, Jesus" that Brighton recorded when she was eight. I put her version on my album, "Christmas Like Christmas Used to Be." Gladys heard it and recorded it on her album, "Where My Heart Belongs."

After we shared stories about our families, talked about music and took a few pictures, it was time to leave.

I was certainly blessed when Gladys' path crossed mine four decades earlier.

I still enjoy writing songs when the mood strikes. Artists continue to record them, for which I'm grateful. I enjoy life with my family on our small horse farm south of Nashville.

I'm close enough to home that I can still get back to Mississippi and Ole Miss to see family and friends a few times a year, and they can come to visit us.

Recently, I found a quote from the 1980s in a *Clarion-Ledger* story. It made me laugh when I read it again. I said it in jest back then, kind of tongue in cheek, but there is truth in it.

"If I never do another thing in my life, I'll be remembered for writing 'Midnight Train to Georgia' and for missing that handoff against Mississippi State. Tell me how many people are lucky enough to say they have two things to be remembered by?"

Acknowledgements

Thank you to Gladys Knight, Bubba Knight, Larry Gordon, Billy Roberson, Richard Roberson, Ray Bedingfield, Don Zimmerman, Archie Manning, Pat Kincade, Leland Russell, Marty Gamblin, Charlie Monk, Dorothy Moore, Teri Brown, Freddie Roberts, Glynn Griffing, Mike Dennis, Louis Guy, Kenny Dill, Shan Weatherly, Sherrie Winter, Elise Black, Don Estes, David Jennings, David Wells, Marty Stuart, Kent Earls, Troy Tomlinson, Frank LiVolsi, Jane Kopf, and Jeff Schrodel.

A special thank you to Dr. Will Norton and the School of Journalism and New Media at Ole Miss, to Langston Rogers and the Ole Miss Athletics Department, and to Larry Wells of Yoknapatawpha Press.

And to Hannah Vines and Bill Rose without whom this book would not exist.

And to my co-writer, Jeff Roberson — I couldn't have done it without you.

— Jim Weatherly

Thanks to my Dad, Jimmy's Uncle Billy, for sharing his knowledge of Pontotoc, Ole Miss, our family, and life. Thanks to Cynthia, Brighton, and Zack, who welcomed me into their home often. It was on one of those visits I had my first contact with Gladys Knight, a phone conversation on a Friday afternoon. The following Monday I saw her on TV. One host on CBS This Morning asked her about the person who wrote her hits. "He's writing a book," she said. I then called Jimmy. "It's too late to turn back now. Gladys just told the world we've got a book on the way."

Thanks to my family - especially Jimmy's sisters Sherrie and Elise, their husbands Ronnie and Scott, Jimmy's brother Shan and his wife Kevin Ann. And to our cousins Tommy, Randy, and Terry - the Wood brothers.

Thanks to so many of Jimmy's high school and college teammates and bandmates, all eager and willing to visit with us. Thanks to his high school football coach, Jim Butler, who died just after we started the book, his wife Betty and son Lance; and to Coach Carl Lowery. A tip of the cap to my supportive friends, including Jules and Jim Foster, Michael Cravens, Ty Allushuski, Adam Ganucheau, Wesley Bell, Mitch Caver, Wesley Hill, Cindy Davis Howle, David Waddell, Jolee Hussey, Pam Manning Shelton, Josh Bogen, Gregg Ellis, Ben Garrett, Chase Parham, Andy Strickland, Don Sheffield, Jim Roberts, David Greenhaw, Charlie McAlexander, Bill McKeithen, Pat Carpenter, Tim Walsh, Carol Easley, Sandra Hamilton, John

Brown, Jack Gadd, Tommy Parker, Hunter Grissom, and Christi Webb. There was also a remarkable visit with Mr. Robin Mathis, legendary radio pioneer at WCPC in Houston, Mississippi.

Thanks to Langston Rogers, Michael Thompson, and Jimmy's teammate David Wells at Ole Miss athletics; to Don Whitten and Chuck Rounsaville, who always gave me freedom to write stories as I saw fit when I worked for them; to Dr. Will Norton, Dean of the School of Journalism and New Media at Ole Miss, who taught me the craft of writing while in college; Curtis Wilkie who helped guide us (and who is part of our family tree from two branches), Bill Rose who edited, and Carroll Moore who put together our proposal.

Thanks to public relations specialist Julie Schoerke, who was always so willing to help, and to publisher Neil White who advised us throughout. This project had no greater friend than Neil.

To Hannah Vines, thank you for your expertise in layout and design, and for your patience throughout the process. To the Journalism School faculty and students at Ole Miss who helped with marketing and publicity, thank you.

Thanks to Gladys Knight, Archie Manning, Marty Stuart, and Dorothy Moore for their important contributions to this book.

And to Larry Wells of Yoknapatawpha Press in Oxford, Mississippi, for publishing us. Thanks for coming on board with us when we needed you most.

Our timing on the book turned out to be right. Two months after we began, we made a trip to D.C. for "We Write the Songs" at the Library of Congress. Jimmy was one of the invited featured songwriters in a talented and accomplished group. There were my own trips to the Motown Museum in Detroit and the Grammy Museum in Cleveland – Mississippi, not Ohio; our journey to New York for his Songwriters Hall of Fame induction, and multiple trips to Nashville, one of them to visit Gladys Knight during the production of Skyville Live.

We tossed around a few titles, but "Midnight Train" seemed the most appropriate. Although shortened from its original song title, it does resonate with those who love American music from the 20th century. In 2011, Rolling Stone proclaimed "Midnight Train to Georgia" one of the 500 greatest songs of all-time.

So, at last, here is Jimmy's story he wanted to tell, just as he wanted to tell it.

—Jeff Roberson

Partial Discography

A Christmas Love Song
The Oak Ridge Boys

A Lady Like You
Eddy Arnold
Glen Campbell
Kamahl

A Married Man's Dream
Lynn Anderson

A Woman's Place
Eddy Raven

All Tangled Up In Love
Gus Hardin & Earl
Thomas Conley

All That Keeps Me Going
Ray Price
Trini Lopez

*Another Dawn Breaking
Over Georgia*
David Frizzell & Shelly
West

*Are We Making Love (Or
Just Making Time)*
Vicki Rae Von

As One As Two Can Get
Jeff Carson

Baby's Blue Again
Bill Anderson

Bad For My Own Good
Reba McIntire
Holly Cieri

Because It's Love
Cooper Getschal

Being Alone
Dorothy Moore

*Best Thing That Ever
Happened To Me*
101 Strings
Acker Bilk
Andy Williams
Anna Wilson (w Ray
Price & Rascal Flatts)
Annie Sandler
Arman Rodriguez
Audrey Scott
Band Of Pleasure
B. J. Thomas
Betty Reid
Betty Winn
Big Miller & Tommy
Banks Orchestra
Bill McIntosh
Billy Daniels
Billy Galvin
Blane Gauss
Bobby Felder
Botticelli Orchestra
Brenda Reid
Cascade Players
Charlie Chase
Chresten Tomlin
Claire Marlo
Corey Sue Ward
Country Road
Danny Thomas
Dean Martin
Deane Waretini
Debbie Tucker
Desmond Pringle
Detroit Soul Sensation
Dionne Warwick
Doris Troy
Ed Tinoso
Eliza
Everett Rucker
Floyd Burton
Francis Yip
Frankie Laine-(DVD)
George Kerr
Gladys Knight & The Pips
Graham BLVD

Greg Hunter & Liz
McComb
Gweneth Douglas
Harris Erbat
Higher Powered
Harmonies
Hissong
Irene Reid
Jackie DePiro
James Cleveland
James Last Orchestraa
Jane MacDonald
Jewel With Love
Joe Koziol
Joe Longthorne
John Davidson
Johnny Lee
Julius Obregon
June Yamagishi
Kaleo Okalani
Kelly Lang
Kenny G. Garrison
Knightsbridge
Larry Shannon Hargrove
Larry Hudson
Larry Trotter
Lindell Cooley
Lena Martel
Love Pearls Unlimited
Marvia Providence
Mariette Wolf
Marrieta
Marti Caine
Matt Lewis
Minister Gale Martin
Monique Demoulin
Myra Walker Singers
Myrna Hague
Nancy Bryan
Niki Harris
Pam Noan
Paris Studio Orchestra &
Singers
Paul Martin
Peter Anthony
Prentice T. Miner

Rachael Asebido
Rainy Day Orchestra
Rainy Day Singers
Ray Boltz
Ray Price
Richard Clayderman
Rick Tanksley
Roger Williams
Ron Trudeau
Russ Taff
Ruth Brown
Salena Jones
Sax & Ivory
Seaside
Side Salad
Sleazesisters
Steve Lawrence
Stevie Cee
Summer O' Love
Super' 74
Super Som T. A.
Sweet Surrender
The Bluesbusters
The Blue Rubatos
The Caravans
The Clark Sisters
The Comptones
The Cruise Family
The Gino Marinello
Orchestra
The Hit Crew
The Levee Singers
The Moonlight Players
The Persuaders
The Reminders
The Rhythm Pals
The Worship Crew
Tony Jones
Top Of The Poppers
Trummy Young
Vivian Blaine
William T Howard
Xyx Top

*Between Her Goodbye And
My Hello*
Arlene Hardin
Gladys Knight & The Pips
Linda George

*Between His Goodbye And
My Hello*
Ray Price

Bring Back My Sunshine
Bobby Angel
Ray Price
Trini Lopez

*Can't Get Your Lovin' Off
My Mind*
Barbara Blue & Phantom
Blue

Carnival Lights Again
The Gordian Knot

Colorado Snow
Ray Price
Nana Mouskouri

Dixie Train
Carl Jackson
Third Time Out

Do It Right
Keb Mo

Does She Need Me
Pearl River

*Don't Stop Believing In
Rainbows*
Bryan Lane

*Everything Reminds Me
Of You*
Danny Thomas
Ray Price

Faithful Companion
Bryan Lane

Find A Little Grace
Bruce Channel
Karl Hinkle
Kenny Rogers

Fire In An Old Flame's Eyes
Donna Ulisse

Genuine Love
Michael Miller

Going Someplace To Forget
David Ball

Gone To Pieces
Brooks Atwood

Gonna Shine It On Again
Bill Anderson

Good Girls
Beverly Mitchell

Happy Birthday Jesus
Gladys Knight
Brighton Weatherly (age 8)

Hat Trick
Tracy Byrd

*He Knows Just Where To
Touch Me*
Dorothy Moore

He Used Me
Mary Taylor
Peggy Lee

Hot Nights
Canyon

*Hot Night In Memphis
(Elvis & The Blue Moon
Boys)*
Billy Burnette

How Can I Make You Love Me
Linda Davis

How'd We Ever Get This Way
Dorothy Moore
Ray Price

*How's The Weather Back In
Tennessee*
Eddy Arnold

I Can't Be Hurt Anymore
The Gordian Knot

*I'd Love To Change Your
Name*
Kenny Chesney

*I'll Be There To Lend A
Helping Heart*
Joe Aylward

I'll Still Love You
Bobby Angel
Marketta Little Wolf
Ray Price
Wanda Jackson

*If I Could Just Find My
Way Back To You*
Dorothy Moore
Dottie West
Sami Jo

If I Could Only Fly
The Gordian Knot

*If I Didn't Have You In
My World*
Anita Perras
Dawn Sears
Doreen & Cash On
Delivery
Houston Wells
Jodie Birge
John McSweeny
Myra Rolen
Vince Gill

*If I Had Lived My Life
Without You*
Bryan Lane
Eddie Arnold

If I Love You
Bryan Lane

Elaine Page
Mike Redway
Sandra Jory
Sandra Schwarzhaup

If I Never Laugh Again
Jim Nabors

If The Truth Were Known
Melissa Kay

If This Ain't Love
Grey Ghost

*If You Ever Change Your
Mind*
Bluefield
Ray Price

In My Frame of Mind
Johnny Bush

Irreplaceable
Bryan Lane

It Must Be Love This Time
Geoff Mullins
Lynn Anderson
Ray Price

*It Must Have Been The
Rain*
Ray Price

It's Gonna Take A Lot
The Gordian Knot

It's My Life
Jim Nabors

*It's Sad To Be Lonely At
Christmas*
Danny Thomas

It Wasn't Me
Monique Demoulin

Jesus Is My Kind Of People
Danny Thomas

Etta James
Gladys Knight & The
Pips
L.J. Reynolds
Ray Price

*Jesus, You're The Best Thing
That Ever Happened To Me*
Reverend James
Cleveland

*Just Enough To Make Me
Stay*
Bob Luman
Ray Price
Sami Jo

Let's Dance
Steve Kolander

Like A First Time Thing
Danny Thomas
Ray Price

Like Old Times Again
Gary Davis Band
Jimmie Davis
Ray Price

*Living Every Man's
Dream*
Danny Thomas
Ray Price

Louisiana Lady
Jim Nabors

Love Finds Its Own Way
Gladys Knight & The
Pips
Ray Price
Graham Blvd
The Soul Lounge Project

*Love Has Made A Woman
Out Of You*
Bobby Goldsboro
Ray Price
Vince & Dianne Hatfield

Love Never Broke Anyone's Heart
Bob Brolly
Dave Hayward
Geordie Jack and Caldonia
Jason McGilligan
Vince Gill
Fool's Gold

Love Thing
Clifford Curry
Dan Seals
Jenny Morris

Loving You Is Just An Old Habit
Dionne Warwick
Dorothy Moore
Hamilton, Joe Frank & Reynolds
Johnny Lee
Ray Price

Lust In A Lady's Eyes
Lee Majors

Lying Here Lonely
Mississippi Rain

Mama, Your Daddy's Come Home
Magnificent Malouchi

Memphis On A Train
Bernadette Tinney

Mercy Descends
Livingstone

Midnight Train To Georgia
Amy Armstrong
Ardijah
Aretha Franklin
Ashleigh Rogers
Banda Old Days & Strings
Bari Koral
Brian Rose Band

Bruce Burton
Carol Smith
Catacoustic Groove
Chie Ayado
Cissy Houston
Claire Poole
Crystal Bowersox
Connie Eaton
Danny Davis Space Sounds
David Clayton-Thomas
Dartmouth Aires
Dee Hemingway
Deja Vu
Eddie Middleton
Eden Brent
Ella Pennewell & Julian Vaught
Emily Reed
Emma Wood
Ephlats
Ferrante & Teicher
Garth Brooks
Gina Symonds
Gladys Knight & The Pips
Graham BLVD
Haviland Stillwell
Hullabahoos
Human Nature
Indigo Girls
Jahsifik
Jai Bandaros
Jasmine Trias
Jasper
Jeacocke
Jennifer Jason Leigh
Joan Osborne
John McClean
Joy Dan Prince
Keisha Brown
Laura
Lynn Anderson
Manilla Rhythm Society
Mano
Martin Ross
Marty Murphy
Meg Birch
Michael Marc
Mix-Masters

Music Factory
Neil Diamond
Nick Ingman Orchestra
Newcastle University Jazz
-----Orchestra
Owen Grey
Oxford Belles
Paris Bennett
Paul Amirault
PMC Blues
Regina Love
Renee Geyer Band
Relaxing Instrumental Jazz Ensemble
Revolving Satellites
Rotel & The Hot Tomatoes Ruth Jacott
Sandra Bernhard
Sandrine
70's Music Guitar Duo
Sharon D. Clark
Shawn Megorden
Smooth Jazz All Stars
Sound Sense
Soul Explosion
Soul Phenomanon
Steve Edwards Orchestra
Super Tamirindo All Stars
Sweet Soul Music Review
Tammy Lynn
Taylor James
Teddy Brown
The Academy Allstars
The Comptoness
The Countdown Singers
The Dresden Soul Symphony The Hangdogs
The Harvard Opportunes
The Hegg Brothers
The Hit Company
The Starlite Orchestra
The Tunes
The Vineyard Sound
The Whiffenpoofs
Thelma Jones
Three Mo'Tenors
3 To Tango
30 Rock Cast

Wendy Robin
Vermettya Royster
Veronica Adams
Vicki Wynans
Widespread Panic
William Blake
Willie Lindo
Willie Neal Johnson &
The New
Keynotes

Mississippi Song
Bill Nash
Dorothy Moore
Guy Hovis
Ora Reed

My Eternal Love
Bryan Lane

*My First Day Without
Her*
Dennis Yost & The
Classics Four
Ray Price

*My Heart Will Always
Remember*
Bryan Lane
Jonathon Willis

My Love For All Seasons
John Rait

Neither One Of Us
A Taste Of Honey
A Touch Of Gold
Akseann
Arthur Greenslade
Orchestra Asha Puthli
Barretta & Rollex
Barry Crocker
Big Miller & Tommy-
Banks Orchestra
Billy Gordon
Bob Luman
Brenda Doumani
Buddy Greco
Carla Thomas

Carolyn Fire
Cecil Holmes
Celia
Charles "Organaire"
Cameron Charmaine
Clamor
Chris "Big Dog" Davis
Cissy Stone
Clint Holmes
David Ladd's Downtown
All-Stars David Sanborn
Deja Vu
Detroit Sound
Duly Noted
Eddie & The Starlites
Edmon Costa
Gina Brown & Anutha
Level Gladys Knight &
The Pips Graham BLVD
Guy Smith
Hall & Oates
Harris Erbat
Horst Seifer & Lake
ing n tequila
Izumi Yukimura
Jackie Trent
Jaya
JAY-R
Jennifer Hudson
Joanne Jackson
Joe Simon
Johnny Adams
Johnny Mathis
Kaleo Okalani
Kelly Lang
Kenny James
Kevin Mahogany
Kim Monroe
Lani Misaluchi
Leba Hibbert
Le Valedon
Lee "Shot" Williams
Linda Davis
Linda George
Lorretta Kendrick
Mahogani
MokuLeo
Maori Volcanics
Miles Jaye

Montel Jordan &
Monifah
Moods
Nicole Henry
Pat Esters
Paul White
Paulette Tyler
Peter J. Martin
Pop Feast
Rare Gems Odyssey's
Charles & Sandy Givings
Ray Boyland & The
Boyland Point Band
Ray Charles
Ray Coniff Singers
Ray Price
Richie Merritt
Rico J. Puno
Robin Kenyatta
Roland Dempsey
Ronnie Bryant
Rose Fostanes
Rosemarie Tan
Ruby Winters
Rhythm 'N' Jazz
Sachal
Sam Levine
Sandra De Sa
Seaside
Sharron
Shawn Dimples Austin
Shine Hayward
Simply Black
Sister Sledge
Studio Allstars
Sudden Move
SVK+G (vintage)
Tecora Rogers
The Castaways
The Fantastic Shakers
The Funk Brothers
The Joint Account
The Manhattens
The Sound Effects
The Spinners
The Superbs
The Temptations
The Texas Blueswomen
Tina Diamond

Trish Lim O' Donnell
Van Ford III
Velvet MacNair
Vernalle Anders
Vikki Carr
Willie Hoskins

Next Time Around
John Schneider
Lenny Valens

No More Rain (In This Cloud)
Angie Stone
The Dreem Teem
Christinti

Nobody Loves Anybody (Like Anybody Wants To Be Loved)
Amarilla

Not A Night Goes By
Tim Malchek

Now That's Love
Bill Anderson
The Kendricks

Ole Kentucky Moon
Ray Price

On A Good Night
Glen Campbell
Susanne Lane
Tim Malchek

Once In A Lifetime Thing
Danny Thomas
Gladys Knight & The Pips
Lee Dresser
Renee Geyer Band
Sami Jo
The Persuaders

One Way Street
The Gordian Knot

Perfect World
Peter Cetera

Rock & Roll Survivor
Brothers Of The Southland

Roses And Love Songs
Bobby Angel
Ray Price

Sails On The Horizon
Bryan Lane

Same Old Song And Dance
Ray Price

Same River, Different Bridge
Lee Greenwood

Scars And All
Jeff Carson

Seeing You Again
Brenda Lee
Danny Thomas
Dionne Warwick
Frank Sinatra Jr.
Ray Price

She Knows Just How To Touch Me
Charlie Rich

She's Gone
Tim Malchek

She's In Dallas
Steve Wariner

Shining Gold, Shining Blue
Cheryl Handy

Silver Moon
Bryan Lane
Toni Jolene Clay

Slow Healing
Calli McCord

Slowly But Surely
Marie Osmond

Smoke From An Old Flame
Steve Wariner

Soft To Touch (But Hard To Hold)
Charley Pride

Some Things Never Change
Danny Thomas
Ray Price

Someday Said The Scarecrow
John Brannen

Someone Else's Star
Bryan White
Carin Clark
Davis Daniel
Graham BLVD
Nashville Voices
Skip Ewing
The Hit Crew

Sometime In Early August
Ray Price

Somewhere Every River Has A Bridge
Mid-South

Southern Loving
Marshall Tucker Band

Still Crazy 'Bout You
Steve Kolander

Still Among The Living
Andy Martin

Storms Of Troubled Times
Beryl Davis
Danny Thomas
Etta James

Gladys Knight & The
Pips
Maxine Weldon
Patsy Sledd
Ray Price
Sami Jo
The Lettermen

Strong Wind Blowing
The Gordian Knot

Susan's House
The Eels

Talk To Her Heart
Steve Wariner

Tennessee Girl
Carl Jackson
The Rarely Herd

The Closest Thing To Love
Mac Davis
Ray Price
Sami Jo

*The Farthest Thing From
My Mind*
Ray Price

The Finer Things In Life
Johnny Russell
Red Stegall

*The Going Ups And The
Coming Downs*
Dorothy Moore
Gladys Knight & The
Pips
Ray Price
Tavaras

The Need To Be
Billy Joe Royal
Danny Barrett
Danny Thomas
Dardanelle
Dionne Warwick
Ester Satterfield

Gap Mangione
Gladys Knight & The Pips
Graham BLVD
Irene Reid
John Fox & His London
Studio Orchestra
Lisa Boray
The Neville Hughes
Orchestra
Ray Price
Sandra Feva
Vikki Carr

*The People Some People
Choose To Love*
Jackie Ross
Patti Boulaye

*The Prince, The Cowboy
And Me*
Johnny Lee
Rangi

The River And The Wind
Tanya Tucker

The World Keeps Spinning
The Gordian Knot

*This Can't Be Anything But
Love*
Katy Benko
Ronna Reeves

This Is A Love Song
Bill Anderson

Til You Found Me
Hannah Belle
Southerland
Lane Brody
Raquel Bitton

To A Gentler Time
Batdorf & Rodney
Danny Thomas
Marketta Little Wolf
Ray Price

Too Many Tears Too Late
Bobbie Cryner
Charly McClain
Carl Jackson

True Love (Finds Its Way)
Brent Lamb

Turn Out The Stars
Ollie Woodson
The Manhattens
Travis Nelson
David Sea

Two Of The Lucky Ones
Michael Peterson with
Bekka Bramlett

Until Forever's Gone
Bernadette Tinney
Daniel Rose
Grace
Kenny Rogers
Tonic Sol-Fa

*Until We Fall Back In Love
Again*
Jeff Carson

Until Your Ship Comes In
Ray Price

*We Just Came Apart At The
Dreams*
Abbie Lynn
Andie Blackwood
Billie Jo Spears
Debra Londen
Dorothy Moore
Rachale Marie
Trish DeRousee

*We Must Be Doing
Something Right*
The Gordian Knot

What Else But Love
Bryan Lane

What's One More Time
Ray Price

When I Run Out Of Road
John Brannen

*When It Snows In
Mississippi In July*
Bryan Lane

When Will I Let Go
Steve Wariner
The Rarely Herd

*When You've Got
Everything*
Lenny Valens

*Where Do I Put Her
Memory*
Burleigh Grimes
Charley Pride
Ray Price
Ronnie Robbins
Kenny Seratt

*Where Do I Put His
Memory*
Gladys Knight & The Pips
Wanda Jackson

Where Peaceful Waters Flow
Danny Thomas
Gladys Knight & The Pips
Jim McDonald
Kenneth Copeland
Ray Price
Rodena Preston
Salena Jones
Sylvie Desgroseilliers
UCLA Gospel Choir

Where Shadows Never Fall
Glen Campbell
W.V. Grant

You Are A Song
Batdorf & Rodney
Danny Thomas

Diane Leslie
Dionne Warwick
Gracie Anne Rivera
Jerry Naylor
Ray Price

*You Can Always Say
Goodbye In The Morning*
Jim Collins
Susanne Lana

You Know How I Feel
Bryan White

*You Made A Memory Of
Me*
Carl Jackson

*You Turn Me On Like A
Radio*
Ed Bruce
Mel Gibson

Your Love Will Carry Me
Bryan Lane

*Your Memory, Me & The
Blues*
Delbert McClinton

You're Seeing Someone Else
Andy Martin

*Wave On, Old Glory, Wave
On*
Billy Dean
Michael Peterson
Blank Check Project,
featuring Pamela Rose

Song Credits

Misty Mississippi Morning
Jim Weatherly, Universal Music

The Rebel Keeps on Rollin'
Jim Weatherly, Universal Music

The Star at the Top of the Tree
Jim Weatherly, Bright Leaf Music

Neither One of Us
Jim Weatherly, Universal Music

Midnight Train to Georgia
Jim Weatherly, Universal Music

Best Thing That Ever Happened to Me
Jim Weatherly, Universal Music

Where Peaceful Waters Flow
Jim Weatherly, Universal Music

The Need To Be
Jim Weatherly, Universal Music

Mississippi Song
Jim Weatherly, Universal Music

Where Do I Put Her Memory
Jim Weatherly, Universal Music

A Lady Like You
Jim Weatherly, Bright Sky Music
Keith Stegall, Sony/ATV Music
Capitol CMG Publishing©1984 EMI
Blackwood Music Inc. and Publisher(s) Unknown. All rights on behalf of
EMI Blackwood Music Inc. and Big
Gassed Hitties administered by Sony/
ATV Music Publishing LLC, 424
Church Street, Suite 1200, Nashville,
TN 37219. All rights reserved.
Used by permission.

Someone Else's Star
Jim Weatherly,
Skip Ewing, Sony ATV Music©1993
Sony/ATV Music Publishing LLC and
Publisher(s) Unknown. All rights on
behalf of Sony/ATV Music Publishing,
LLC and Basuare Music administered
by Sony/ATV Music Publishing LLC.
424 Church St, Suite 1200, Nashville,
TN 37219. All rights reserved. Used by
permission.

Where Shadows Never Fall
Jim Weatherly, Bright Sky Music
Carl Jackson, Universal Music

Find A Little Grace
Jim Weatherly, Bright Leaf Music
Bob Welch, Moraine Music
Round Hill Music

If I Had Lived My Life Without You
Jim Weatherly, Bright Leaf Music

Hot Night in Memphis
Jim Weatherly, Bright Leaf Music

Wave On, Old Glory, Wave On
Jim Weatherly, Bright Leaf Music
Wood Newton, Rope-A-Note

My Heart Will Always Remember
Jim Weatherly, Bright Leaf Music
Jonathon Willis

To A Gentler Time
Jim Weatherly, Universal Music

Photo and Image Credits

Page 5 – Pontotoc depot photo: Charles Nicholas, *Commercial Appeal*, Memphis

Page 31 – Peewee football photo: *Pontotoc Progress*

Page 33 – High school football: *Pontotoc Warrior* yearbook

Page 43 – Football photo: courtesy Ole Miss Athletics

Page 54 – Basketball photo: *Pontotoc Progress*

Page 55 – Football photo: courtesy Ole Miss Athletics

Page 58 – Invitation photo: Pam Manning Shelton

Page 63 – Football photo: courtesy Ole Miss Athletics

Page 69 – Walk of Champions arch photo: Jeff Roberson

Page 84 – Football Photo: courtesy Ole Miss Athletics

Page 86 – 1962 Ole Miss football plaque photo: Jeff Roberson

Page 90 – Football photo: courtesy Ole Miss Athletics

Page 97 – Photos in flyer: Terry Wood Photography, Tupelo

Page 107 – Football photo: courtesy Ole Miss Athletics

Page 113 – Football photo: courtesy Ole Miss Athletics

Page 117 – Football photo: courtesy Ole Miss Athletics

Page 135 – Gordian Knot photo: Ron Joy/Belle Joy Schwartz Estate

Page 143 – Gordian Knot photo – Ron Joy/Belle Joy Schwartz Estate

Page 153 – Nancy Sinatra photo: Frank LiVolsi

Page 156 – Nancy Sinatra photo: Frank LiVolsi

Page 158 – Gordian Knot group photo: Frank LiVolsi

Page 167 – The Factory photo: Ron Joy/Belle Joy Schwartz Estate

Page 171 – Gordian Knot and Fred Astaire photo: Getty Images/NBC Universal

Page 181 – Jim Weatherly photo: Shan Weatherly

Page 184 – Jim Weatherly photo: Shan Weatherly

Page 187 – Jim Weatherly photo: Brighton Weatherly

Page 196 – Jim Weatherly photo: Shan Weatherly

Page 207 – Larry Gordon and Jim Weatherly photo: Sam Emerson

Page 213 – Jim Weatherly photo: Shan Weatherly

Page 226 – Gladys Knight and the Pips and Jim Weatherly photo: Robert Failla and Daniela Failla

Page 249 – Jim Weatherly and Dorothy Moore photo: Shan Weatherly

Page 251 – Lyceum at Ole Miss photo: Jeff Roberson

Page 255 – Charley Pride, Jim Weatherly, Gov. Cliff Finch photo: Hubert Worley

Page 265 – Jim Weatherly photo: Hubert Worley

Page 274 – Edith Weatherly and Jim Weatherly photos: Hubert Worley

Page 298 – Ole Miss Alumni Hall of Fame photo: Ole Miss Alumni Association

Page 301 – Songwriters Hall of Fame induction: Songwriters Hall of Fame photo

Page 308 – Brighton Weatherly, Gladys Knight, Zack Weatherly photo: Jeff Roberson

Page 310 – Jim Weatherly and family at home photo: Jay Wilkinson

Front cover photos: Michael Gomez and courtesy Ole Miss athletics

Back cover photo: Brighton Weatherly

Other photos in the book are from the Weatherly family collection. The Ole Miss sports photos also appeared in the Ole Miss yearbooks of the era.

Credits

"A Nightmarish Ending for Spook Murphy's Dream" – Dan Jenkins, Sports Illustrated, September 28, 1964 – pages 109-110

Bubba Knight excerpt from "Motown: The Golden Years" – by Bill Dahl – page 215

Daryl Hall quote – pages 217-218

Goldmine magazine excerpt from the 40th anniversary of "Midnight Train to Georgia" story – pages 224-225

The Daily Guru excerpt on "Midnight Train to Georgia" – Joel Friemark – pages 227-229

Charley Pride: "Where Do I Put Her Memory" Quote from Rolling Stone's "40 Saddest Country Songs of All Time" List. Copyright © Rolling Stone LLC 2014. All Rights Reserved. Used by Permission. –page 253

Quote from Jay-Z's Foreword in Rolling Stone's Special Interest Publication '500 Greatest Songs of All Time.' Copyright © Rolling Stone LLC 2010. All Rights Reserved. Used by Permission. – page 292

Mariah Carey excerpt from Gladys Knight and the Pips induction – Rock and Roll Hall of Fame – page 296

Jeff Roberson, a Baldwyn, Mississippi, native and Ole Miss alumnus, lives in Oxford, Mississippi. He has spent most of his professional career as a sportswriter at the Ole Miss Spirit and the Oxford Eagle while also teaching and mentoring future writers and sportswriters. Jeff's father, Billy, and Jim's mother, Edith, were siblings.

CPSIA information can be obtained
at www.ICGtesting.com
Printed in the USA
LVHW030016120221
679034LV00003B/301